UNIVERSAL COMPATIBILITY IS ALMOST HERE

As computer communication becomes a major priority in industry and commerce, high-speed computer links will rely less on guesswork and more on substantive detail and faster decision-making. Whether you're a business professional, computer hobbyist, electronic bulletin board operator, or home worker, you will learn:

— 3 common communications problems

— The rules, protocols, and standards of each system

— How to "direct connect" and integrate data

— Information on local area networking and micro-mainframe links

— The latest in state-of the-art connections between IBM PCs, compatibles, Apples, Macintoshes, Kaypros, Tandy, and other computers

— And much more!

DIRECT CONNECTIONS

ARIELLE EMMETT is Senior Editor of *Computer Graphics World*. Her articles have appeared in *Personal Computing, Omni,* the *Village Voice, Saturday Review,* and *Ms.* She lives in Hewitt, New Jersey.

DAVID GABEL, formerly Senior Editor of *Personal Computing,* is a frequent contributor to electronics and computer magazines such as *PC Week, Software News,* and *Electronic Buyer's News.* He lives in New York.

DIRECT CONNECTIONS
Making Your Personal Computers Communicate

by Arielle Emmett and David Gabel

A PLUME BOOK
NEW AMERICAN LIBRARY
NEW YORK AND SCARBOROUGH, ONTARIO

NAL BOOKS ARE AVAILABLE AT QUANTITY DISCOUNTS WHEN USED TO PROMOTE PRODUCTS OR SERVICES. FOR INFORMATION PLEASE WRITE TO PREMIUM MARKETING DIVISION, NEW AMERICAN LIBRARY, 1633 BROADWAY, NEW YORK, NEW YORK 10019.

Copyright © 1986 by Arielle Emmett and David Gabel

All rights reserved

 PLUME TRADEMARK REG. U.S. PAT. OFF. AND FOREIGN COUNTRIES
REG. TRADEMARK—MARCA REGISTRADA
HECHO EN HARRISONBURG, VA., U.S.A.

SIGNET, SIGNET CLASSIC, MENTOR, ONYX, PLUME, MERIDIAN and NAL BOOKS are published *in the United States* by New American Library, 1633 Broadway, New York, New York 10019, *in Canada* by The New American Library of Canada Limited, 81 Mack Avenue, Scarborough, Ontario M1L 1M8

Library of Congress Cataloging in Publication Data

Emmett, Arielle.
    Direct connections.

    1. Microcomputers. 2. Software compatibility.
3. Computer interfaces. I. Gabel, David. II. Title.
III. Series.
QA76.5.E5625   1986   004.16   86–5258
ISBN 0–452–25649–6

First Printing, August, 1986

1 2 3 4 5 6 7 8 9

PRINTED IN THE UNITED STATES OF AMERICA

For Nathalie Donnet Emmett and George Heidenrich
A.E.

For Ilse
D.G.

CONTENTS

Acknowledgments xi

Introduction: The Computer Interconnect Dilemma 1

Chapter 1—Computers Obey the Rules 7
 • The Communications Game • Protocols and Standards • What Can Go Wrong • Some Rules in Detail

Chapter 2—Understanding the OSI Model 15
 • Rules of the Game • A Case Study Preview • Step-by-Step Connection: Compaq Plus and Kaypro 4—Modem to Modem • Layered Communications • Communicating with Micros: A Model Subset • A Step-by-Step Connection • What Can Go Wrong

Chapter 3—Three Communications Challenges 39
 • An Overfull Memory Buffer • Practical Solutions • A Speed-Matching Problem • Handshaking, Control Codes, and Other Mysteries

Chapter 4—The Problem: Computers Don't Talk Alike 55
 • Incompatible Operating Systems • The Invention of CP/M • Incompatible Disk Formats • The Communications Solution • Incompatible Communications Hardware • Incompatible Applications Programs • ASCII Code

Chapter 5—Modems and What They Do 71
 • Kinds of Modems • Modem Speed • Modem Protocols • Inside a Modem

Chapter 6—The Modem Decision   85
• Preliminary Considerations • The Phone Company • Transmission Accuracy • Using Communications Software • Communications Parameters • Hooking Up a Modem • Transferring a File

Chapter 7—Using a Modem Without Using the Phone Line   107
• The OSI Model Again • Why Get Another Telephone for Communications? • How Modem-to-Modem Works • Troubleshooting the Connection

Chapter 8—Modem Connections: Introduction to the Case Studies   115
• Practical Considerations
• Modem Connection Case Studies
    Apple II + to Apple IIe
    Apple IIe to Macintosh
    Apple IIe to IBM PC
    IBM PC to Apple IIe
    Apple IIe to Compaq Plus
    Kayporo 4 to Apple IIe
    Apple IIe to ATEX TLM (DEC PDP-11) system
    Radio Shack TRS-80 Model 100 to Apple IIe
    Radio Shack TRS-80 Model 100 to Compaq Plus
    Radio Shack TRS-80 Model 100 to Osborne I
    Commodore 64 to Apple II +
    Commodore 64 to Apple II + (Direct Connection, Modem to Modem)
    Sanyo MBC 555 to Compaq Plus (2400 BPS)
    Compaq Plus to Apple IIe (2400 BPS)

Chapter 9—The Direct Connection   159
• The EIA Serial Interface • How to Make RS-232-C Work • The General Solution • The UART

Chapter 10—A Direct-Connect Methodology   175
• The Physical Link • Diagnostic Strategies: Getting Physical • Quick and Easy Solutions • The Higher Levels of Communications

Chapter 11—Direct-Connect Case Studies   195
• Radio Shack TRS-80 Model 100 to Apple II + • Tandy 2000 (or Compaq Plus/IBM PC XT-Compatible) as Host; Radio Shack TRS-80 Model 100 as Terminal • IBM PC to Apple Macintosh (Including a *Word Star* File Transfer) • Cable Requirements for the Macintosh and IBM PC • Apple Macintosh to Radio Shack TRS-80 Model 100 • Compaq Plus to Apple II +

Chapter 12—File Compatibility   221
 • Binary Files and Other Mysteries • "Different" Text Files • Spreadsheet Files • Other Situations

Chapter 13—Networks   229
 • Networking Introduction • A Proto Network • From Ideal to Real • Trade-offs • Size, Scope, and Topology • Points of Failure • Software vs. Hardware Compatibility • Costs and Flexibility

Chapter 14—The Micro-to-Mainframe Link   251
 • The Mainframe Connection • Basic Dilemmas • Needs and Standards • Essential Terminology • Physical Connection • Types of Conversions • Common Characteristics • Limitations • Applications Interface Links • Universal Links • The Future? • One Final Word

Appendices   267
 A. ASCII Code Chart   267
 B. Keyboard Conventions for ASCII Codes   271
 C. RS-232-C Pin Assignments   275
 D. File-Transfer Software Vendors   279
 E. Local-Area Network Vendors   283
 F. Micro-to-Mainframe Link Vendors   289
 G. Communications Software Vendors   295
 H. A Communications Diary   301

Bibliography   313

Acknowledgments

Direct Connections would not have been possible without the generous contributions of hardware, software, and written materials from the following publishers, manufacturers, dealers, and research institutions:

Action Research-Northwest, Agent Computer Services, Inc., Alpha Software Corporation, Apple Computer, Inc., AT&T Bell Laboratories, AT&T Information Systems, Bizcomp Corporation, Bridge Communications, Inc., Bytcom, Inc., Coherent Communications Systems Corporation, Commodore Business Machines, Inc., Communications Research Group, Compaq Computer Corporation, CompuServe, Inc., Computer Discount of New Jersey, Context Management Systems, Cork Control, Inc., Corvus Systems, Inc., Cullinet Software, Inc., Datapoint Corporation, Datec, Inc., Digital Communications Associates, dilithium Press, Electronic Industries Association, FOG, Fox Research, Inc., Hayes Microcomputer Products, Inc., The Headlands Press, Inc., Informatics General Corporation, Information Service Strategies, InformationWEEK Magazine, International Business Machines, ITOM International Co., Kaypro Corporation, Lexicon Corporation, Lindbergh Systems, Microcom, Inc., Management Science America, Inc., Micro-Module Systems, Inc., Microstuf, Inc., MultiTech Systems, Newark Public Library, Novation, Inc., Personal Computer Products, Persoft, Inc., Radio Shack (division of Tandy Corporation), Radio Shack Computer Center (Paramus, N.J.) Source Telecomputing Corporation, Standard Microsystems Corporation, Televideo Systems, Inc., The On-Line Computer Telephone Directory, Ungermann-Bass, Inc., U.S. Robotics, Inc., Vertex Systems, Inc., Wang Laboratories, Inc., Woolf Software Systems.

In addition, we'd like to express appreciation to the following individuals who provided research materials, technical, and editing assistance:

Mike Andres (West Milford, N.J.), Jim Cambron (Kansas City, Mo.), David Crellen (San Diego, Calif.), Timothy Dygert (Columbia City,

Ind.), Mario Eisenbacher (West Chester, Pa.), A.G. Fraser (Murray Hill, N.J.), Jorge Gardos (Philadelphia, Pa.), Ron Halshyn (Washington, D.C.), George Heidenrich (Briarcliff Manor, N.Y.), Charles Leighton (Oxnard, Calif.), Claire Lichack (New York, N.Y.), Ernest Mau (Aurora, Colo.), Michael McKillip (Chicago, Ill.), Wes Merchant (Washington, D.C.), James Moran (Bayville, N.Y.), Bradley O'Brien (Franklin Lakes, N.J.), Gregory Pearson (Norwood, Mass.), Omri Serlin (Los Altos, Calif.), V.A. Vyssotsky (Murray Hill, N.J.).

Special thanks to Thomas O'Flaherty, Information Service Strategies, Wood-Ridge, N.J., for patient reading and editing suggestions; Katinka Matson (John Brockman Associates), our book agent; Stephen Ross, for photography; and Joseph Esposito and Jill Grossman, our supportive editors at New American Library.

Finally, love and thanks to our families, and to Gerry and Ilse especially, whose understanding and encouragement always kept us on target.

A.E. & D.G.

DIRECT CONNECTIONS
Making Your Personal Computers Communicate

INTRODUCTION: THE COMPUTER INTERCONNECT DILEMMA

Needs and Applications

Personal computers ought to exchange data and programs with ease and efficiency. Unfortunately, they don't yet. That's why we wrote this book.

Chances are you're making tough choices about your productivity—electronic choices, in many cases, choices that may rework the map of your professional life. You've heard that personal computer communications may enhance the productivity of your business. But your hardware and software choices aren't simple. What if you need a mix of personal computers—portables, transportables, even several different desktop models—to support all your business tasks? Will you have problems swapping data from one computer to another? Can you transfer software programs from a 3¼-inch microfloppy to a 20-megabyte hard disk? Do you require links to mainframes? Can you develop simple, inexpensive cabling systems to ease communications? Or must you sacrifice the flexibility of your computing environment to make all your computers talk alike?

You've heard horror stories about "the incompatibility problem." X computer jabbers incoherently with Y; your field-service officer loses ten important reports trying to transfer them from his portable computer to the IBM PC XT in corporate headquarters; the manual that comes with your portable doesn't include a troubleshooting checklist. You can't figure out how to connect up the cables from your Kaypro to your Radio Shack; you need to "cross that wire" and "jumper those pins" and there are no solid directions and fewer schematics. No matter how carefully you choose your computers, it seems there's a hitch somewhere. You have to troubleshoot the connection, and there is always the balancing act between flexibility, on one hand, and ease of data swapping on the other.

What do you do if your Apple can't read CP/M disks? Or your IBM PC XT won't interface correctly with your TRS-80 Model 100 portable? Or your brand-new Macintosh in the Los Angeles office won't download its *Multiplan* spreadsheets to the Compaq Plus computer in New York?

Basically, you've got three alternatives. If you've already accumulated a collection of unlike personal computers for your business or home, you can get rid of them—at a loss—very fast. Another alternative, especially if you've only reached the stage of deciding about a computer purchase, is to call in a specialist in computers, asking him to network as many identical personal computers as you need. Your third choice is to read this book and find out the benefits of making most of your computers suddenly capable of fast, accurate communications, through modems, serial cables, or more advanced high-speed networking schemes.

Obviously, personal computers should be able to talk to each other: communications in the last twenty years of the century, and beyond, will be a major priority for industry and commerce racing ahead to transmit information and to capitalize on its newness. A Wall Street broker, for example, will get a jump on what Toshiba and Nikon are doing by monitoring sudden upswings in buy and sell activity, as well as analysts' forecasts, through the Dow Jones News/Retrieval Service, a service that can be accessed by using a personal computer, a modem, and communications software. Examining the data, the analyst can save them, perform technical analysis, and then "stuff" them into an electronic mailbox of a client for same-day pickup. Alternatively, the broker can transmit tips to a colleague through a local computer network right within the building, or use the data to upgrade files stored on the corporate mainframe.

Whatever the application, high-speed computer links will make decision making a faster process based on less guesswork and more substantive detail. But once data are transferred, each piece must also be sifted, interpreted and "custom fit" in ways that make sense to the user and the business. Here personal computers and software can be an advantage over mainframes or minicomputers: the software is tailored to the end-user. Different forms fit different functions; one manager prefers a *SuperCalc* or Lotus's *1-2-3* to another spreadsheet; a business writer fancies an elegant word processor with indexing, communications, and database-management functions. An information systems manager, by contrast, prefers a report writer and mainframe data extraction tool. Each of these software pieces might, potentially, be linked together, and their data integrated and swapped back and forth between systems in a departmental work group or an entire corporate office.

How is the question. There are ways of interconnecting personal computers that involve hardware or hardware/software combinations, switching devices, or just the software by itself, as well as a phone link or hardwire connection. With these tools and some know-how, you can learn to develop simple communications systems within your department, or use outside providers. You can find the right services to help network dozens, even hundreds of personal computers in a local area network. Or you can get yourself a modem and access more than a thousand databases and free electronic bulletin boards.

This book shows you how, step by step. We begin with a premise: personal computer communications is based on systems of rules—rules that display no logic or consistency outside of their own realm. Like the rules of a sports game, the rules of microcomputer communications must be followed strictly, to the letter. But the hitch is discovering just what the rules are, since more than one set of rules are operating during communications at any one time.

Rules, Protocols, and Standards

Our first two chapters are devoted to laying a foundation for understanding communication rules, including the complex sets of rules, called protocol, required to make a transmission work. In Chapter 1 we review basic concepts; in Chapter 2 we show how a model of communications can be used to identify and troubleshoot connections; in Chapter 3 we illustrate three communications challenges—difficult, but not uncommon problems that anyone attempting direct personal computer transfer of data might encounter.

In Chapter 4 we go to the heart of the matter: explaining the origins of software and hardware incompatibilities, the differences in computer languages, operating systems, and disk and file formats. Once this foundation is built, we proceed in Chapters 5–8 with telecommunications solutions. Chapters 5–7 examine the modem connection; Chapter 8 consists of a series of case studies showing exactly how to connect and transmit data between major brands of personal computers using standard communications equipment and software. In it we cover state-of-the-art connections between IBM PCs and compatibles, Apple II series computers and Macintoshes, Kaypros, Tandy products, DEC PDP-II minicomputers, and others.

In Chapters 9–11 we develop Phase II communications, what's known as the "direct connect" or "hardwire" technique. This form of communications bypasses a modem entirely, transferring files and programs across each computer's serial port. We explain the basics of the port, the different implementations of signals on the port, and provide a methodology for direct-connecting and troubleshooting serial connections. Chapter 11, again, provides how-to case studies of direct serial connections between the chief personal computers in the marketplace.

Chapters 12–14 tackle three distinct topics: file incompatibility problems, local area networking and switching schemes, and finally, the micro-mainframe connection. We survey existing technologies and explain the issues of cost, selection criteria, and compatibility problems both for small groups and large organizations.

Anecdotes, personal experiences, and practical examples are sprinkled throughout the text to illuminate the theory, and we provide useful appendices that include the ASCII code chart, RS-232-C signal control lines, file transfer programs, and communications network product manufacturers.

There are two ways to use this book. If you're experienced with computers, then proceed to Chapters 8 or 11 for case studies with computers similar to yours. Or you can read straight through, to get more background and understanding of the principles involved.

All the technologies presented here are feasible and, in most cases, inexpensive. While there are indeed some computer connections yet to be made practical for the average consumer, we do know that hundreds of new products have been released as of this writing to make the terms "universal compatibility" and "easy communications" much closer to reality. We are not claiming the reality is here. But we do believe that you can get computer communications working for you, so that you can get onto your other business as quickly as possible.

CHAPTER 1
COMPUTERS OBEY RULES (MORE THAN ONE SET AT A TIME)

- The Communications Game • Protocols and Standards • What Can Go Wrong • Some Rules in Detail

COMMUNICATIONS BASICS

ASCII Code: A way of encoding characters for transmission that virtually all microcomputers and minicomputers understand.

Baud: Speed of data transmission. One baud is one signal change per second. At 300 baud, transmission occurs at 300 bits per second. At 1200 bits per second and faster, because of the way the bits are encoded, the speed in baud is slower than the bit rate.

Communications Port: The totality of the hardware and software that establishes the physical connection for communications and handles the minute operations necessary for successful communications.

Duplex: A term that refers to the bidirectionality (or lack thereof) of data communications. Often used to mean Echoplex.

Echoplex: The directions in which characters are echoed. Terms are confusing, but a computer set for full duplex (see above) echoes received characters to the communications line, but does not echo transmitted characters to the local screen. A computer set for half duplex behaves in the opposite manner.

Parity Bit: A bit added to a character to be transmitted that is used for error checking.

Protocol: A set of rules governing the format and timing of messages in data communications.

Start bit: A bit inserted before a character is transmitted to signal the start of the character.

Stop bit: An added bit that signals the end of a transmitted character.

The Communications Game

Computers obey rules, but the rules are complex. Like the rules of a sports game that make strict sense to the participants but possibly no sense at all to an outsider, microcomputer communications rules succeed only if they are followed strictly, to the letter. Part of the challenge in linking computers is discovering just what the rules are, especially since more than one set of rules operate during communications at any one time.

Protocols and Standards

Sets of rules governing the interaction between communicating computers are known as *protocols*. When protocols become widely implemented, published, and accepted in the computer industry, they may become communications *standards*. In human interaction, protocols and standards govern the ways we recognize and behave toward each other. Diplomatic procedures like the seating arrangements at a dinner party or the rules for formal introductions, all form an etiquette of interaction. Microcomputer communications work in much the same way—though it should be noted that the analogy breaks down in that people can spontaneously reinvent their protocols when the situation requires it, but computers can't. Exchange of information between computers succeeds because of a strict agreement on the part of both parties to follow a prescribed set of procedures.

When we decide, for example, to make two computers transfer files, both sender and receiver obey the same communications protocol. Protocols define exactly how computers exchange data; they specify when to send a message, how to frame the data so that the next computer can process them, and how to send electrical signals across a computer's communications port to modems and, ultimately, to other computers.

At the other end of the line, rules specify to the receiving computer how to acknowledge the incoming data and when to request a retransmission if the data are garbled. In fact, there are several sets of rules that ensure that the details of the physical link, the hardware, and the details of the data transmission itself are compatible from one end of the communications channel to the other.

Problems with computer communications occur when users don't know all of the rules. For example, the physical link between computers—the wiring—may be set up in such a way that the signals between sender and receiver conflict, even though each computer is transmitting according to a consistent set of rules. In much the same way, communications software, which controls the message swapping between computers, may not recognize subtle differences in hardware. Thus two different makes of computer, even though they may be running the same communications software package, may not exchange files and data at all.

Manufacturers, for their part, have contributed to the problem by taking liberties with communications standards developed by major industry standards groups, such as the Electronic Industries Association (EIA) and the Comite Consultatif International Télégraphique et Téléphonique (CCITT). For reasons we discuss in the next chapter—some of which are historical, some expedient—manufacturers have simplified the rules or bent them just a bit to suit the peculiar demands of their systems' hardware. For example, when microcomputer manufacturers design their communications hardware port, the "standard" RS-232-C (or derivative) serial interface, a means for connecting auxiliary computer equipment (e.g., modem, printer), they may bend the rules governing electrical signals that cross the port just enough to confuse the connecting computer. By the same token, communications-software producers may add programming codes to make their software unique or proprietary. They may do this for good reasons: to protect transmitted or received files, for instance, or to improve message flow control. But whatever the reason, the result is that no software without that particular protocol can talk to it. When these problems crop up, the result is a computerized Tower of Babel.

What Can Go Wrong

Computer babble takes many forms. You might see garbled data or an abruptly ended transmission, or nontransmission, or the failure to get a dial tone, or the appearance of nonsense characters due to incessant telephone noise. Consider the following examples from actual experience:

- An expert Osborne 1 user in New York plugs into GTE Telenet's Telemail, an electronic mail service. He gets a mixture of unintelligible and legible characters on his computer's screen.
- A street-maintenance supervisor in Oxnard, California, sets up a modem and telephone connection between his division's Apple II+ and a computerized fuel-dispensing terminal in an equipment garage. He loses more than 50 percent of the fuel transactions each time the fuel terminal transfers its information to the Apple II+.
- A computer reviewer in Aurora, Colorado, tries to transfer data directly from a Morrow Micro Decision 1 microcomputer to an Apple II+. He succeeds in hardwiring the machines properly through the RS-232-C serial port, but gets nonsense on the receiving computer screen.
- A writer in New Jersey tries to transfer a computer program from a Radio Shack TRS-80 Model 100 to a Compaq Plus computer. Half the program comes across clearly. The other half is mangled as the Compaq flashes distress signals and displays portions of its file directory.

These are just a few of many examples of communications problems we will examine and troubleshoot. The problems are confusing at first. Why should a Telemail user get a mixture of unreadable and legible characters on the screen? Why should a transmission from a fuel terminal to an Apple II+ result in 50 percent good data, stored on an Apple floppy disk, and 50 percent lost data? Why should information be destroyed in a transmission between a Morrow Micro Decision 1 and an Apple II+, much less a Radio Shack Model 100 and an IBM-compatible computer?

The answers to these questions arise from a misapprehension of hardware and software capabilities, as well as a misunderstanding of communications rules and their variants. These rules apply to many levels of communications, from hardware and the communications networks to applications programs and the ways these programs format data for use by a receiving computer. In every case, some violation of rules, either on the operator's part or the computer's part resulted in a weak or faulty data connection.

We should be able to solve these connection problems if we can just find out what all of the rules are. But there's a catch: not only do manufacturers and their products implement rules we know nothing about, but there are instances in which even the most reliable hardware and software may seem to distort or work against the rules we do know. When you have a bug in a communications connection, you've got to go in and troubleshoot your system. You've got to attack each layer of protocol in hardware and software, one by one, to find the bug and eliminate it. In essence, you have to develop an understanding of the rules and how they work, and what can go wrong with equipment that may be faulty, or may even be operating properly but in a way that you don't understand.

To find out if a connection will work, you have to try it. When you try, you should be prepared to analyze any problems you encounter against your own concept of a good computer connection. Where are the weak and vulnerable points of the connection? Once you've identified the problem, you'll have one of two general options for solving it: either change the rules consistently to match your equipment or change the equipment to match a consistent set of rules. Either way, communications rules must prevail.

Some Rules in Detail

What kinds of rules are we talking about? You probably have seen some rudimentary rules in communications software menus and the manuals for the bulletin boards and on-line databases. The manual for The Source, for example, tells you to set up your system to meet the following technical requirements:

300 or 1200 baud
Full duplex
No parity
8-bit ASCII code
1 stop bit

The top line, which specifies *baud*, lets you choose either one of two speeds of transmission. (The Source, as of this writing, does not handle 2400 bits per second.) By making sure that your choice is compatible with the speed of your modem, you are getting your computer to obey a rule that is part of a communications scheme The Source's large computers understand.

Full Duplex is a bit more complicated. Duplex refers to the ability to carry on a two-way conversation. When you talk on the telephone, you speak in full duplex; that is, you and the other party on the line can speak at the same time. In contrast, conversations on CB radios take place in half duplex; either of the parties in a conversation can speak, but the other must listen. Most modems popularly in use today are full-duplex modems, so the requirement for full-duplex operation seems obsolete. But what is important is that the user recognizes a rule: both computers must communicate in the same duplex mode, full or half. Otherwise the computers may transmit back and forth using double letters, so the word "HELLO" would look like "HHEELLOO."

The other settings, "No parity, 8-bit ASCII code, 1 stop bit," specify rules that govern exactly what the data characters will look like coming over the communications line. *No parity*, for example, tells the sending computer *not* to add a special error-checking data bit (called a *parity bit*) to each data packet. No parity means, in essence, that each computer agrees on a protocol in which a specific type of error-checking method is not used.

A setting of *8-Bit ASCII Code* tells your microcomputer to package your data in 8-bit segments. An information bit, we recall, is represented in your computer as a 1 or 0 (actually a difference in voltage). Eight bits means that eight different voltages make up a single character. Each 8-bit character is encoded in such a way that it conforms to a specific numeric translation table called ASCII (American Standard Code for Information Interchange). ASCII can be understood by virtually all microcomputers as well as by large on-line systems like The Source and CompuServe. Once we are set for 8-bit ASCII code, we add a special data bit, called a *stop bit*, to frame or mark each data segment so that The Source's host computers can identify it as a discrete unit.

So now we know that these technical requirements, sometimes called communications parameters, are actually specifications for rules that control a data transmission. Under ordinary circumstances—and ordinary is a matter of definition—we would install our modem, load communications software, and go through a series of menus that let us specify whatever rules are necessary to make the transmission work. When we have a large and well-organized information utility like The Source, or if we subscribe to various bulletin boards or electronic-mail services that provide complete documentation and error checking, chances are we can get the rules to work without a hitch—or too many hitches, that is. In a similar fashion, with a little practice and tinkering, we should also be able to set up solid and reliable modem or hardwire communications between microcomputers of the same make: an Apple-to-Apple connection, for example, or an IBM PC to IBM PC, or a Radio Shack TRS-80 Model 100 to a Tandy Model 2000.

These are the ordinary situations. However, there are extraordinary situations that go beyond simple computer connection and can cause the real trouble. To get to where we can solve all of the more difficult connections, we have to understand some theory, and that's what our next chapter takes up.

CHAPTER 2
UNDERSTANDING THE OSI MODEL

- Rules of the Game • A Case Study Preview • Step-by-Step Connection: Compaq Plus and Kaypro 4—Modem to Modem • Layered Communications • Communicating with Micros: A Model Subset • A Step-by-Step Connection • What Can Go Wrong

COMMUNICATIONS BASICS

Control Characters: A set of predetermined, nonprinting characters that format data and control the flow of messages to a remote device.

Data: The information transferred in a communications session.

EBCDIC: An 8-bit code used in mainframe computers for communications.

Handshaking: Signals that control the flow of data.

Interface: A physical interconnect boundary shared between computers, modems, and printers.

Layers of Communication: The structure of the OSI Model.

OSI (Open Systems Interconnect): A general model of the data communications process.

Rules of the Game

Computers communicate according to several sets of rules, which dictate the character and sequencing of the communications event. Many small steps make up the big event we call data transmission; transmission is successful when sender and receiver communicate according to compatible sets of rules implemented in hardware and software.

A personal computer communications session begins when communication software instructs a computer to dial another device; either a computer or intelligent terminal. The calling computer uses a hardware device, the modem, to take the phone "off-hook" electronically to get a dial tone. When modems on each end of the line begin sending signals that request clearance for data transmission, a path for data is cleared. Sender and receiver then begin swapping information about the files to be transferred, and the amount of empty disk space available for reception. Finally, when the data are sent and written on the receiver's disk, the receiving computer sends acknowledgment signals, indicating the data transmission is complete. All of these steps are governed by prescribed sets of rules; the sum of rules defining the format and relative timing of message exchange between computers is known as *protocol*.[1]

Protocol may also refer to more sophisticated sets of rules governing message transmission between multiple computers on a communications network. These rules govern access to the physical channel, opening and closing of communications sessions, checking of errors, and many other features.

---

[1] Protocol is rather loosely defined in microcomputer communications. Some experts refer to protocol only as the communications settings (such as stop bits, parity, baud rate, duplex, and character length) that define the agreement on how two computers will communicate. These settings are controlled in a communications-software menu.

Protocol, in effect, governs two major domains: software and hardware. It governs the way communications software is written. Protocol is implemented in software as a series of step-by-step instructions (in the form of code) that tells the computer exactly how to communicate with another computer.

Protocol is also implemented in hardware. It is a set of rules that specifies the ways in which the hardware handles signal voltages—raising and lowering them in a prescribed sequence to control the beginnings and endings of a communications session.

When communications protocols are gathered into one place, or one set, they may be designated as *communications standards*. Standards represent a common agreement to exchange information in the same way; in computer communications, standards organizations, like the International Standards Organization (ISO), CCITT (Comite Consultatif International Télégraphique et Téléphonique, an international agency), and the Electronic Industries Association (EIA), commonly make standards recommendations to the computer industry and attempt to promulgate a limited number of them so that computers may speak a common language—implementing the same sets of rules to communicate.

The officially designated standard for personal computer communication is EIA-232-D, a derivative standard based on the earlier EIA recommendation, RS-232-C. The EIA-232-D standard specifies the electrical characteristics that make up the communications interface on modems, computers, and many printers. The standard dictates the rules for asynchronous data communications, the kind that is used by personal computers over ordinary telephone lines. It also specifies the mechanical characteristics of a 25-pin interface connector, assigning particular electrical signals to each of a number of standard pins.

Rules, then, govern not only software and hardware, but also different realms of functionality. The two most essential functions are transfer of data and control of the data stream. Sets of rules (grouped together as protocol) implemented in hardware and software thus dictate the nature of *data signals* and *control signals*. Data signals are just what they sound like: voltages that transmit bits of information. Control signals are specialized signals generated by the hardware and software that regulate message flow control. Often they are called "handshaking" signals. Both types of signals, data and control, cross an interface during an effective microcomputer communication.

A Case Study Preview

How does a communications session work? We can illustrate the basics by showing a link between a Compaq Plus (IBM PC XT-compatible) and a Kaypro 4 personal computer. In the case study below (which represents a compact version of the case studies in communications we present in Chapters 8 and 11), we show how to connect these two different computers using modems, but without using telephone lines. This type of direct connection can be accomplished successfully with certain kinds of personal computers linked together with an ordinary phone cord, provided that rules of communications are followed.

Step-by-Step Connection: Compaq Plus and Kaypro 4—Modem to Modem

The main issue in a direct modem-to-modem connection is to simulate the sequence of actions that will make the calling modem connect itself to the telephone line. It isn't always easy to do that. One modem has to have its answer tone turned on; the calling modem has to expect the tone. After the calling modem completes a dialing sequence, it samples the line to detect the presence of an answer tone. Once it detects the tone, it turns on its originate tone. When the answering modem detects the originate tone, the connection is established.

Equipment

Compaq Plus Computer	Kaypro 4 Computer
Computer with two disk drives (one hard and one floppy), 256K memory	Computer with two floppy disk drives, 64K memory
Bytcom 212AD modem	Built-in modem
IBM Asynchronous Communications Card	Modular phone cord
RS-232-C Cable	
Modular Phone Cord	
Software	
Telpac (U.S. Robotics)	*SuperTerm* (supplied with Kaypro 4 computer)

Procedure

Connect the modular phone cord from one modem to the other. If you have more than one connector on a modem, as is the case with the Bytcom 212AD, make sure to plug into the connector that normally connects to the phone line. Boot the communications software in both computers. On the Kaypro 4, choose Dial from the main menu, then Online. The Kaypro automatically turns on its answer tone, and waits to detect the originate tone from the Bytcom 212AD modem.

On the Compaq, enter terminal mode, and type RETURN twice. The attached modem interprets RETURN as a signal that indicates an impending user command. The modem prompts the user for a command. Type the words SET UP. This makes the modem automatically set its communications parameters to match those of the RS-232-C port to which it's connected. Then dial any number—1 will do. The Kaypro screen will go blank, indicating a connection. The Compaq screen displays the "On-Line" message, indicating that the connection is complete. Type a few words on each keyboard to verify that the computers are connected. If you get no characters, change duplex (Compaq) or echo (from the Term option on the Kaypro 4). Do the same if you get double characters. If you get garbage characters on the Kaypro screen, check the baud setting, word lengths, and parity-bit settings to ensure all communications parameters (rules) match on both computers. When everything is working properly, you have completed the connection.

Notice all the "ifs" followed by remedies. How do we know to try those particular remedies? How will you know? The questions to ask, and the answers that you can deduce, are all buried in the intricacies of the communications process itself.

Layered Communications

The rules are implemented in *layers*. Layering is a mental construct; layers refer to levels of function, procedures ranging from the exchange of hardware handshaking signals (signals that cross the RS-232-C serial interface) to the transfer of computer files.

In mainframe communications and networking, the procedures for putting together computer networks have been codified into a set of layered design rules, known as *network architectures*. In microcomputer communications, layering is a way for programmers and designers of protocol to segment communications functions and give them some semblance of order and modularity. Particular sequences or *layers of protocol* are sometimes needed to ensure the accuracy of data transmission from beginning to end.

There is a very comprehensive model of data communications to help us understand the layering concept. Called the International Standards Organization (ISO) Open Systems Interconnect Model (OSI), this architectural scheme was designed by a prominent standards organization to support data communications functions. The model combines many of the finest features of commercial computer network architectures, such as IBM's SNA and DEC's Digital Network Architecture (DNA/DEC-net). But its significance to us is that it provides a useful framework to talk about any kind of data communications, including communications between microcomputers and between micros and mainframes as well. With the knowledge of the OSI model, we can figure out what computer connections entail, and what happens when each machine tries to connect to another that uses slightly different communications rules—different communications protocol.

Connection Bulletin

You can see how layered communications work in microcomputers immediately by turning to the step-by-step connection experiment (Apple IIe/Macintosh) on page 125. The experiment uses *ERA 2*, a software package and modem from Microcom, Inc. (Norwood, Massachusetts), both of which implement the popular Microcom Networking Protocol (MNP), a layered communications protocol that adheres closely to the structure of the OSI model.

One of the most intriguing features of *ERA 2* is that it tells you which layer of the MNP protocol is operating at any given time. If you are ready to swap files between an IBM PC and an Apple IIe, turn to page 128, where we demonstrate another MNP transfer using modems and communications software.

The OSI model is essentially a seven-layered architecture, as shown on the left of Figure 2.1: each layer supports different, but interrelated, communications functions, some of which run simultaneously and some in sequence.

ARCHITECTURAL MODEL

	OSI		MNP
7	APPLICATION	⎫ ————————	FILE TRANSFER
6	PRESENTATION	⎭	
5	SESSION	————————	SESSION
4	TRANSPORT		
3	NETWORK	————————	NETWORK
2	LINK	————————	LINK
1	PHYSICAL	————————	PHYSICAL

Figure 2.1 Not all of the layers of the ISO model need be implemented in microcomputer communications. Here is the version that Microcom uses. (Illustration courtesy, Microcom, Inc.)

The functions are extremely diverse. In mainframe communications, they include:

- Access to and establishment of a communications channel
- Conversion of data into digital form with modems
- Error checking (ensuring that groups of bits, known as frames or packets, arrive intact at the receiving node)
- Sending messages to the correct computer or peripheral on a network
- Incorporating such devices as fast circuit switches and communications multiplexors (multiplexors allow multiple-computer access to the same communications channel)
- Bypassing failed network stations
- Accommodating different memory buffer sizes of different machines
- Regulating message flow control rates
- Providing end-user file translation, format, code, and protocol conversion

The logical way to organize functions is to group them by similarity, assign them to an architectural layer, and then implement them in hardware and software. The highest layers, in software, control transfer of files, conversion of file formats, and character translation, while the lower layers interface to the physical transmission medium.

The OSI model provides the model for organization (see Figure 2-1). The left column represents the general model; the right (really a subset of OSI) describes the structure of micro-to-micro communications. A section by section explanation of the structure, as depicted in the figure, follows:

1. The physical layer represents a set of rules governing physical connection. The rules define all the electrical and mechanical aspects of connecting, maintaining, and disconnecting the physical medium for transmitting data. In concrete terms, the layer includes communications hardware, such as modems, the RS-232-C serial port (and other types of ports), communications lines, the signals they generate, as well as software to control and drive the hardware.

2. The data-link layer is built on the foundation of the physical link. This layer establishes a channel of communications between computers and controls access and use of that channel. The link protocol also provides instructions to the transmitting computer on how to frame the data in each message. The layer also assures the proper sequence of transmitted information, and checks the integrity of received messages.

3. The network-control layer is necessary for routing messages in complex communications networks. This layer specifies ways to control the flow of messages. Network protocol also designates procedures for establishing more than one communications circuit at a time over the same physical channel, a process called *communications multiplexing*, so that a computer can communicate with several other computers at once.

4. The transport layer regulates the communications session once the channel has been established. It provides what's known as "end-to-end" reliability over packet-switching networks—telecommunications networks that shuttle data in small blocks or "packets" of up to 2000 bits. Transport protocol allows computers to exchange data reliably and in sequence along these networks, regardless of the computer type or where they are physically situated.

5. The session-control layer provides a protocol to regulate the establishment and termination of connections. It adds information in the data packet, ensuring that pertinent systems information is transmitted back and forth, and provides for message-unit flow control and dialogue control. Session protocol also signals nonrecoverable errors to the transmitting computer, and bridges the gap between the transport layer and the communications program running in the computer as it communicates.

6. The presentation layer. Puts the data into forms that can be understood and manipulated by a human operator. Presentation rules translate encoded data from a transmission into a display format that

can be used by receiving computer screens and printers. It also provides services such as character code translation (e.g., translating ASCII into mainframe communications codes like EBCDIC, an ASCII-like code that uses 8 bits) and terminal emulation. The protocol also designates means of compacting, expanding, encrypting, or decrypting data. It provides a data structure for file transfers.

7. Finally, the applications or user layer provides rules for specific computing tasks. File transfers, sharing of resources, access to remote files (over communications links), execution of a processing task on the remote machine, handling of file-writing errors, database management, and network management are services incorporated in this layer of protocol.

The boundaries between any architectural layer are called interfaces. A given layer may only communicate with the layers immediately above and below it; that is, each layer performs services across an interface to the layer above, and uses services from the layer below. There is no direct dialogue permitted between non-adjacent layers. This limitation ensures the independence and modularity of each layer, so that programmers can alter functions in a single layer without significantly affecting other architectural layers.

When two computers communicate using OSI, functional elements in each layer communicate in a pairwise fashion across the physical transmission medium. In other words, modems communicate with modems, ignoring the content or meaning of the data they transmit. Data-link elements—instructions that frame data bits into discernible units—communicate directly with each other, controlling the flow of messages and assuring that frames are sent successfully across the connection. Network and transport elements, and so forth, address their counterparts, addressing and routing messages. Session control elements in sender and receiver manage the dialogue, sending pertinent systems information back and forth. Finally, presentation and application layer elements do the necessary data translation on each end of the line, converting data files for transfer and decoding and encoding files for the human operator.

Protocol controls each of these pairwise interactions. Originally, the OSI protocols and interfaces were written to encourage the development of a universally accepted communications architecture, one that would allow major vendors like IBM, DEC, and Honeywell to convert their products and protocols to the OSI scheme. Unfortunately, most manufacturers have maintained their own proprietary architectures; their layers of protocol are not identical. Certain mainframe software packages, for example, implement error-checking and message flow control functions in a lower architectural layer than other packages. Some mainframe packages eliminate certain functions altogether or provide special enhancements. Still others use programming techniques that depart from the modular or subroutine approach suggested by the OSI model. Not surprisingly, these different approaches boil down to different communication protocols. The result is incompatibility between different networking architectures, unless manufacturers choose to develop interfaces, commonly known as gateways, between them.

The OSI model thus represents more of a conceptual device than a strict standard for communications. While protocols for layers 1 to 3 have been fleshed out and generally agreed on (the standard for layer 3, for example, is implemented in CCITT's packet-switching protocol, X.25), work on the higher layers will continue for a number of years, leaving the implementation of higher layer protocols open to interpretation.

Programmers, however, still use the model as a way to divide a dizzying number of communications functions into manageable paths. The model has also been adapted to microcomputer communications; some packages today compress the OSI seven-tiered structure into three or four layers of function.

These functions are defined above in our micro model, which is based on the Microcom Networking Protocol (MNP), developed by Microcom, Inc. MNP is closely patterned after the OSI communications model; it is one among several competing communications protocols in the personal computer marketplace. Dozens of major software, hardware, and networking vendors have licensed it, though, so MNP has a chance to become a *de facto* communications standard. Whether or not MNP achieves that success, though, the model that emerges from its architecture is applicable to microcomputer communications functions in general. Packages may implement the layered functions differently, but most adhere to three or four major groups of functions.

First, there is the physical-link layer—hardware, modems, connecting cables, the RS-232-C interface, and all other physical components of connecting. This link must always be present in any communications. Next comes the data-link layer. The data-link here specifies how the software frames data bits into recognizable segments and does certain kinds of error checking and data-flow control. The third layer, the session layer, which manages the communications event by communicating internally with the data and file transfer layers, enables each computer to trade pertinent systems and file information. Finally, there's a file transfer layer, which incorporates a number of functions of both the presentation and applications layers in the general model, including file-translation techniques—ways of formatting data files so they are acceptable to the receiving computer.

Communicating with Micros: A Model Subset

These four layers, then, constitute the world of microcomputer communications. All rules and sequences can be explained by referring to these four functions.

Notice, though, that networking and transport protocol layers have suddenly evaporated. Why? By and large, networking protocols are not incorporated into microcomputer software unless the computers are part of a local-area network. In general, microcomputers are equipped only to do simple, point-to-point transmission along a single data channel. (Microcom, however, has implemented a new network layer protocol for some of its microcomputer modems that send and receive electronic mail.)

Transport layer protocols, the other missing link, were originally designed to check the integrity of data being shuttled along packet-switching networks. They haven't been incorporated in microcomputer software because programmers say the codes required would slow the package's running speed too drastically.

What remains, then, are the essential protocol layers that do the job of accurately sending batches of data from one computer to the next. Notice we say *accurately*. Many of the less sophisticated microcomputer communications protocols establish only a rudimentary data link and then send out characters in what's known as *terminal mode*, a mode that will accept data files regardless of what kind of shape they're in.

The more sophisticated protocols don't do that: they check for errors and provide other communications features, such as file translation (resolving incompatibilities between files swapped between different systems) and multiple file transfer. Packages that implement the more sophisticated protocols also offer lower level terminal mode to perform unmonitored communications. But their trademark is the higher level protocols—protocols that ensure reliable communications. You've probably heard some of the names of these protocols: BLAST, Transend, XMODEM. They compete for market presence with products implementing MNP, X.PC (a Tymnet link protocol), Modem 7 (a variation of XMODEM), and dozens of others. Each of these protocols offers a unique way for checking for errors and pacing data flow, among many other functions. The downside is that products implementing different protocols don't communicate, except in the lowest level, terminal mode.

A Step-by-Step Connection

Let's try a quick file transfer between an Apple IIe and a Macintosh using all the power of the Microcom Networking Protocol. As you connect, your screen will flash a STATUS message showing each stage of your link: physical connection, link request message, session request, and file transfer.

Special Features

MNP's primary advantage over other systems is that it resolves file incompatibilities and ensures error-free transmissions of data between virtually any microcomputer, mini, or mainframe implementing MNP. The software (*ERA 2* or other packages implementing the protocol) automates log-on and file-transfer procedures, allowing you to store that information under special "user function" files, which can be accessed and sent with a single keystroke.

Equipment

Macintosh Personal Computer with one microflopp disk drive and 128K memory	Apple IIe Computer, two disk drives 64K memory, DOS 3.3
MacModem and ERA 2 Software (Microcom, Inc.)	*ERA 2* Modem and Software (Microcom, Inc.)
Modular phone cord	the Apple IIe with
Modular jack	RJ 11 telephone jack

Procedure

Install *ERA 2* modem in an available slot inside the Apple IIe (or II+) and attach the telephone connector to the two-pronged plug located on the modem card. Now attach the modular connector to a phone cord, and plug the other end into the telephone wall jack.

Install MacModem by plugging one end of the connecting cable into the Macintosh phone socket and the other end into the MacModem socket. Attach the phone cord from the MacModem phone socket to the telephone wall jack.

Now boot your software and prepare for connection. Insert *ERA 2* in the Apple IIe, and the MacModem software disk in the Macintosh. Double click the MacModem icon. Choose the Display/Change Configuration option on the first menu you see on the Apple IIe. On the Macintosh, choose SETUP. You then drag down the menu with the cursor to COMMUNICATIONS, and then release the button on the mouse. You will see the communications-settings dialogue box. Select the speed and set it, then select parity and set it. When you are finished, click on the OK box, which will take you back to main menu.

On the Apple IIe, after initial boot, press RETURN, and the program will ask you to specify your modem slot number, dialing default (a tone or pulse), and the number and location of disk controller cards, clock cards, and the like. Answer the questions, press ESC when finished, and return to main menu. Your configuration will be automatically written to a disk file.

You are now ready to send and receive error-free text or binary files. Specify your own communications settings on the Apple IIe. Select your parity, bits, baud rate, duplex, flow control (X-ON/X-OFF) and other communications settings to match the remote system. You can change these in the Display/Change Communications Settings, which is accessible through option (3) of the main menu: Display/Change Terminal Setup.

Now enter Interactive Mode, and choose the menu option that lets you dial up the remote computer, Open Apple D, or set your modem to auto answer with Open Apple A. On an Apple IIe or a Macintosh, the dialing option will ask you to type in a phone number. The modem will automatically dial when you press RETURN. A status line indicates that the connection is established. Type back and forth in terminal mode to make sure your settings are compatible. Press Open Apple-L on both computers to initiate reliable link mode. This will automatically correct transmission errors as you type back and forth. When ready, press Open Apple F to begin an error-free file transfer. Type S to send a file, and R to receive one. If you are sending, the system will ask you to specify your file name, file type (message, text, or binary), and the name under which the remote computer will store your file. After you specify the remote file name, *ERA 2* will begin sending the file. A status screen monitors the connection until transfer is complete. You will then be returned to Interactive Mode.

On the Macintosh, pick Transfer option, and pick the kind of file transfer you want. Choose send or receive from the transfer menu, and click it. For example, you can select Send using MNP. A dialogue box, with a scroll box, will appear with a list of the files that can be sent. Then pick Send and the transfer will commence. Another dialogue box will keep you informed of the status of transfer, showing progress from physical-link establishment to file-transfer completion.

Unfortunately, a lot of communications protocols don't work this way. Some don't have as many layers (the session protocol exists in a comparatively small number of packages), and still others aren't programmed in a layered fashion at all, meaning their code is more or less linear, with very few subroutines. That difference, necessarily, will affect the way the software handles transmission functions. A linear protocol can't be expected to understand a protocol that communicates in a highly layered format. That in itself may spawn communications problems. But how do you begin to diagnose them? First, simple physical-layer protocols deal with the particulars of hardware configuration: modems, the RS-232-C interface, connecting wires, and telephones. In a typical PC-to-PC communication, physical protocol governs exactly how a computer is physically hooked to a modem through eight or more connecting wires defined by the RS-232-C interface standard. The modems, in addition to receiving data and control signals across the interface, convert digital information—a series of electrical voltages—into audio tones for transmission over a telephone line. This information is reconverted back to digital form by the receiving modem. Establishing this basic physical link requires that a particular series of actions be taken, all of which are dictated by the physical-link protocol.

As we mentioned before, the calling modem takes the phone "off hook" electronically and waits for a dial tone. Once it gets a tone (some modems can actually "hear" the tone; others wait a prescribed number of seconds before dialing), it emulates a standard telephone set in dialing the number of the intended destination address. The receiving modem now gets a ring signal, which its internal circuitry can detect as a request to connect to the line. It now goes off hook, transmitting a "connected" message. At this point, as dictated by the protocol, a series of greetings known as handshaking signals are exchanged. Hardware generates these signals; they flow across the RS-232-C interface from computer to modem and back again. The signals allow both computers and modems to monitor each other's readiness to send and accept data.

All of this happens because of the physical-link protocol. The proto-

RELIABLE FILE TRANSFER

```
  <----------------- FILE TRANSFER ----------------->
        <------------- SESSION ------------->
              <------- LINK ------->
```

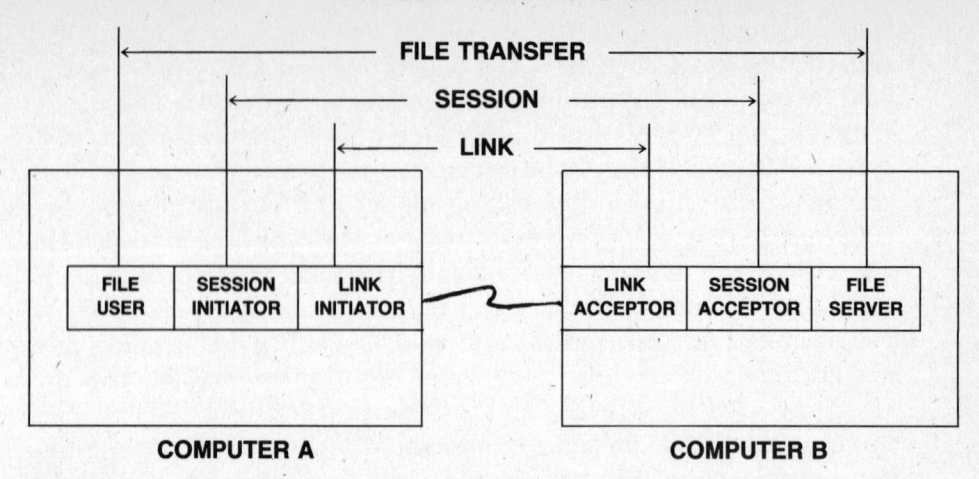

| FILE USER | SESSION INITIATOR | LINK INITIATOR | | LINK ACCEPTOR | SESSION ACCEPTOR | FILE SERVER |

COMPUTER A   COMPUTER B

Figure 2.2 These MNP protocols combine in a verified information transfer with MNP to provide reliable data transfer for a variety of computers. (Illustration courtesy Microcom, Inc.)

col defines the signals that computers and modems send back and forth. Thanks to the fact that physical protocols are standardized among the three Bell families of modems—the 103, 202, and 212A low-speed asynchronous modems—most microcomputers, in North America at least, can agree on basic physical connection. Modems with different protocol standards are in existence, and flourishing in Europe and other parts of the world. They conform to specifications by CCITT or individual manufacturers, such as Racal-Vadic. These modem protocols are not compatible with those of the standard Bell modems.

But what happens when communications become more complex, to include, for example, pacing of data, error checking, and sending of files between dissimilar computers? It's necessary at that point to employ the more sophisticated types of protocol available in software, like those shown in Figure 2.1. The programming instructions that define data-link functions go into action as soon as the physical connection is established. They establish whether the session will be full or half duplex, how many messages can be sent before an acknowledgment is required, how much data can be put into a single message, and what kinds of codes the link layer will use to cap each data message so that the receiving computer can understand it and clock it in. (Here we get into start, stop bits, and other forms of data flagging and framing.)

In most cases the user of the program specifies the link-layer rules by choosing menu options in the software before transmitting, rather than having the computers carry out some sort of automatic negotiations. Once these rules have been ironed out, the data-link protocol starts the data transfer and acts to regulate the flow of data and to monitor the phone line for noise. Control characters—a set of predetermined, nonprinting characters generated by the software or by the user on the keyboard—handle data pacing. In many microcomputer software packages, for example, the data-link protocol lets the program understand that a CTRL-Q (control key and Q key held down at the same time) keystroke combination means to start transmission, while CTRL-S means to halt a transmission temporarily. This is the famous protocol called X-ON/X-OFF. Another is called ACK/NAK (Acknowledge/Not Acknowledge). This latter protocol lets a receiving computer send an *acknowledge* control character to the transmitter, indicating a block of data was received correctly. Naturally, a *not acknowledge* character tells the transmitter "try again."

These kinds of simple pacing techniques are vital to the data link. They enable both sender or receiver to halt a transmission temporarily to take care of some other pressing matter. For example, a receiver might need to take a few moments to write the contents of a full memory buffer to a disk, so that its memory has space to store more incoming information. You also need pacing protocols between computers and printers, since, again, printers may write out data much more slowly than computers send those data. So computers must have some way of halting when the printer's memory buffer is full.

The data-link protocol also checks for errors. Some packages use primitive "parity checking" methods: the transmitter, acting on the command of the human operator, adds an eighth data bit to a 7-bit character, so that the sum of all the information bits is either even or odd. The receiving computer, set to accept data in "even" or "odd" parity, checks each character to see if the sum conforms to the specification. Still more complex and reliable error-checking protocols rely on *checksums*, mathematical sums tacked to the back of each data block that enable sender and receiver literally to check the sum of the bits to make sure they're identical at the transmitting and receiving ends. Still more complex methods employ *cyclic redundancy checksums (CRCs)*. In this technique, all the bits that represent data are operated upon according to a polynomial function and then divided by a constant; this task is performed by sender and receiver. The results are compared. If they match, the data block has been successfully transmitted; otherwise, a message is sent back to transmitter to send again.

A data link can only go so far in controlling the terms and pacing of transmission, however. A still more sophisticated layer of protocol, the session layer, has to manage communications functions that prepare for file transfers. A session protocol takes information from the human operator, specifically the names of the files chosen to send, and does all the internal communications work to get those files split up and sent out properly. Some session protocols (Transend is an example) stand between the data-link layer and the file-transfer layer. They get the human instruction, call on the file-transfer layer to read those files off the disk, and break them up into a manageable number of blocks, which are then sent out, one by one, by the data-link protocol.

In some packages, session protocols go still further: they provide, get, and keep required information about each computer system in the connection. For example, how do sender and receiver format their data files? Is space available on the receiving end for new files? What kind of information can be transmitted (e.g., a binary or ASCII text file)? How many files will be sent, and what types of computers are being used? Previously, much of this session management information was controlled by the human operator, but now some session protocols—MNP is an example—do it automatically. They may even be able to specify what kind of system should be communicating on the other end and establish a level of transmission service, such as a high-speed synchronous transmission or a low-speed asynchronous transmission.

But even with all of this power, microcomputer protocols would be incomplete without a file-transfer layer. Aside from responding to commands from the data and session protocols, the file-transfer protocol handles procedures for sending, receiving, and even appending an existing file at the other end of the communications link. Some file-transfer protocols allow a host computer to manipulate a distant computer's files: to delete them, to add to them, to call up a directory. Still others may offer the capability of resolving incompatibilities in file structure and even in hardware. This is done by implementing protocols that design and execute a *virtual file format*—a format that enables both sender and receiver to read a data file and convert it to whatever form is used locally. Such a protocol is used when sending files from an Apple IIe to an IBM PC, for example, or an IBM to a UNIX-based minicomputer. Both sender and receiver must implement the virtual file store rules to make this element work.

File transfer is thus considered the end result of all the transmission work. Once it's completed, the file-transfer protocol sends an end-of-file message to the receiving computer, which acknowledges receipt of the data and confirms that they were stored properly. Additional end-of-session and end-of-link messages may also be sent back and forth to close those respective connections. The file-transfer protocol may then defer, internally, to the session-layer protocol, which flashes a message on screen to the operator that the file transmission is complete. This provides an option to drop back to a lower level, terminal mode, for example, or to pick another file and begin again.

All these protocols, then, govern the complex interactions of a microcomputer transmission. There is tremendous variation in function from one package to the next. If we look at two protocols, Transend for Apple-to-Apple connection, and MNP in Microcom's *ERA 2* software and modems, they appear, structurally at least, to be similar. Both contain a file-transfer protocol, some kind of session protocol, and a packet-handling or data protocol. These protocols build on standard physical connections.

Nevertheless, a look at the layered structure of these two protocols shows some interesting results.

MNP	Transend
File Transfer	File Protocol
Session	Session
Network (in some products)	***(null)
Link	Link
Physical	Physical

In reality, the protocols are not similar at all. The big difference between them is that Transend is designed to send and verify data only between "like" hardware systems—Apple to Apple, or from IBM PC to IBM PC. It contains no instructions to handle hardware differences between dissimilar computers. MNP, a still more complex format, contains different session-layer protocol and file-transfer capability. Thus it can design virtual files to send back and forth between dissimilar computers.

The difference between the two is suggestive of protocol incompatibilities across the communications board. Competing protocols now deliver, within their own sphere of influence, so to speak, specialized services ensuring the integrity of data, the transfer of multiple files, even the conversion of file formats into virtual files. But because the protocols are proprietary, they cannot readily communicate. In the cases of Transend and Microcom, at least, you must have the identical software on both ends to take advantage of all the sophisticated protocols. Otherwise, you might as well go back to dumb-terminal mode, which has no error checking and will transmit only ASCII files. This is the most "plain vanilla" of all computer communications.

It would probably be impossible to write a conversion program to make Transend talk to MNP in a high level, verified mode. The differences in programming are just too great: functions and services, in general, must be incorporated into the same protocol layer. Moreover, the more sophisticated the protocol, the less likely it is to work with other protocols. And the more sophisticated you want the connection to be, the more things can go wrong.

What Can Go Wrong

You might get a hardware handshaking problem that will stop your transmission dead in its tracks. You may get a transmission going partially, only to find that crucial control codes are being screened by your computer's software. These control codes, codes, which are part of the data-link layer protocol, prevent your computer from formatting data correctly. You may get a mixture of illegible and legible characters on the screen if one of your communications parameters—a stop bit, a parity bit, for instance—is set incorrectly.

The problems could be more invidious. What happens when your computer starts to send a file of data in a verified mode and stops dead after your first character gets transmitted? Is it your hardware, your software, or both? Could it be that one of your communications settings is incorrect? Is it a file-transfer-layer protocol problem, or a link-layer problem? And what about message flow control, which is usually a characteristic link-layer problem? What happens when a transmitting computer doesn't read a control code sent by the receiver? It could refuse to transmit, or it could spew out loads of data, even though the receiving computer is signaling it to stop. That's a definite link-layer problem, a message flow control problem. The characteristic sign of that problem is that the receiver loses chunks of data during the transmission, according to a pattern, but not all the data.

And what about a session-layer problem, or a file-transfer problem? A session that can't ascertain the available disk space on a remote computer might send a file, only to find it's not received. A file-transfer protocol that can't format data to the requirements of the receiving computer might send along a good file that translates into nonsense characters.

Indeed, there are literally dozens of problems. Many pertain to data flow control, to matching of speeds between computers, and to readjusting communications parameters in the software. Some pertain to hardware peculiarities, to computer languages, to the ways computers read disk files. Before we begin to solve these problems, we need to discover which layer in the communications model is vulnerable. Finding vulnerabilities is not that hard: problems in each layer leave characteristic traces, as we'll soon see.

Learning to identify and solve hardware and software problems is the subject of our next chapter. We'll look at three case studies of computer-connect problems, and how three people solved them by isolating problems in hardware and software, and in each layer of protocol. We'll show you how they developed a plan of attack, moving from general understandings to specifics, and from intuition to a solid grasp of the rules.

The RS-232-C Blues

In the last chapter we hinted that both history and expediency have played a role in the adoption of communications standards and protocols. One particular standard, known as RS-232, an interface standard for connecting computers and modems together in asynchronous mode, is a case in point. Developed in 1969 by the major North American standards group, the Electronic Industries Association (EIA), RS-232 was designed to bring coherence to the interconnect universe. Subsequently revised (a "C" was tacked on to indicate the revision), the newer version, the RS-232-C, became the version that most microcomputer manufacturers in North America adopted. Notice we say *most*. A number of manufacturers implemented only subsets of the standard in their communications equipment. In many cases, the equipment was incompatible with other manufacturers' equipment, so when users tried to interconnect dissimilar computers together, using the so-called RS-232-C-compatible interface, they had a horrific time of it. What had evidently been designed to clear up confusion ended up spawning even greater problems.

Manufacturers argued early on that the standard was basically English language gobbledygook, defining interconnections for a very narrow range of communications equipment, mostly for specialized applications. Most of the standard, they claimed, wasn't useful for microcomputer communications. Standards makers retorted that manufacturers were implementing too many interpretations and hand-me-down versions of the RS-232-C. Many were using proprietary and lockout marketing strategies to keep customers buying exclusively in their product line.

Whatever the truth, the end result is that dissimilar computers often do not implement the same rules for connecting auxiliary equipment. EIA and CCITT, as vigilant standards groups, have attempted to make amends by developing yet other standards that might prove more attractive than RS-232-C. Indeed, many are designed to correct the defects of RS-232-C and to define yet other interfaces for different kinds of modems and networks. Now there are literally dozens of standards—RS-366, RS-422, RS-423A, RS-449, V.10, V.11, V.24, V. 28, X.21, X.21 bis, X.26, X.27. Most are gathering dust on the shelf. EIA in 1985 developed yet another standard, EIA-232-D, to replace RS-232-C and bring it more closely in line with international standards developed by CCITT and ISO. But whether manufacturers will rekey their interfaces to the newer standard remains open to question.

Indeed, standards have always been like isolated stepchildren, needed but ignored. Standards makers have no power to enforce standards; they release recommendations and documents; the computer industry either adopts or ignores them. Standards are made by consensus. RS-232-C, for example, is the only serial communications standard the microcomputer world widely implements; for several years, it has been the reigning interconnect standard. It is unlikely that EIA-232-D, which represents essentially minor modifications of RS-232-C, will immediately take hold.

The EIA standard's full title is *Interface Between Data Terminal Equipment and Data Circuit-Terminating Equipment Employing Serial Binary Interface,* which means that EIA is describing a means of connecting terminals, data terminal equipment, with modems, data circuit-terminating equipment, using a serial exchange of data. In EIA-232-D, certain definitions of communications equipment are broadened to include data circuit-terminating equipment in digital services. Serial exchange is a way of sending out data bits one at a time, through the communications port to the modem.

The RS-232-C standard has four parts: (1) a section dictating the voltage characteristics of each electrical signal on the interface; (2) the mechanical characteristics of the connectors (here the section dictates that plug and receptacle character of the interface—the receptacle must be on the DCE; pin number assignments on the plug are included); (3) a functional description of the signals on the interface, in which twenty-one signal definitions are given; and (4) a list of fourteen subsets of these twenty-one signals that are used in different types of modems. The new EIA-232-D document makes additions to RS-232-C: it includes, for the first time, an explicit description and diagrams of the 25 pin subminiature D serial connector, adds specifications for three new interface leads—local loop back, remote loop back, and test mode— and rekeys certain definitions to broaden the applicability of the standard to current equipment requirements.

In the main, though both EIA-232-D and RS-232-C cover such things as the protocol for answering calls and modem control for reversing the direction of transmission in a half-duplex link. In addition, they give names to all the important signals of the interface, many of which don't apply to microcomputer communications.

Manufacturers of microcomputers, usually design their hardware so that only a fraction of the signals will be used. They do, in general, adhere strictly to the signal voltage levels specified by the RS-232-C standard. Most will also design their connectors so that male plugs fit female receptacles of the modem. Beyond that, however, manufacturers may choose to design their connectors only to allow a certain subset of those twenty-one signals to pass through. Because many of the signals specified by EIA are superfluous to microcomputer communications, a number of manufacturers omit them altogther. Most concentrate only on eight or fewer major signals that allow data to be both sent and received (pins 2 and 3 are used for this purpose), as well as some handshaking signals that pass back and forth between computer and modem to regulate data flow. These eight signals—and subsets of those eight—form the basis of most microcomputer signal connections. They form the bedrock of the physical-link-layer we've talked about. Different implementations of those signals result in computer babble and headaches for you, the consumer.

Knowing that much background, though, is probably enough to get you started on practical interfacing solutions. It's not necessary to worry too much about other standards: they exist on paper, but not much in the real world. RS-232-C is the closest there is to a microcomputer serial standard, and that isn't very close to a real standard. But it is all we have to work with.

Indeed, trying to implement RS-232-C is like designing a narrow gauge track for a railroad system when the country is evolving rapidly toward supersonic travel. RS-232-C is a stopgap, no more. Eventually it will be replaced by standard digital interfaces—perhaps ISDN (Integrated Services Digital Network), a communications system designed to support simultaneous voice/data and video over a single line, which is now being tested in selected telecommunications sites around the United States. By the 1990s, ISDN may be the reigning interconnect standard; for now, though, RS-232-C, and its derivatives, continue to be of chief concern to users of personal computers.

CHAPTER 3
THREE COMMUNICATIONS CHALLENGES

- An Overfull Memory Buffer • Practical Solutions • A Speed-Matching Problem • Handshaking, Control Codes, and Other Mysteries

COMMUNICATIONS BASICS

Dial-up Line: A telephone line on which you dial for access to other lines. A leased line is a point-to-point line.

Line Feed: One of the control characters in the ASCII code set. Line feed moves the cursor on the terminal screen down one line when it is received. The action is analogous to feeding one line of paper in a printing terminal, hence the name.

Overtyping: A condition that occurs when a typist moves faster than the typing device can accept the keystrokes. This also happens when information is coming too fast from a communications channel.

Polling: A means of handling multiple communications devices connected to a single transceiver. The transceiver signals each device in sequence to allow it to transmit, if there is any information to send.

Speed Matching: Making sure that the speed of transmission is slow enough for the receiver to handle the data that are being received, considering that the receiver must perform certain overhead functions.

Upload: Sending a file from your computer to another. Download is just the opposite.

The following case studies illustrate the analysis and correction strategies used to solve three separate computer interconnect problems: (1) an overfull memory buffer; (2) a speed-matching problem between two computers of dissimilar hardware design and operating systems; (3) a problem of matching hardware handshaking signals and inserting control codes in transferred text.

An Overfull Memory Buffer

Apple II+: Communicates with Veederoot Fuel Master System, Loses Data

Synopsis: A popular-brand fuel-dispensing terminal equipped with a microprocessor and basic communications capability is connected via modem and dial-up line to an Apple II+ personal computer. The object is to download 1000 recorded fuel transactions from the terminal to the Apple II+. Data will then be loaded into *dBase II* on the Apple for manipulation and report writing.

Problems: Transmission proceeds clearly, but the Apple II+, equipped with a *Data Capture 4.0* communications program, loses more than half the data each time 1000 transactions are downloaded. The pattern of loss shows that forty transactions are lost each time *Data Capture* writes the contents of its buffer, 20 kbytes, to a disk file.

Details

In Oxnard, California, about 60 miles north of Los Angeles, Charlie Leighton and the Public Works Department were experiencing major difficulties getting an automated fuel-dispensing terminal to communicate successfully to a street division Apple II+. The terminal, a Fuel Master System, manufactured by Engineering Systems, Inc., of Tempe, Arizona, and marketed by the Veederoot Fuel Company of Hartford,

Connecticut, had been installed in an Oxnard equipment maintenance garage. It was the kind that recorded vehicle identification by reading codes off a plastic card the driver would insert each time he pulled in for a fill-up. Once the truck's current mileage was recorded, the terminal automatically activated one of several fuel pumps, dispensing fuel, recording the total number of gallons, date, and time of day. Leighton, a General Supervisor in the Street Division, was assigned to download these data to his division's Apple II+ personal computer. As many as 1000 transactions, each of which took up 58 bytes of memory, would be transferred from the terminal to the Apple during a single transmission. At the end of the month, he would merge the weekly records into a database program and present a report on fuel consumption. He was keeping track of 300 city vehicles.

Equipment

Apple II+ (48K RAM) Computer with two 5¼-inch floppies
Apple Super Serial Card
Racal-Vadic modem
16-byte memory card

Data-Entry Terminal
Fuel Master System equipped with a 300-baud auto-answer modem
Phone Line

Software

Data Capture 4.0 communications software for Apple II+ (Southeastern Software, New Orleans)

Communications software for fuel control unit burned into ROM.

First Results

When Leighton attempted the transmission, using his Apple II+ and modem to dial up the fuel terminal, he established a clear physical connection and was able to download data successfully. But because of the limited memory space of the *Data Capture 4.0* capture buffer, a kind of holding tank that captures incoming data, the communications program was able to record only 20 kilobytes of information—344 fuel transactions at a time— before automatically writing that data to a file, called Overflow-1, on disk.

During disk access, the light on the disk drive turned on, indicating the communications program was emptying its memory buffer. Meanwhile, the Fuel Master System continued to transmit data, but *Data*

Capture, busy with disk access, ignored the new data coming in. When Charlie surveyed the saved fuel-transaction files on his Apple disks, he found that he had lost roughly forty fuel transactions during each disk access. The total amount of data lost during any one transmission was roughly 4.6 kbytes.

Analysis and Correction Strategy

What had caused the problem? Charlie's immediate analysis pointed to an insufficient memory in the Apple II+. With 48 kbytes of available memory space, and only 20 kilobytes of capture buffer memory when equipped with *Data Capture 4.0* software, his Apple II+ couldn't capture the full 58 kilobytes of fuel-transaction data sent by the Veederoot Fuel Master System. The situation was worsened by the fact that the Veederoot terminal continued to transmit during each disk access. The new, incoming characters were flushed from Charlie's small modem-input buffer before *Data Capture* knew they came in.

Charlie's investigations of the problem indicated he could correct it in part by expanding the Apple's available memory space to capture more data from the fuel terminal. A second approach, however, pointed to a better solution: Why not find out the reason why the Veederoot system had continued to transmit when *Data Capture* accessed the disk drive? For some reason, the Fuel Master System was not monitoring the status of *Data Capture* during disk access and thus data were being lost.

A Broader Diagnostic

This proved to be the crux of the matter. We learned by contacting George McClelland, President of Southeastern Software, that the fuel terminal, for some reason, was failing to acknowledge a message flow control protocol that *Data Capture* used. This protocol, known as X-ON/X-OFF, allows *Data Capture* to signal the other computer that its capture buffer is full. Under normal circumstances, the receiving computer would get the X-OFF signal, a CTRL-S command, and temporarily halt transmission during disk access. It would once again resume transmission after it got an X-ON signal, a CTRL-Q, indicating *Data Capture* had cleared its buffer and was ready to receive more data. This simple method of data pacing would have prevented any loss of fuel transactions during the transmission.

Unfortunately, this Veederoot terminal is among many communicating devices that don't understand X-ON/X-OFF. In terms of our OSI communications model, it was lacking a simple data-link-layer protocol. All of Charlie Leighton's otherwise complicated problems boiled down to that. If both computers had acknowledged a message flow control protocol, his problem would have been solved.

Practical Solutions

At first Leighton opted to get around the problem by ignoring protocol altogether and working exclusively from the Apple end. He decided to expand the Apple's memory to capture larger chunks of data. The manual for *Data Capture 4.0* recommended one way to do it: by using a small programming routine, called a DOS (disk operating system) move routine. The program transports the operating system from its normal location in memory to yet another location—a RAM extension of 16 kbytes more than the Apple II+'s normal 48 kbytes. This maneuver frees an additional 10K of available memory, bringing the total capture buffer memory to 30 kilobytes. The additional space allowed the Apple to save an extra 200 transactions during each transmission. That partially solved the problem. But Leighton still had to go back and pick up the missing fuel data in separate transmission sequences.

The incompleteness of the strategy, though, prompted him to investigate other maneuvers. After much searching and discussion, he learned that an independent company had already written an Apple software program that would communicate directly, and effectively, with the Veederoot Terminal. The program, called *Automated Fueling System*, by Cork Control, Inc., of Missoula, Montana, automatically dials up any number of fuel terminals and polls them for fuel transaction data. It then uses a sequence of commands that packs the data into a shortened form and dumps them to the Apple memory. When data are sent, the flow is controlled through a simple control character protocol, ACK/NAK (Acknowledge/Not Acknowledge). In this protocol, the Apple sends a control character, CTRL-F, to the Veederoot terminal, indicating it has acknowledged a particular data transaction. The Apple sends a not-acknowledge control character, CTRL-U when it fails to read a transaction. That solves the problem of disk access if transmissions are exceptionally long. For example, if the Apple must write the contents of its buffer to a disk, it flashes a not-acknowledge signal to the fuel terminal; the terminal will keep transmitting the same data until the Apple is finished writing out its memory buffer. This prevents the Apple from losing any of the transmitted data.

Like the X-ON/X-OFF protocol, ACK/NAK is essentially a *software handshaking* protocol, a simple protocol designed to control message flow in the data-link layer. It is the one protocol that the Veederoot Fuel Master system understands. To get a transmission going, Charlie had to find a piece of Apple software that could match that protocol. Luckily, a company had already done it.

This points up a moral of sorts: if you can identify the problem, you can probably find someone who's either written a program to solve it, or can write a program to solve it. You don't need to write a program yourself if you don't know how. Users groups and vast public domain libraries, in addition to commercial ventures, offer a wealth of software that can help you solve your connection problem.

The chief issue, though, is accurate diagnosis. In this case study, a pattern of lost data indicated a breakdown (or lack) of important software flow control protocols. These protocols can prevent an overfull memory buffer from losing part of its contents. Overfull buffers and lack of control codes are common connection problems.

Two strategies for solution are feasible in such a case, however: either expansion of the receiving computer's buffer, through a DOS move or RAM expansion card, or use of a simple stop/start or acknowledge/not acknowledge protocol to pace the flow of data. Most microcomputer packages are equipped to handle at least an X-ON/X-OFF protocol. And many are now equipped with still more sophisticated protocols to pace data and check their accuracy.

A Speed-Matching Problem

Morrow Decision 1 Outpaces Apple II+

Synopsis: An Apple II+ is connected through an RS-232-C serial port to a Morrow Decision 1 using a jury-rigged adapter cable. The cable is wired so that send and receive signals (pins 2 and 3) are crossed, which permits both computers' transmitted data to feed directly into the receive wire of the other computer. Ground wires (pins 1 and 7) are mated without being crossed, and all other handshaking lines are tied together (pins 4, 5, 6, 8, and 20). Early tests show this cable configuration establishes a successful physical link.

Small programming modifications in BASIC are made to let the Apple receive text directly from the RS-232-C port and buffer it into memory.

The object is to enable the Decision I to transmit simple ASCII text files to the Apple memory buffer. These are then written out in a disk file.

Problem: As transmission begins, illegible characters, referred to as garbage, fill the Apple screen.

Details

In Aurora, Colorado, Ernest Mau, a computer writer, editor, and documentation specialist, was trying to get his Morrow Decision I, an S-100 bus CP/M computer, to communicate with an Apple II+ in the same basement office. He had a specific goal in mind for the connection: Mau wrote profitable word-find puzzles on the Morrow, and he wished to merge these with the excellent graphics capabilities of the Apple. So he decided to generate the puzzles on the Morrow and transfer them in ASCII text file format across the RS-232-C serial ports of each computer. His Apple DOS's *Toolkit* graphics program could then be used to illustrate the puzzles.

Having had extensive experience in direct connecting dissimilar computers, Mau had little trouble modifying a cable to connect to each computer's serial port. His initial setup included the following:

Equipment:

Apple II+ Computer	Morrow Micro Decision I
California Computer Systems 7710a Asynchronous Serial Interface card	Equipped with RS-232-C serial Printer Port
100-foot adapter cable with two DB-25 connectors bolted back to back (male to female).	Cable connection described above

Hardware handshaking signals (4, 5, 6, 8, and 20) were nullified by shorting them out. This solved the problem of hardware signal control across the RS-232-C interface. As Mau explained it, "It just eliminates the handshaking capabilities from the interfaces by making each computer think each handshaking line is present at all times." Mau found this cable configuration to be "an almost universal connector for intercomputer communications among several different machines."

Once the physical link had been completed, Mau expected that he could send standard files at a speed of 1200 baud—roughly 150 characters per second—without a modem. That equalled the speed of most of the fastest modems in the microcomputer market at the time, and also saved him the hassle of tying up phone lines in his house.

Mau, however, had no communications software to handle the transmission. Consequently, he had to modify a BASIC program on the Apple slightly so that it would accept incoming data directly from the RS-232-C serial port, load it into memory, and finally write out a disk file when done. Mau achieved this goal by modifying a *MAKE TEXT* program provided on the Apple DOS 3.3 diskette. He was able to make simple changes that would allow the Apple to accept characters from the port rather than from the keyboard.

First Results

With these changes in place, Mau thought he was set for the data transfer. He had chosen the simplest and easiest file format—ASCII text files—a universal file format that is understood by virtually any microcomputer, no matter what make. Even with these precautions, though, Mau got "nothing but garbage" on the Apple screen. "The Apple was misinterpreting the ASCII codes from the Morrow," he said. What was the cause?

Analysis and Correction

Mau retraced his steps. Since he was knowledgeable about communications, and boasted a programming background, he had already made sure that his Apple knew where to look for incoming data. He didn't think there was anything wrong with his modification of the *MAKE TEXT* program or with his cable connection. Instead, the screen garbage had a characteristic appearance that made him suspicious.

"I knew what I was sending to the Apple was clean material," he said, "but it wasn't being received clearly." Mau suddenly remembered that the Apple screen display had a quirk to it: it could be overtyped or overwritten if Mau forgot himself and typed at the keyboard too rapidly. Was it possible that the screen was being overtyped by characters coming in too rapidly from the RS-232-C port?

Mau checked the transmission speeds of each computer. Both the Morrow and the Apple's communications port were set to send and receive data at 1200 baud. Yet the Morrow indeed seemed to be transmitting data faster than the Apple screen display could handle.

Broader Diagnostic

There's no question that Mau's computers were suffering from a speed-matching problem. Despite the overt match between transmission rates, 1200 baud, data were still arriving too quickly, given the Apple's peculiar screen display. A definite hardware limitation—the Apple's screen speed, the rate at which it turns data into visible characters on the screen—had turned good data arriving at the port into garbage on the screen. Mau really had only two alternatives to fix the problem: either speed up the Apple screen or slow down the Morrow. By far, the easier approach was the latter.

Practical Solutions

It was a relatively simple matter to write a program in BASIC to slow down the data transfer. Delays could be inserted after each line of text. "I put in a delay loop," he said. "There would be a delay after Morrow would send a line of data, which simply allowed the Apple to catch up." Though Mau had to write a small program to accomplish this task, sending data line by line, and inserting pauses after each line, he noted that this is often a built-in capability of communications software packages. Simply by accessing a menu, an operator can elect to send text character by character, or line by line. That solves a great number of speed-matching problems generated by hardware.

Indeed, speed matching is a common problem in microcomputer communication, especially when computers connect directly through serial ports. On one level, simple pecularities in one computer's hardware (a screen speed display is an example) will affect data transport in the physical layer. Garbage characters will appear in the data stream because of hardware distortion. Protocols, then, are needed to control speed and to match speed. These protocols affect the data-link layer: they are basically flow control protocols. A delay after a line is a way to get one side to slow down so the other side can keep up.

Handshaking, Control Codes, and other Mysteries

An Osborne I sends partial files to a Radio Shack TRS-80 Model 100, but control characters are misinterpreted or stripped out.

Synopsis: An Osborne I is connected on separate occasions to the

Radio Shack TRS-80 Model 100 portable computer using (1) direct modem cable without phone line, and (2) RS-232-C direct-connect cable. Separate programs are used to control each connection. The objective is to send Radio Shack text files to the Osborne for massaging with *WordStar* word processing and other applications programs.

The first modem cable connection, at 300 baud, allows the TRS-80 to transfer data to the Osborne's buffer successfully, but the Osborne fails to write the contents of the data to a disk file. Data transfer in the other direction is yet more difficult and cumbersome. In the direct cable connection, the Osborne I will not accept standard ASCII text files and control codes, and appears not to recognize the TRS-80's end-of-file control characters during the connection. Separate keyboard control characters must be entered. In the direct cable connection, hardware handshaking signals may be missing, which prevents the Osborne I from recognizing end-of-file signals from the other computer.

Details

In Briarcliff Manor, New York, software consultant George Heidenrich was attempting direct data transfer between his portable Radio Shack Model 100 and an Osborne I. Heidenrich, who did a great deal of writing on the Model 100 while traveling, wanted to transfer files easily back and forth to the Osborne, and also to a Xerox Memory-Writer correspondence-quality printer. This would let him format data files and programs using the most appropriate software and output equipment available.

First Tests

A preliminary test of the Osborne's telecommunications capability indicated the machine was functional. Heidenrich, relying on documentation provided by a client, used a standard modem connection (the Osborne comes equipped with a modem) to access GTE Telenet's Telemail electronic mail service. Having first gotten a screenful of garbage and legible characters, Heidenrich realized that communications parameters in his software program, *AMCALL*, from MicroCall Services of Laurel, Maryland, were not set correctly. He experimented with parity checking until he completely cleared the problem.

After telecommunications with public databases, Heidenrich began his direct-connect experiments in earnest. He first attempted a direct transfer of data from his Radio Shack Model 100 to his Osborne I using a modem connecting cable, which plugs into each machine's modem port. These ports are separate and distinct on each machine from the RS-232-C serial port, which is distinguished by its 25 pin or hole connector. Heidenrich's modem connection simulated an actual communications data transfer through a telephone. "All I want to do is get a carrier tone going from one modem to the other, and I want the other to hear it," he said.

The initial transfer set up was as follows.

Equipment

Radio Shack TRS-80 Model 100 (portable computer with 24K)

Osborne I (transportable computer) 2 disk drives, 64 kbytes memory

Software
TELCOM (built into Model 100)

Set to answer a call

AMCALL (MicroCall Services, Laurel, Maryland)

Set to "O" for originate call

Communications Parameters Setup

Radio Shack
300 baud, 7 bits, no parity, one stop bit, X-ON/X-OFF enabled.
(The code appears on the Radio Shack screen as M7N1E, which translates to Modem, 7 bits, No parity, 1 Stop bit, X-On/X-Off enabled.)

Osborne I
(Same settings on *AMCALL* menu; 8 bits on each will also work).

Parameters were set identically, so that physical- and data-link protocols would match. Heidenrich also specified "O" in the *AMCALL* menu for originating the call. By entering an @ command and pressing the return key, he enabled *AMCALL* to send a high-pitched carrier signal to the Model 100. Model 100, recognizing the signal, buzzed. Heidenrich then pressed a RETURN key and F4 on the Model 100, allowing it to enter Terminal Mode. The Osborne flashed a message showing the connection was established.

First Results

Once this happened, Heidenrich was rippling with delight. He could type back and forth on either the Model 100 or the Osborne, and the characters appeared on the other computer. No line feeds were sent, however. They appeared to be stripped out, and he had to enter line feeds separately by using a CTRL-J command on the Osborne, which enabled the computers to space the entry of each line.

When Heidenrich decided to send a Model 100 file to the Osborne, he set the parameters accordingly. Pressing an ESC-R keystroke command on the Osborne, which prepared it to receive a file, he pressed an F3 key (File Upload) on the Radio Shack, specified a file name, and a width. Pressing a RETURN keystroke enabled the Model 100 to send the file at whatever width it took. The upload light on the Model 100 turned on, indicating the file was being sent. Characters streamed across the bottom of the Osborne screen. No extra line feeds or carriage returns had been added.

Checking the Osborne disk file directory, Heidenrich discovered that the file had not been recorded. After much experimentation and reading of the Model 100 manual, he typed in a separate CTRL-Z keystroke on the Model 100 keyboard. This closed the file and enabled the Osborne I to write it to disk.

Analysis and Correction

"Evidently, the Model 100 never sent an end-of-file character to the Osborne during the ordinary transmission," Heidenrich observed. The end-of-file character had to be input separately, by hand. It was also possible that the Osborne was missing, or failing to properly interpret, some of the Model 100's automatic control characters sent in the data stream. The control characters are generally used by each computer to control the formatting of files. The fact that line feeds were missing during the connection indicated that some control characters were being screened out. The problem could be solved easily, however, by entering separate control characters, for example, CTRL-J, CTRL-Z, from the keyboard once the transmission was complete.

Reverse data transfer (Osborne to Model 100) proved to be a still greater problem. The Osborne would send text only line by line, waiting for a CTRL-Q command from the Model 100 to enable it to continue sending. The Model 100 never sent the command, and it could not be sent manually from the Radio Shack keyboard. If

Heidenrich entered separate CTRL-Q keystrokes on the Osborne keyboard, though, text could be sent. But this method proved unsatisfactory, since he had no desire to stimulate transmission manually after each line.

A Second, Direct Cable Connection

Heidenrich decided to attempt a fast, serial transfer of data by hardwiring the RS-232-C ports of each computer. He used an adaptor cable he built himself. The pin configuration worked as follows: Transmit and receive lines ran straight through from the Model 100 to the Osborne without a crossover. The Osborne is configured as if it were a modem for communications. Ground wires were also mated directly. Handshaking lines were more of a problem. Heidenrich, following a recipe specified by FOG (Daly City, Calif.), an Osborne user's group, nullified pins 4 and 5 on the Model 100, as well as pins 6, 8, and 20. He left all the corresponding pins on the Osborne alone, meaning they were not connected. This allowed both computers to receive and transmit as the other computer had cleared it for transmission. More explicit details of connections like these are in Chapter 10.

A software connection that would work was another problem. Heidenrich could not use the *AMCALL* program because it was designed only to work with modem connections, not with RS-232-C serial ports. He had to find some other means for getting the Osborne to accept data—and control codes—from its serial port. The answer Heidenrich found was a program called *PIP* (Peripheral Interface Processor) which resides in the Osborne's CP/M operating system. This program, as Heidenrich explains it, "talks to the physical device, the RS-232-C port, directly from the operating system." That enables the operating system to process the control characters embedded in the Model 100 text.

Set Up and First Results

To set up communications, Heidenrich needed to use a program in CP/M called STAT, which told PIP exactly how to talk directly to the RS-232-C serial port. The commands established a basic physical connection. Model 100 *TELCOM* parameters were set to send and receive data out the RS-232-C port at 1200 baud, 8 bits, no parity, one stop bit, X-ON/X-OFF enabled. Heidenrich entered a terminal mode command to allow the Model 100 to communicate with the Osborne. He pressed the upload key, specified a file name, a width, and pressed carriage returns on both the Model 100 and the Osborne. Once again, a CTRL-Z keystroke was needed on the Model 100 to send an end-of-file instruction to the Osborne. Line feeds, however, were not sent, only carriage returns. Separate commands were entered on both the Osborne and the Model 100 to close the file and write it on the disk. In the reverse direction, the Model 100 was able to receive data, but with errors. PIP continued not to recognize end-of-transmission control codes.

Diagnostic

The Osborne and Radio Shack Model 100 problem proved extremely complex. Even with the PIP program, modified to accept data from the serial port, Heidenrich found that control characters from the Radio Shack computer were still being screened out during transmission. To solve this problem, he had to find exactly which control characters PIP was looking for and then embed those characters in the text in order to save the Model 100 file. A similar strategy would be needed to get files transferred in the reverse direction, from the Osborne to the Model 100.

Heidenrich hasn't hit paydirt yet; he's still looking for a better solution. He suspects that his direct-connect cable is responsible for at least some of his problems. Without the correct hardware handshaking signals, neither computer can properly monitor the status of the other. This affects the physical link protocol, including the establishment and termination of a connection. That problem is compounded by a hardware or software screening of control characters in the data stream. Heidenrich is working on this by changing communications parameters affecting the PIP program. He is experimenting with setting the PIP parameters to accept non-ASCII files. This is a "trick" that may allow the Osborne to accept many of the Model 100's control codes.

CHAPTER 4
THE PROBLEM: COMPUTERS DON'T TALK ALIKE

- Incompatible Operating Systems ■ The Invention of CP/M ■ Incompatible Disk Formats ■ The Communications Solution ■ Incompatible Communications Hardware ■ Incompatible Applications Programs ■ ASCII Code

COMMUNICATIONS BASICS

Instruction: A string of bits that causes a microprocessor to perform some action.

Instruction Set: The collection of all instructions acted upon by a particular microprocessor.

I/O Slot: An electrical connector connected to a personal computer's input/output structure that allows connection from the computer to the outside world.

Operating System: The program in a computer that contains instructions for interaction with all the peripherals connected to the computer.

Interface: A general term meaning either the act of connecting two machines together, or the physical means by which the connection is accomplished.

RS-232-C Standard: The recommended standard for serial communications promulgated by the Electronic Industries Association (EIA). It is being renamed EIA-232-D.

Port: The gateway through which data pass from the computer to the outside world, and from the world to the computer. A port is actually a combination of hardware and the software that makes the hardware perform its function.

Each of the men in Chapter 3 had a particular problem with computer communications. To find solutions in hardware and software, they had to subdivide the components of the problem and then isolate a faulty element within one or more of the components. Engineers use this technique all the time in diagnostic work. They develop models of a problem, and portions of the model represent faulty components under study.

As we've already seen, there's a model for computer communications, the OSI Open Systems Interconnect Reference Model. If we use this model, then we can take the complex difficulties that these three encountered—or any set of communications problems, for that matter—and dissect them to determine where within the layered approach the problems are occurring. This gets us through the complexity somewhat and into solving the problem.

Data communications is complex, though, and the OSI model requires several architectural layers to explain all that happens during a transmission. In this chapter we discuss why the complexity exists and, where appropriate, relate it to representations in the model.

Basically, there are three major reasons for problems in personal computer communications. These include incompatibilities in operating systems, incompatibilities in the implementation of the communications hardware (and some software), and incompatibilities in the applications programs that the computers are running. Let's take a close look at each of these to see just what the incompatibilities imply.

Incompatible Operating Systems

There are several operating systems that run on personal computers today. On some computers, the operating system is almost transparent, so a user needs to think little about it. Such operating systems are those buried in the BASIC language of inexpensive home computers—the Commodore 64 is a good example—and the operating system that handles all the complex chores that make the Macintosh computer the wonderful graphics machine it is.

Other computers—the IBM PC is a perfect example, as are the Radio Shack TRS-80 Models I through IV computers—have operating systems more closely tailored to mainframe or minicomputer operating systems. And, of course, before the advent of the IBM PC, there was a *de facto* standard operating system for business microcomputers, called CP/M, which stands for Control Program for Microprocessors. CP/M, another operating system that mimics those running on minicomputers, is still in wide use today. Of course, the users of IBM personal computers and compatible computers are familiar with PC-DOS, and its more generic version, MS-DOS. PC-DOS was developed specifically for the IBM PC.

The operating system contains all the basic intelligence of the machine. By that we simply mean that the operating system contains all the instructions for printing a character to the monitor screen, writing information to disks, inputting data through a local communications port, and so forth. Just as our bodies have a basic set of instructions they follow with no additional input from us—breathing, for example—computers have no need of instructions other than those in their operating systems to perform basic functions. Commands must be input to initiate these basic functions, of course, because a computer, being a nonsentient machine, can do nothing without external commands. But once a command has been received, the computer follows the instructions in its operating system to carry out the command.

At this point we can ask a logical question: Why do we have operating systems that are so different, given that they are such fundamental programs?

There isn't a really satisfactory answer, but here's a stab at one. When the personal computer industry was new, there were no microcomputer operating systems. An operator made a computer do something by loading in a series of instructions through the use of front-panel switches. The instructions were a series of binary digits, as they still are today, and each different series of digits meant a different operation to the microprocessor. Of course, two microcomputers having different microprocessors needed different sets of instructions put in through these switches. Different microprocessors took dissimilar actions when presented with a particular set of digits that makes up an instruction. Thus two different processors were said to have different instruction sets.

The Invention of CP/M

Then along came Gary Kildall, who was working at the Naval Postgraduate School in Monterey, California. He wrote CP/M to run on the 8080 Intel microprocessor, which was a popular processor for microcomputers at that time, particularly those used in business.

CP/M quickly became a general-purpose operating system. It is currently published by Digital Research, the company Kildall founded. CP/M is general-purpose because its hardware requirements are open; that is, it doesn't make any difference which hardware you connect to the computer system, because the software operating system, which controls the hardware, handles that control requirement through the use of logical devices. A logical device denotes a general function of the microcomputer; the device is one that the operating system knows how to handle. A physical device, in contrast, is the specific piece of equipment chosen to perform the function designated in the logical device. For example, CP/M defines the device RDR: as something that acts like a card reader, and it has instructions for obtaining information from card readers.

Other early computers, by their very nature, had no need for such a general operating system because their hardware requirements were simple. Apple II personal computers, for example, originally used no disk drives, so their first operating system was in ROM-based BASIC. As demand for disk drives with Apples increased, though, Apple DOS was written to handle interaction with the drives. Still, there was no requirement for other peripherals that was too large for the original operating system, closely linked with BASIC, to handle. So CP/M machines interpret instructions differently from Apples. The differences between them exemplify an early parting of the ways in computer design. In fact, as different personal computers with dissimilar microprocessors and applications proliferated, the operating systems that contained their basic instructions multiplied as well. So today we have a hodgepodge of operating systems: MS-DOS, Apple DOS, CP/M, TRS-DOS, among others. They are different and incompatible. But even their incompatibilities would not be a problem were it not for the fact that every different operating system writes information to a floppy disk in a different way.

Incompatible Disk Formats

This is really the heart of our problem. If it weren't for incompatible disk formats, which stem from operating-system incompatibilities, then there would be no real problems making computers communicate. Similar operating systems and identical disk file formats would actually reduce the need for communications solutions (telecommunications or serial cable) because operators could easily insert their data and program disks in one computer and then another; each computer would be capable of reading (and writing to) a disk without further difficulty.

Ernie Mau, for example, who wanted to transfer files from a CP/M-based Morrow Micro Decision I directly into the Apple II+ would have been able to insert one disk from the Morrow drive directly into the Apple drive, eliminating the need for a hardwired solution. Charles Leighton, by the same token, would not have needed a telecommunications setup; he simply would have transferred his disk from the Veederoot fuel terminal directly into his personal computer.

George Heidenrich's problem was more complex. He wanted to transfer the Radio Shack TRS-80 Model 100 word processing files to his Osborne so that he could format and then print them. Had the operating systems and file formats on the disks been identical, he would have had no problem. But in reality, the Model 100 stores information in internal memory, not on a disk drive (there is a drive available for this computer as an option), so a direct disk transfer wouldn't have been possible anyway.

The Radio Shack/Obsorne connection points up an adjunct problem to file format incompatibilities: these are incompatibilities in disk size. The problem gets more acute as you allow for more computers, some of which, like Macintosh, don't even use the same size disks, let alone identical disk formats. But, as we've already seen, there is a way to get information from one computer to another, even when the disks are not alike. The solution is computer communications.

The Communications Solution

Communications software will handle the interface between the different operating systems and the communications medium as defined in the session-control layer of the communications model. Remember that this layer of the model contains those rules that handle the interaction between the transport layer and the operating system. This means that communications software takes care of the disk incompatibilities by performing all the translations, clocking, timing, reading, and writing needed on both ends of the communications line to make each computer compatible with the line. Then the computer handles the information it transmits and receives as its operating system tells it to do.

We should point out that there are programs available on some computers that allow those computers to emulate the drives of another machine with their own disk drives. For example, the Kaypro 4 has a utility program in its CP/M operating system allowing the user to specify different disk formats (all CP/M formats, but slightly different from one another) for both of the computer's disk drives. Thus the Kaypro 4 can read the disks written by some other CP/M computers, and can write disks for later reading by those other computers. The Kaypro, however, can't handle Apple disks or IBM PC disks: it requires a separate program to handle the information transfer between these dissimilar machines. (A list of such programs appears in Appendix D.)

What's needed is a much more general solution to the communications problem. To get to that solution, we have to go still further, to incompatibilities in communications hardware.

Incompatible Communications Hardware

As we mentioned in Chapter 2, there's a standard for digital communications hardware used in the United States. It's called RS-232-C, which is being modified and renamed EIA-232-D. This standard was developed for one purpose only, to enable different manufacturers to make terminal devices that connect properly to modems. The early terminals were printing terminals, while later the so-called "glass-Teletype" terminals, the ones with CRT screens, came about. In the standard, all such terminals fall under the generic name *data-terminal equipment* (DTE). By the same token, modems were meant to communicate with the outside world over the phone lines, so they were called *data-communications equipment* (DCE) in the standard. DCE has now been modified to include a larger range of equipment, known as *data-circuit terminating equipment*, but for our purposes DCE will suffice.

The standard was developed for the express purpose of defining the way to connect terminals to modems for communications over phone lines. That's all well and good, but here's the problem. No one envisioned the personal computer at the time the original RS-232 standard was developed. So should a personal computer be a DCE or a DTE? The RS-232-C—the C is a revision level—standard doesn't say. Consequently, some computers' communications ports are set up as DCE, and others are DTE. Moreover, if you allow a personal computer to be equipped according to the standard, then what about other devices? What about printers, for example? Because a printer was intended to run in accordance with the standard, it is called a receive-only (RO) terminal. We therefore know what to do with a printer— it's a terminal—so it's a DTE, and it communicates with a DCE.

But does that mean that personal computers are, or should be, DCE? And if so, what does that imply about connecting a personal computer to a modem, which is clearly a DCE?

Well, these problems are really close to insoluble. Straightening them out would take a massive effort of a standardization committee, and the cooperation of all manufacturers involved. Standards committees meet all the time, but their work is complicated and time-consuming. And when personal computers came out, everyone wanted to make them communicate. There wasn't enough time to iron out all the difficulties. So manufacturers made do with what they had. In fact, as we mentioned earlier, they implemented those parts of the standard that made sense to them, leaving out what seemed superfluous to their own implementation.

Almost all computer makers used, or said they used, RS-232-C-compatible communications devices. What they didn't specify was the particular subset of the standard for hardware they had implemented. So competing—and incompatible—subsets of the RS-232-C standards became rife in the personal computer marketplace.

We'll talk a lot more about the RS-232-C standard in Chapters 9–11, including its implementation in computers and how to figure out what particular flavor of interface your computer has. If you're anxious to dive into this arcane subject, then be our guest. But it might be best to hold off a moment and see how these incompatibilities are represented in the layers of the OSI communications model. In this way, we can deduce a consistent means of attacking the communications problems we'll find.

RS-232-C implements portions of the physical-link layer and the data-link layer of the communications model. These layers are at the very base of the communications connection, so you can imagine that if two computers should communicate with one another, yet have different implementations of these basic link protocols, communications would be a problem. In effect, the two computers will not be following the same sets of rules in these bedrock layers.

The Other Communications Port

All this talk of RS-232-C would lead you to conclude that this is the only communications standard for small computers, and that's not true. There is another standard called the Centronics Parallel standard that is also widely implemented in personal computers and printers as well.

RS-232-C is used to define serial communications—communications that happens one bit at a time. Bytes, eight bits, are sent one bit after another, with bits added to those required for information transmission to tell the receiver where the information starts and stops.

Parallel transmission happens a byte at a time. In a parallel-transmission scheme, there are eight signal-carrying wires, compared with the one in a serial scheme.

The Centronics Parallel standard is implemented in parallel printer ports that come with many computers. The IBM printer adaptor, for example, is a Centronics-compatible port. The IBM Asynchronous Communications Adaptor, in contrast, is an RS-232-C-compatible serial port.

And what, you ask, is a port? A port is actually the sum of the hardware and software implementing a communications standard. It is like a portal, or gateway through which data passes to and from the outside world.

Since the RS-232-C link, and the ports that implement the link are so important, they are also the first consideration in any attempt to make communications between computers work. It is not always true, but often true, for example, that computers are configured as DTE. Two DTEs cannot communicate with one another without modifications to the physical-link layer of the communications system: the wiring of pins on the physical interface, in other words, and the electrical signals that cross the interface.

You will recall that physical and data-link problems—problems associated with the RS-232-C standard—were the first problems that Ernie Mau and George Heidenrich had to overcome on their way to a communications solution. In Mau's case, in particular, he had two computers, configured as DTE, that would not communicate with one another without modifying the physical link. (More about physical interfacing in Chapters 9–11.)

Incompatible Applications Programs

But physical and data-link problems, principally incompatibilities in hardware, in other words, pale in relation to incompatible applications programs. Applications compatibility is the last hurdle in data communications.

Once the information has gone from one computer to another, once the data-link-layer problems of timing and message flow control are solved, once the physical link is intact and compatible from end to end, once the session-control layer and the transport layer have performed the actions they must, there still is the problem of actually seeing the data that have been transmitted (after all, you have to see the information, courtesy of the presentation layer of the model) and then having your program do something with the data that the presentation layer lets you see.

This latter problem is quite simple to illustrate, although it can be difficult to solve. Suppose that data are kept somewhere in a database format. The separate data items in a record are separated by the comma (,) which is called a field delimiter. Suppose these data are sent to another computer that has a different database program running, and that program expects the data items to be separated by a space— not a comma—as a field delimiter. What happens when it reads in the data that came over as a result of a data transmission? You can imagine the answer. Not encountering a space, and not recognizing the comma as a field delimiter, the database program in the receiving computer tries to read all the data items in the first record into the first field of that record, and that just won't work.

Charlie Leighton had something of this problem. To solve it, he had to shift the information that came from the fuel terminal through a couple of programs to make the formatting work properly, finally, in his ultimate application. Applications compatibility is a real challenge.

We should point out that there are some subtler, deeper parts to this problem. For example, how does the receiving computer and its applications programs understand the data that have been communicated in the first place?

ASCII Code

American Standard Code for Information Interchange (ASCII) solves that problem in most cases. Data are normally transmitted as ASCII-coded text files, and personal computers, and almost all applications programs, understand ASCII. There are some exceptions. With some programs you have to ensure that you're sending the proper kind of ASCII-based characters into the communications line. We'll discuss these in detail in our modem and direct-connect case studies.

ASCII code is a 7-bit binary code used to represent every letter of the alphabet, as well as the necessary punctuation marks. There are 128 possible combinations of the binary digits 1 and 0 using ASCII code. It's employed in a large number of communications applications. We have an ASCII code chart included in Appendix A. There is another code, an 8-bit code called EBCDIC, for extended binary-coded decimal interchange code, which is used in IBM mainframe communications. It has 256 possible code combinations. EBCDIC is not used in personal computer to personal computer communications.

ASCII is thus commonly used to transmit data between personal computers. But data are one problem, and transmitting programs is another.

Some programs are stored in machine code—strings of 1s and 0s. BASIC programs, for instance, are stored in a short, compacted form called a *tokenized form*. If you were to read these programs as they are stored in a computer or on disks, they would make no sense, unless you employed the services of several code-translation charts. Because such translations are needed, sending a program from one computer to the next calls for more care than simply transmitting a letter or memo. Various error-checking protocols are employed to transfer programs or other plain binary data whose sense cannot be reconstructed from context. ASCII-coded documents, in contrast, can be reconstructed from context. You simply read a plain-English document, transmitted in the ASCII-code format, and you can make sense of any mistransmitted characters.

So ASCII code is an almost universal data interchange code. Though some programs can also read data in binary form, most of these can pick up data in ASCII text form as well. Files encoded in ASCII are thus often referred to as text files. Operating systems and applications programs understand data that have been encoded in ASCII. But what are the components of a character represented in ASCII?

We've noted that ASCII requires seven bits to represent information. But still other bits are added to the 7-bit representation of a character to solve the problems of sessions and transport-layer control.

The added bits are called stop, start, and parity bits. We've already discussed these bits in Chapter 2. There is always one start bit for each character, and there can be as many as two stop bits. Moreover, there can be a parity bit, used to check for errors. Thus a character sent into a communications line as ASCII code can have as few as nine or as many as eleven bits. Obviously, the session-control layer at both ends of the communications line must be set to expect only a certain number of bits per character, or else communications will not be interpreted correctly.

But if interpretation at the sessions level is correct, and data are flowing properly, and their representation as numbers and letters is correctly displayed on the screen, there is still the problem of the applications compatibility. The database transfer is one example of a problem. Spreadsheet programs provide us with another.

Suppose, for example, that a manager wanted some portion of a spreadsheet to be provided in a form suitable for inclusion in a letter. Specifically, assume that the manager was in one office of a company and needed certain data added to a letter to the president, and that information was in a spreadsheet file in another office. No problem, you think. The manager can very simply transmit the file from the other computer to his own, and then just insert the data, letting his word processor handle the merging process.

It won't work. The files are incompatible.

)D10:@SUM(D5...D8	The file on the left is a file
)C10:@SUM(C5...C8	of sales data for a company
)B10:@SUM(B5...B8	saved by a spreadsheet
)A10:"TOTAL	program on an Apple II computer.
)D9:/ – =	The data items in the file are
)C9:/ – =	saved with additional items
)B9:/ – =	of information appended to them.
)A9:/ – =	For example, the 9500 entry at
)D8:9500	cell location D8 has that
)C8:9400	address preceding the data
)B8:9100	item. When the *VisiCalc* program
)A8:"REGION 4	sees that data item coming into
)D7:9000	the computer, it knows that 9500

)C7:8900   is to be inserted into the cell
)B7:8700   located in column D and in row 8.
)A7:"REGION 3
)D6:7780   Other data items are preceded by
)C6:7700   their spreadsheet addresses as
)B6:7500   well.
)A6:"REGION 2
)D5:9750   The final items in the data
)C5:9100   stream represented by this file
)B5:9900   are information *VisiCalc*
)A5:"REGION 1   needs to set up the spreadsheet
)D3:/FR"MAR   display the way the user wanted
)C3:/FR"FEB   it.
)B3:/FR"JAN
)C1:"MODEL   Another program can either
/W1   use this information literally,
/GOC   exactly as it appears, or mis-
/GRA   understand the address informa-
/GF$ tion and use it incorrectly.
/GC9
/X!/X)A1:)A1:

Figure 4.1 Incompatible files.

The illustration of Figure 4.1 shows a file that was saved from a spreadsheet. The data in the file represent information about the first quarter's sales of some company, broken down by region and then totaled. If this were the information that you wanted to include in a letter to the company president, then you can see that there's no way you can load it into a word processor and expect it to print in a format that will make sense to another person. A word processor will treat the information in exactly the way that you see here, that is, it will take the data as strings of information with no interpretation.

In reality, of course, the strings of characters include data, but they also include instructions to the spreadsheet program in which the data were developed. For example,)B7:8700 is interpreted by this particular spreadsheet program as "GOTO cell B7 and there insert the value 8700." The other character strings are interpreted in similar ways. The instructions tell the spreadsheet program how to format the information in a way that will make sense to humans. But a word processor has no such formatting instructions, so it treats the strings of characters as just that, and presents them in a manner that is very difficult to understand.

This is a comparatively small problem, showing applications incompatibility, but it nicely illustrates our point: in all their ramifications, applications incompatibilities are significant. They are the driving force behind the movement toward ever more integrated computer applications.

Integration is one way around the problem, but there are others. In the particular case that we have illustrated here, the solution is quite simple. We simply print the spreadsheet file, but instead of using a printer to print the file to paper, we print it to disk. The file is sent to the disk as though it were being sent to a printer, complete with formatting, spaces, line feeds, and the other niceties needed to make the data really convey information.

A word processor can then merge the file as it has been printed to the disk for inclusion in a letter to the company president, as shown in Figure 4.2.

```
                   JAN           FEB           MAR
  REGION 1      9900.00       9100.00       9750.00
  REGION 2      7500.00       7700.00       7780.00
  REGION 3      8700.00       8900.00       9000.00
  REGION 4      9100.00       9400.00       9500.00
  ------------------------------------------------
  TOTAL        35200.00      35100.00      36030.00
```

Figure 4.2 Spreadsheet files can be printed by a word processor. This model was printed to disk. Printing effectively follows the spreadsheet's formatting instructions, leaving a spreadsheet that a word processor can print. But the basic file isn't compatible with a word processor.

These sets of incompatibilities, then—operating system and disk format, hardware, and applications—cause many of the foul-ups in communications, and also the convoluted layering of the communications model. Applications incompatibilities, in particular, are the ones manufacturers have paid the least attention to as of this writing. Consequently, applications require the most innovative solutions on the part of users. These are solutions that no one can prescribe in detail in advance, since programs and communications needs vary widely. Also, you won't see the need for an applications solution until the data have already arrived at the receiving computer and you prepare to down load them into a program.

But to get to that point, you have to get on the air and make computers communicate. There are several ways of doing this: through a modem and telephone lines, through modems without telephone lines, or with a direct computer-to-computer connection.

The modem is often the simplest solution, and we detail its use in the coming chapters.

CHAPTER 5
MODEMS AND WHAT THEY DO

- Kinds of Modems ■ Modem Speed ■ Modem Protocols ■ Inside a Modem

COMMUNICATIONS BASICS

ACIA: An integrated circuit (also called SIO or UART) that handles the data conversions and manipulations necessary for serial communications.

Auto-Dial/Auto-Answer Modem: A modem that can dial the phone and respond to a ring signal automatically.

Bandwidth: A figure of merit for a communications channel that describes the amount of information the channel can carry. The greater the bandwidth, the more information the channel can carry.

Bus: A collection of wires used to carry electronic signals from place to place.

Flag: A term, in computer programming, synonymous with indicator. When a flag is "set" (usually by changing the value of a bit to a logical 1), it indicates that some condition, like the presence of a data carrier, is valid.

Frequency: The measure of speed of oscillation of a time-varying electronic signal.

Frequency-shift Keying: The modulation scheme used in Bell-103-compatible modems. Different data values are represented by tones at different frequencies.

Phase-shift Keying: A modulation scheme in which the phase (the mathematical integral of frequency) is changed to reflect a different information content.

A modem is absolutely necessary for your computer to be able to communicate over the telephone line.

The telephone system wasn't designed for data communications. Except for special data lines, telephones were designed to carry voice signals only. The human voice varies in tone from one individual to the next because voices have different fundamental frequencies. (*Frequency* refers to how fast a periodic waveform is changing.) A sine curve is a periodic waveform; it repeats itself after a set space of time called the *period*. Frequency is the measure of how quickly the periods occur. Frequency is, in fact, the inverse of the period.

While there is a great range of frequencies with which humans can communicate, the information contained in voice communications can be transmitted economically by using relatively few of these frequencies. Thus the telephone company long ago decided that it had no need to use cables and amplifiers for telephone communications that were capable of transmitting a wide range of frequencies—or even very high frequencies for that matter. As a result, the voice telephone system is said to have a *limited bandwidth*, bandwidth being a term that describes the range of frequencies a system will transmit without attenuating, or weakening, the signals at those frequencies.

Computers, however, require wide-bandwidth transmission. The signals that computers use, the 1s and 0s that make up internal computer code and also make up ASCII code, have high-frequency components, and if they were to be input to a telephone line as they are, the high-frequency parts of the signal would be attenuated, while the low-frequency parts would not. If you were to look at the signal that came out the other end of the line, you'd see a signal that didn't look at all like the signal that was injected into the line at the start. The computer on the receiving end would very likely not get the information that was intended for it.

Thus there has to be a device that will convert the computer's internal signals into signals the phone line can handle, and then reconvert the phone-compatible signals back to computer signals at the other end. The device that does this is the modem.

Modem stands for MODulator/DEModulator. *Modulation* is the process of changing some characteristic of a signal—either its size, called *amplitude*, or its frequency, or its *phase*, which is related to frequency in the same way that distance is related to velocity. Amplitude modulation (AM), is a popular modulation scheme used in radio and television broadcasting. Frequency modulation (FM) is used in those media as well. In these modulation methods, a high-frequency signal, called a *carrier*, because it carries information, is changed in accordance with the information that the carrier is to transmit. Demodulation is the process of recovering information from a modulated signal. It is the reverse of modulation.

Modems use other kinds of modulation. Some modems, the low-speed ones, use frequency-shift modulation. It works like this: a modem that's on the telephone line, ready to communicate, is transmitting an unmodulated carrier. If you listen to the phone line, you'll hear a steady tone. The tone carries no information with it—it's just a noise. To make the tone carry information, we have to change it. With frequency-shift keying (or modulation), the frequency of the tone is changed to a different frequency when information is present. There's one frequency for a mark—a low signal or 0—and a different one for a space—a high signal or 1.

When a 1 bit comes into the modem for transmission down the telephone line, the modem changes the pitch of its carrier to that assigned to it for a 1. Conversely, when a 0 bit comes in, the modem changes pitch to that assigned for a 0. Thus if you were to listen to a phone line that is carrying computer information, you'd hear a series of beeps of different pitch, as the information is sent to and fro on the line, assuming that the information is being sent slowly enough for your ear to resolve the differences in pitch. Low-speed personal computer communications are slow enough that you can hear the tones change.

So that's what a modem does. It changes the digital pulses a computer uses into audio-frequency tones that can be sent over the telephone lines, and then at the other end, it changes the audio tones back into digital pulses the computer can use.

Kinds of Modems

There are many different kinds of modems. Even if you already have a modem, you probably don't understand all the options that other modems have. Modems can be divided into two broad categories:

Figure 5.1 The LEX-11 acoustically coupled modem from Lexidata. Note the rubber cups on the top of the modem. You put a telephone handset in the cups. Clearly, this isn't designed for a princess phone. (Illustration courtesy Lexidata, Inc.)

direct-connect modems and acoustic-coupled modems. There are many subdivisions of these major categories.

The simplest kinds are the modems that don't directly connect to the telephone lines. Rather, acoustic modems, like the one in Figure 5.1, have rubber cups mounted on them into which you place your telephone handset. The audible tones that the modem produces are sent to a small speaker in the rubber cup; these are picked up by the telephone handset's mouthpiece. The reverse happens with incoming data—the modem receives the audible tones coming over the telephone line from the earpiece of the telephone, because there's a small microphone mounted in the rubber cup into which the earpiece is inserted. Modems like this are called acoustic coupled modems.

Other modems are called direct-connect modems. These are devices that use common phone plugs to tie them to the telephone lines.

Acoustic-coupled modems have no need to dial another phone number; you can do that yourself before plugging the telephone's handset into the rubber cups on the modem. If you're waiting for a call from another computer, you can pick up the telephone, verify that

Modems and What They Do 75

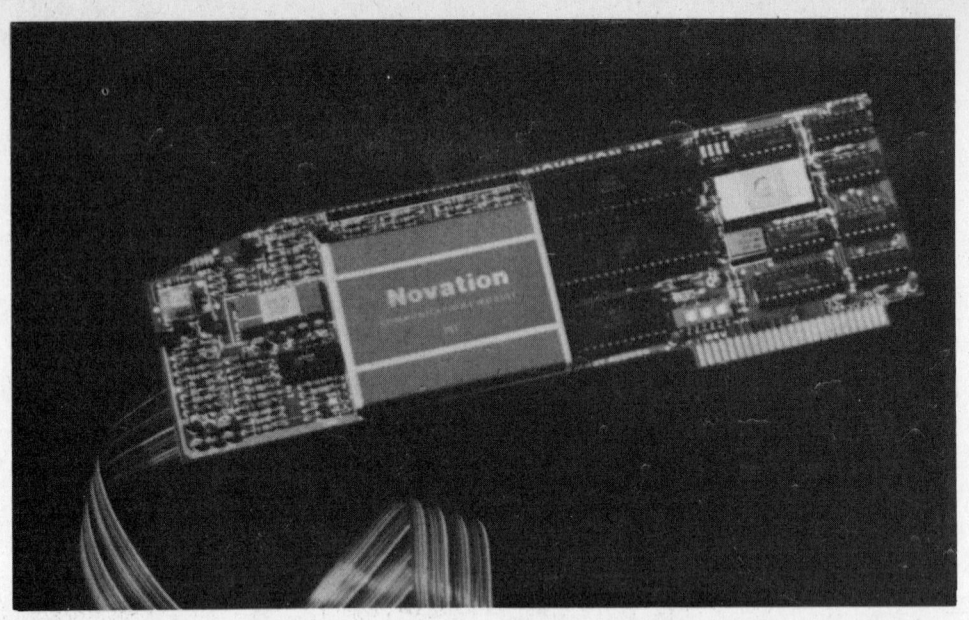

Figure 5.2 This Novation modem is a card modem for the Apple II. (Photo courtesy Novation, Inc.)

there's a modem on the other end of the line, and plug the handset into the cups; there's no need for the modem to answer the phone, either.

A direct-connect modem, like the one in Figure 5.2 on the other hand, has to be able to dial and answer. It's going to be on the phone line all by itself, with no telephone instrument to help it communicate. A modem that can automatically answer a phone and dial is called an auto-dial, auto-answer modem. This kind of modem is more expensive than the ones that require you to do all the dialing and answering work.

Some modems connect into the telephone itself, and yet require you to do the dialing and answering manually. This kind of modem has the advantage of both low cost and data accuracy exceeding that of acoustic-coupled modems.

Data accuracy, or transmission accuracy, is a subject we'll explore further. Accurate transmissions are vital if you have sensitive data to move from one place to another. For example, if you're moving data, such as binary numbers, which you can't easily decipher yourself, then you need accurate transmissions. Some communications software takes the need for accuracy into account by adding error-checking information to each byte of data. But accuracy has to start with the communications hardware, which includes the telephone system. Hardware can degrade the quality of the received or transmitted signal, so that software has to check to see if it's correct. If hardware were perfect, there would be no need for error correcting in software.

Acoustic couplers try to seal out the ambient noise—the noise that is present in the environment of the coupler—by using the rubber cups to seal the handset into the coupler. But as the cups wear, or if the coupler is jolted, then the coupler can leak, which can degrade the transmission accuracy. That's why a direct-connect modem will provide more transmission accuracy than will an acoustic-coupled one.
On the other hand, acoustic-coupled modems have a major advantage—portability. You can use them wherever there's a telephone, even if the telephone happens to be in a booth on a busy street corner. You can't do that with any other kind of modem.

Modem Speed

Once you know about the types of modems, then there's still another question that has to be at least considered: modem speed.

Possible speeds are set by various standards-setting bodies. Then modem manufacturers build products to these standards. It is often thought that there are only four data-transmission speeds, 110 baud, 300 baud, 1200 baud, and 2400 baud. But there are actually a large number of possible speeds for data transmission. You only hear about those mentioned because they happen to be the speeds supported for the voice network by the old Bell System. A Bell-103 modem would transmit and receive at 110 or 300 baud, while a Bell-212A modem would transmit at 300 or 1200 baud. New 2400-bits-per-second (bps) modems will run at all the speeds mentioned.

Transmission Speed

Data-communications speed is measured in baud. A baud, spelled this way, is not a woman of easy virtue; rather it is a measure of bits per second—actually, flux changes per second. To use the term baud rate is redundant, because baud is, by definition, a rate.

The Modern Dictionary of Electronics, by Rudolph F. Graf (Howard W. Sams & Co., Inc. 1977) defines baud as "A unit of signalling speed derived from the duration of the shortest code

> element. Speed in baud is the number of code elements per second."
>
> Unless the modulation scheme is exotic, which, for personal computer, low-speed communications, it isn't, then the speed in baud is equal to the number of bits transmitted every second. But don't be misled by this statement. There are as many as 12 bits to every character sent over a communications line. Thus the speed in baud must be divided by the number of bits per character to determine the transmission speed in characters per second. If you are sending 12 bits per character, then at 300 baud you're transmitting 300/12 or 25 characters per second.

We should mention, by the way, that a 1200-bps modem such as the PC-compatible card modem in Figure 5.3 modem uses a different modulation scheme than does a 300-baud modem. The faster device uses phase-shift keying; it doesn't change the frequency of the tone to indicate a 1 or a 0. It also sends more than one bit of information for every signal change, so the speed in baud is not equal to the bit rate. Three hundred-baud modems, in contrast, use frequency-shift keying, which does change the tones you'd hear on a phone handset. If you listen to a 1200-bps transmission, however, you won't hear the tones change.

These transmission speeds are easily within the capability of the voice-phone network. Remember that we said that the network has a limited bandwidth. The smaller the bandwidth, the slower digital communications must be if the communications are to be reliable. So the limited bandwidth of the phone network means not only that we have to install a modem to make our computer communicate over the lines but we must also transmit at limited speed to use the lines reliably.

How limited is that speed? Most computers with serial interfaces, and that's almost all personal computers these days, can transmit and receive information as fast as 19,200 bps, provided that a lot of software conditions in the operating system are met. But we've been poking along at 1200 or 300, for the most part, simply because the phone system can handle that speed, and modem manufacturers don't have to add a lot of sophisticated electronics to improve speed. We should point out, though, that 2400-bps modems are appearing on the scene, and they'll become more and more available as the cost of electronic components continues to decrease and error-checking protocols become easier to implement.

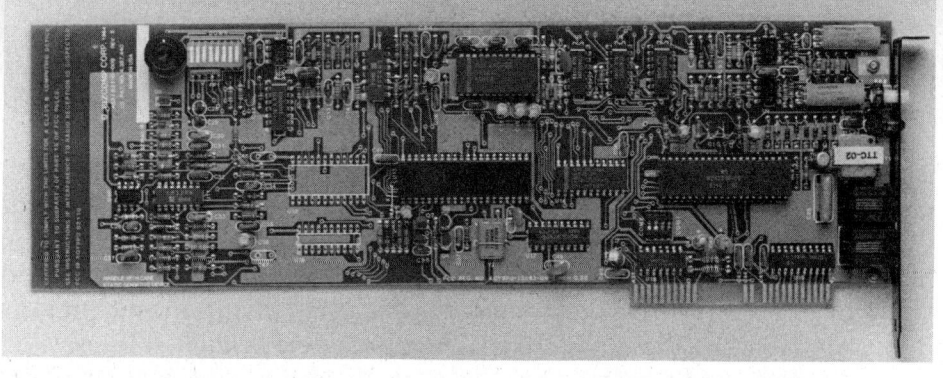

Figure 5.3 The Bizcomp PC: Intellimodem, a card modem for the IBM PC and compatibles. This modem is Bell-212A-compatible. (Photo courtesy Bizcomp, Inc.)

Modem Protocols

We've already noted that protocols are nothing more than the rules by which some interaction can take place. Modems have protocols for communications. If the modem is of the acoustic-coupled type, then its protocol is pretty simple. It sends its appropriate carrier signal (called the *originate carrier* or the *answer carrier*) to the other modem as soon as it detects the receipt of the other carrier. On many modems of this type, you have to physically set a switch that tells your modem whether it is originating the call or answering it.

On the other hand, a direct-connect modem has to determine first of all what's going on, who's calling whom, and what it's going to do about it. If the modem is calling, for example, it has to be programmed to send an originate carrier into the phone line when it detects an answer carrier coming in over the line. If it's waiting for a call, then it must, as soon as it detects the ring signal coming in (a short pulse of high voltage on the phone line), pick up the phone (by closing a "hook switch") and send an answer carrier. The two carriers are of different frequency, so they can exist on the line at the same time. If you have ever heard an auto-answer modem answering the phone and hooking up, then you have heard the two different tones that are, in effect, the different carrier frequencies, originate and answer.

If the modem is operating in half duplex, then there's another set of protocols that comes into play. Half duplex is, as we've already pointed out, a communications mode in which only one computer can talk at a time. When computers use half duplex, then they operate with rules that manipulate signal lines that connect the computer to the modem. When a modem transmits in half-duplex mode, it uses these lines to determine when it can send information, and to tell the other computer that it (the other computer) is free to send information over the line. The computer changes the state of these lines as a result of information it gets from its communications program, or as a result of ASCII characters that come over the line. Most modems you'll come across don't operate in half duplex. They follow the Bell-103 standard, which is a full-duplex standard. On the other hand, most communications software allows you to toggle a parameter called Duplex. That parameter really refers to a different phenomenon called echo, not duplex. Local echo, often called half duplex, means your computer screen will display characters you type; that is, you can see exactly what is going out from your computer onto the communications line. Remote echo, erroneously called full duplex, in contrast, means your computer does not automatically display characters to your own screen; it relies on an echo of the character from the remote computer.

The modems use such communications protocols to get ready to transfer data. These rules are properly called hardware protocols because they are implemented completely in the communications hardware. After the hardware protocols are done, then it's the time for software protocols to take over. They are discussed in the next chapter.

Inside A Modem

All these hardware protocols are fulfilled inside the modem. Which rules are observed depends on the kind of modem. Modems have different internal designs, and they fulfill three major functions. First, the data have to be converted to the proper format for transmission. Then, the data must be converted to the audio tones that are sent over the line. Finally, the actual transmission takes place. If the modem is receiving, the opposite sequence occurs, and the functions are the inverses of those described. Some modems do this all in one place, in one electronic circuit, while others assign functions to different locations.

Telephone lines are serial transmission media; that is, they can only handle one piece of information at a time. You can think of the words you speak into the telephone as discrete chunks of information. Each of these chunks follows another into the line, and they come out the other end one at a time, in sequence.

If we want to move digital information, made up of alternations, or pulses of voltage that represent bits of information, then the bits have to move sequentially, or serially down the phone line, just as voice signals do. And there's the rub, because the information that's inside a computer travels in parallel, not in serial. That is, inside the computer, data move over what's called a data bus. A bus is a collection of wires, in electrical terms, and the data bus is a collection of eight, sixteen, or thirty-two (sometimes more) wires along which data can travel. When the CPU calls for the data in a particular location in an Apple II computer, for example, it gets 8 bits of data at a time; the data have traveled from memory to the CPU in parallel.

The CPU sends data in parallel to a location where a modem will transmit them. But before these data can be handled by the modem, they have to be converted from parallel data to serial data by a device called a parallel-to-serial converter. This is one part of a more global device called a serial communications port, or an RS-232-C port or, in some computers, an asynchronous communications port, as we've already mentioned.

Many people look at a particular D-shaped connector on the back of a computer and assume that this connector is the serial port. Others look at a circuit card and say that is the port. Neither idea is correct, although both are close to being correct. The port is really a concept. It's like a theoretical gateway between the computer and the outside world. Some ports are one-way ports, like printer ports; some are two-way ports, like ports to which modems connect. But ports aren't connectors or circuit cards. Rather, they are the whole implementation of the standard, or set of rules, by which information flows through the port: where the information is, what form the information will take, what the voltage and/or current levels will be, etc. An RS-232-C port is a port that follows the rules of EIA's recommended standard 232. At some point, new computers should implement portions of the newest EIA standard, EIA-232-D, an improved serial port specification.

Some modems are external to the computer. Where do they get the information they are to send over the telephone line? They get it from an RS-232 port inside the computer, either one the manufacturer built in, or one that the computer owner bought and installed. Some modems, though, called card modems, go right inside the computer itself. The Hayes Micromodem IIe and the *ERA 2* modem from Microcom are examples of card modems, the first for the Apple IIe computer and the second for the IBM PC or the Apple II series. These cards handle parallel-to-serial conversion, formatting, modulating, and transmitting all in one shot; they implement RS-232-C port functions and don't require a separate serial card.

If the modem isn't a card modem, though, then the parallel-to-serial conversion, the formatting in accordance with communications protocols (number of stop bits, parity, number of data bits—sometimes called *framing*), and the electrical conversions of data in accordance with the RS-232-C standard are accomplished in a separate circuit card that implements the functions of the RS-232 port.

The RS-232 card will have an integrated circuit on it that goes under a number of different names. The most common is probably UART, for Universal Asynchronous Receiver/Transmitter, although it's also called ACIA (Asynchronous Communications Interface Adaptor) and SIO (Serial Input Output), depending on which semiconductor company manufactures it. They all accomplish the same function, namely, to frame the data to be sent and to recover the received data coming into the port This integrated circuit has a certain number of memory locations on it, called *registers*, where it stores status indicators, called *flags*. Flags indicate things like the presence or absence of a detected remote data carrier or whether the user wants to add parity bits to the characters being sent. Based on the status of the flags, the UART can do different things, such as adding different numbers of stop bits or setting other flags to warn of trouble in the data transmission.

When you initialize a communications port with your computer, there are default values of the communications parameters that are loaded into the registers on the communications chip. You can then change them later through software.

There may also be a small microprocessor on the serial card or it might be in the modem box, if the modem is in a separate box. Figure 5.4 shows such a modem. This microprocessor (sometimes called a microcontroller) operates on a program that's stored in ROM to allow it to do such things as auto dial, and, perhaps, run its own internal terminal program. It will be this microprocessor, running the modem program stored in ROM, that will determine just how smart a modem that's touted as being "smart" really is. A high degree of programmed intelligence in the modem isn't necessary for communications to occur, since the communications controller, the UART, has the programming necessary to make communications happen.

So this is a modem, and that's the way it works. Using a modem, it turns out, is the simplest way of getting two computers to communi-

Figure 5.4 Radio Shack's Bell-212A-compatible modem for high-speed data transfers. (Photo courtesy Tandy Corporation)

cate. Modems can be used to call from one computer to the other when the computers are running on two different phone lines. They can be used to make two computers communicate without hooking the computers up to the external phone system. They are easy to use, and we review exactly how they're used in the next chapter. Then in Chapter 7, we describe how to connect computers through modems, but leaving the phone company out of the picture.

CHAPTER 6
THE MODEM DECISION

- Preliminary Considerations • The Phone Company • Transmission Accuracy • Using Communications Software • Communications Parameters • Hooking Up a Modem • Transferring a File

COMMUNICATIONS BASICS

Capture Buffer: The area that a communications program reserves in memory to retain the data that are transmitted and received during a communications session.

DB-25 Connector: The connector that became the *de facto* standard (and soon should be the published standard) for electrical connectors that implement the RS-232-C interface.

Firmware: Instructions for a microprocessor that are placed in read-only memory. Like software, firmware can be changed, but with difficulty. But it is installed like a hardware memory device; thus it is neither hard nor soft, merely firm.

Intelligent Terminal: A terminal that is capable of more functions than just the reception and transmission of data. An intelligent terminal can store data on floppy disks, for example.

Noise: Any of several kinds of random signals that can be present in a communications channel. Noise degrades the integrity of data communications.

The chief considerations in choosing a modem are functionality and cost. What kind of modem do you really want? How fast should it go? Should it be a card modem, or should it be one with a separate box that can be attached to any number of computers through a standard RS-232-C serial interface? How much should you spend?

Preliminary Considerations

The two principal kinds of modems, as we noted in the last chapter, are the acoustic-coupled modem and the direct-connect modem. The first is easier to operate, but gives you fewer functions and is less costly. Acoustic modems are easily connected to the phone line, assuming you have the ordinary telephone desk set. Princess phones and all their variants won't work, as they won't fit into the cups.

There is one other disadvantage to acoustic-coupled modems. After some period of time, you might start to get errors in transmission simply because the rubber cups that grab the telephone handset will leak. When that happens, outside sound can get on the phone line, and that's death for transmission accuracy. All you need is one wrong bit in a 7-bit ASCII character and the character is received or transmitted incorrectly. The crash of a lamp on the floor or a slammed door can give you that wrong bit. But if you're not planning for heavy-duty use, and data-transmission accuracy isn't a real problem, then an acoustic-coupled modem might be just the choice.

If you opt for a direct-connect modem, though, you'll have more functions to play with. Most of these modems will provide you with auto-answer and auto-dial capability, the ability to change speed in software, automatic hanging up of the phone, and more. To use these functions, of course, you have to know how to access them, and how to use them once you've gotten access.

Direct-connect modems can be card modems or separate devices. Card modems are made for specific brands of computer, while stand-alone modems can be used with any computer that has an RS-232-C port. In general, if your computer has an I/O bus (the bus will look like a series of black female plugs with gold contacts somewhere near the rear of the computer), then you'll need an RS-232-C circuit card to connect to your modem. If you have a computer that's the all-in-one-piece kind, look on the back panel of the computer and see if there's a plug labeled "RS-232-C." Most portables, Macintoshes, Lisas, TRS-80s, and so forth, have these ports already installed in the computer. If the port isn't installed, you'll need one, whether your modem will be a direct-connect type or acoustic-coupled.

How fast should the modem be? If you decide to go the low-priced route and spring for an acoustic-coupled modem, then this question is already answered for you: it will not work at more than 300 baud. That translates into 25 to about 40 characters per second (cps), which sounds pretty fast. Consider, though, that slow dot-matrix printers run at 80 cps, and slow daisy-wheel printers poke along at about 25 cps. Either one of them seem to take an eternity to finish a job once you get used to computer speeds. So after a while a 300-baud modem will seem slow.

It will seem even slower if you use your modem for long-distance computer-to-computer communications and then look at the first phone bill AM (after modem). Calling from New York to somewhere in California and spending 20 minutes on the phone every day during working hours can give you a jolt. The way around this, of course, is to use a 1200-bps modem, the newer 2400-bps series, and, if you're a business user, the ultra-high-speed asynchronous "smart" modems that now run at up to 10,000-bps rates over dial-up (not specially conditioned) phone lines.

The Ultra-Fast Modems

By mid-1985, leaders in the data communications field had introduced expensive, but highly intelligent modems capable of transmitting over voice-grade phone lines at speeds eight times faster than 1200-bps modems, and with complete error checking.

One such modem, Irma FastLink, developed by Digital Communications Associates (DCA) and Telebit Corp., was introduced in July 1985. Touted by its manufacturers as transmitting at speeds of up to 10,000 bps in asynchronous mode, FastLink was the first of a new generation of modems that begin to approach the speed and efficiency of synchronous modems used in mainframe networks.

> The Irma FastLink is equipped with intelligent features. It automatically downgrades speeds in increments of 100 bps or less when necessary to accommodate poor transmission lines. The modem uses two microprocessors and a new packet technology to transfer information and monitor the status of the phone line. The packet technology and special signal processing capabilities of the modem increase usable bandwidth on normal phone lines by 50 percent. The modem can also communicate with Bell-103 and 212A standard 300-baud and 1200-bps modems, and is driven by software developed by Microstuf Inc., actually a modification of that company's popular communications program, *Crosstalk*.
>
> Irma FastLink was more expensive than most personal computers at its introduction. But as such technologies become commonplace, and as competition increases, prices will drop, and a much more sophisticated, high-speed technology will flourish in the business personal-computing environment.

The effect of high-speed modems is simple to understand. A 1200-bps modem—still the most common high-speed modem for ordinary dial-up use in the mid-1980s—transmits and receives data four times faster than a 300-baud unit. So if your application calls for lots of time spent on the phone with your computer jabbering away long distance, then the additional cost of a 1200-bps modem (prices vary, but figure slightly more than twice as much for a 1200-bps unit as for a 300-baud direct-connect modem) may be worth it in phone bills saved.

You have to be careful here, though. It's probably fair to say that most people spend more time entering data on their keyboards than they do with the computer actually communicating. This is particularly true if they're communicating with a public data utility, like The Source of Dow Jones News/Retrieval. Such utilities charge premiums for connecting to them at 1200 bps on top of the normal 300-baud connect-time charge. It really makes little sense to pay the extra money for a 1200-bps modem and then pay extra connect-time charges for databank use so you can sit and think about your menu choice while the meter is running. That's like putting high-octane gas into a car that runs fine on regular. The message? Check out your application so you'll know if the cost of a high-speed modem is really worth it.

There's another way to save on long-distance bills. If you're going to communicate with another personal computer over the long-distance lines, use one of the services that competes, at reduced rates, with the

AT&T services. This can work, but you should realize that some of these services offer lower quality service (noisier and with echoes) than AT&T does. In addition, most of them need Touch-tone dialing, which means that an auto-dial modem that will access these services must be able to perform tone dialing. Not all of them do.

A card modem sounds like a good idea, because the whole thing goes inside the computer where you never see it, as we've shown in Figure 6-1. It doesn't take up additional desk space, and that's a real advantage, given the size of most computers. But there's a disadvantage here as well. If you get a card modem, then it will be specifically for your computer and no other. If at some later time you decide to trade up, and you don't get a computer that accepts that particular card, then you have to buy another modem as well as another computer. If you have a separate modem, then at most all you'll need is a different RS-232 card.

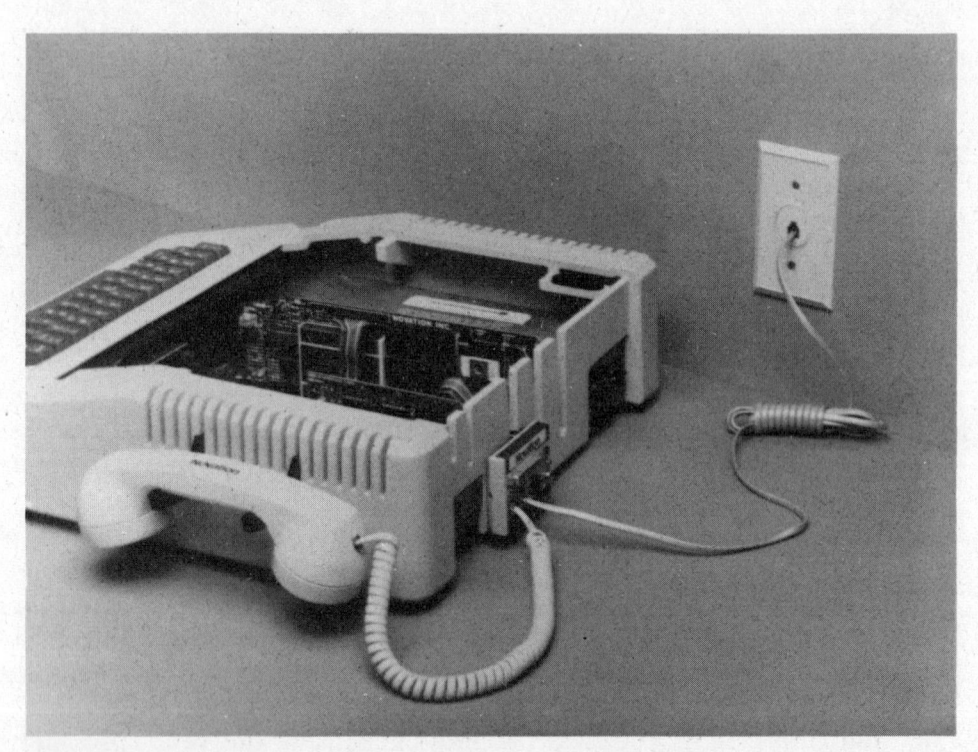

Figure 6.1 A Novation modem mounted inside an Apple II+. The card modem has everything needed for data communications over the phone. A modular phone socket allows simple plug-in to the phone network. (Photo courtesy Novation, Inc.)

The Phone Company

With the recent AT&T divestiture, you don't deal with a giant monolithic telecommunications company anymore but with a local phone company that provides the lines into your home or office. What you do beyond those lines is up to you, provided that you comply with good installation practice and notify your serving phone company of the equipment that you have connected to the line. Specifically, you have to tell the company the FCC registration number of any privately owned equipment you install, and you must inform the company of the ringer equivalence. This is an internal phone-company specification, and it will appear on the data plate of the equipment you want to install. Beyond that, you're the boss. You can even install your own phone wiring if you want to.

Most modems for personal computers (one is shown in Figure 6.2, for an Apple IIe) that you buy off-the-shelf come equipped with modular phone jacks. Modular jacks are wonderful devices that allow you to plug into the telephone network as though you were plugging in a lamp. Push–click, and that's all there is to it, provided you have modular receptacles in your house, or office.

What if you don't? Then you have two choices. The first is to get some modular connections and replace whatever connection you have with modular phone jacks. This isn't terribly hard. Modular jacks are sold in retail stores that have phones and phone equipment, and the packages include instructions for installation of the modular connectors. Or the phone company will do it for you, for a price. This option works well if you're installing the modem in your home where changing the phone wiring makes a lot of sense.

On the other hand, if you're in the office, you may have another problem. You'll probably have an older system that uses huge cables, containing many twisted pairs of wire attached to a multibutton phone on your desk. If that's the case, then there is no connection for a modular phone, and you can't just run out and replace the multibutton phone set. Or, you could have a more modern computerized phone system that has the modular connector, but is expecting a multibutton phone to be connected to that modular jack. If you plug a modem into such a system, then nothing will work as far as your phone is concerned. The system will probably have to be reconfigured, and/or you may need to have a separate line installed to handle your computer.

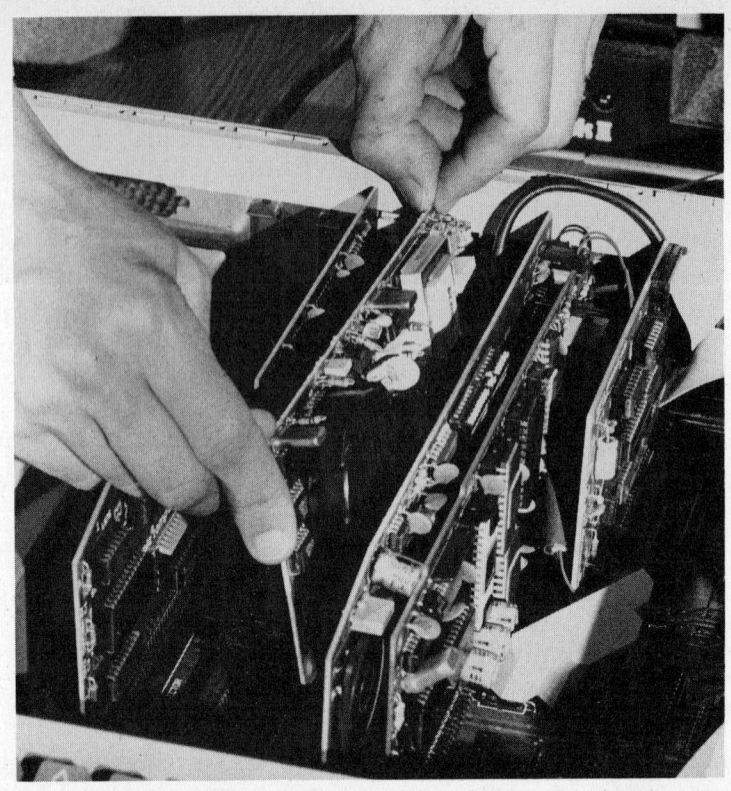

Figure 6.2 Installing a Hayes Micromodem IIe inside an Apple computer. The card modem is being put into I/O slot 3. (*Photo: Stephen Ross*)

The huge-cable situation is easier to handle. Simply go out to your local eletronics store and get an adaptor for your multiline phone. You disconnect the large metal connectors that connect your phone to the cable coming from the wall, insert the adaptor between the connector halves, and put the whole assembly together again. The adaptor has a switch on it to allow you to select one of four lines going into a multi-line phone. It effectively connects itself to the phone line selected by the switch, and has a modular connector in it that will handle a modem, an answering machine, or a phone speaker.

While we're on the subject of multiline phones and electronic phones and such, we should point out one little fault with these things. If you have Call Waiting—a nice feature that will cause a beep in your telephone if you're on the line and another call comes in—beware. Receiving a call while your computer is on the line is a problem. The modem will interpret the beep as a loss of carrier from the other computer and will automatically hang up, if it has an auto-hangup feature. If it's an acoustic modem, the incoming beep will almost certainly cause scrambled data. If you're operating with a phone in an office and can forward your calls to another station, do so before you get your computer on the phone. If you can't, you may have to just grin and bear it. It's annoying, we know. It happens to us all the time, so we try to keep our modem usage to nighttime, after normal business hours when we don't expect to receive incoming phone calls.

The point to remember is simple. Just because you have a modem doesn't mean you'll be able to plug it in and everything will work out fine. It usually will, but if you have multiline phones, or you don't have a built-in RS-232 port, or you don't have modular telephone connectors, then there may be problems. We can't tell you what specific remedy to apply in every situation—there are too many of them. But we have told you the remedy in the most common situations we know about. The rest of the physical interface to the phone company is a matter for you, and your phone-company customer-service representative, to decide.

Transmission Accuracy

We once received a long document in New York that had been sent from California, a part of which read something like this:

> Wh5n5v5r you boot your comput5r, you should 5nsur5 that th5 door of the floppy disk driv5 is clos5d.

Obviously, that wasn't the real document, but you get the idea. Every "e" in the real document received had been changed to a "5." It so happens that "e" and "5" are closely related in ASCII code. The ASCII code for "e" is 101 in decimal, or 1100101 in binary while ASCII "5" is 53 in decimal, or 0110101 in binary. Look at what happened as the message winged its way from California to New York. The bits in the letters "e" got changed subtly; the most significant bits were altered. The least significant bits were, apparently, unchanged. The characters looked like "5" to our computer, and that's how they were displayed on the screen. We don't know why it didn't happen with other characters, and we suspect we never will. Thunderstorms over the Midwest, or rainwater in a local phone line can cause noisy transmissions. And noise in a digital transmission line can change the information you're getting, even if you have a direct-connect modem that has better inherent transmission accuracy.

Such changes however, may not make any difference at all. The document received from California was radically changed, yet we had no trouble reconstructing the sense of the phrases that had been mangled. Textual material can usually be deciphered from context. Not so, however, with other kinds of data transferred over the phone lines, like binary data, or a BASIC program. Even numerical data are an example.

Businesses send streams of numbers from one place to another every day. It's almost impossible to tell from context whether a number should be a 3 or a 4 or a 5. There's a 1-bit difference between the ASCII code for these numbers. ASCII 3 is 51, or 0110011, 4 is 52, or 0110100, and 5 is 0110101. Therefore, it's very easy to confuse the ASCII representation of one of these numbers with the representation for another. Since you can't tell what the number should be from context, then you have to have some way to determine what the number was as it came from the transmitting computer. That calls for error detection and correction by some means or other.

If it's difficult to tell one number from another from context, imagine how much more difficult is the task of deciphering a binary file from context. Here's a short part of a program listing for an Apple computer as it's stored in binary form. It's part of a routine that moves DOS from one location in memory to another.

```
00 40 40 04 AD D2 03 C9
9D F0 20 A0 13 B9 13 40
20 F0 FD 88 10 F7 60 C4
CE D5 CF C6 A0 D3 CF C4
```

and so forth. . . .

These strings of letters and numbers are hexadecimal digits, which represent binary digits, which in turn represent instructions and data for the computer to operate on. The digits represent a machine-language program. As you can see, there is no apparent logic to the message they contain, hence there is no intuitive way that a human can decode the message. Since this is a representation of a program, it must be completely correct if a computer is to execute the proper instructions.

A Short Aside: What on Earth is a Hexadecimal Digit?

People commonly use numbers that have a base of 10. Such numbers have ten digits to represent the numbers 0 through 9. Computers use binary numbers, those that have the base 2.

---

94   DIRECT CONNECTIONS

Binary numbers have two digits to represent the numbers 0 and 1. Converting numbers from binary, which computers understand, to decimal, which people are used to, is tough, so computer gurus use an entirely different number scheme to represent binary numbers—hexadecimal numbers.

Hex numbers, as they are called, have a base of 16. They have 16 digits to represent the numbers 0 through 15. Since we only have 10 symbols used to represent numbers, the symbols A through F were pressed into service to represent hex digits 10 through 15. A represents 10, B is 11, C is 12 and so forth.

Most computers have some sort of utility program in their operating system that allows you to look at portions of memory. Apple's monitor program has it. In CP/M it's the dynamic debugger that contains this facility. MS-DOS has the capability in the DEBUG utility. These programs display the contents of memory, in the locations you select, represented in hex digits. You should understand that what you see is not what's in memory. You see the hex representation of the memory contents. Below are some decimal, binary, and hex equivalents.

Decimal	*Binary*	*Hexidecimal*
0	0000	00
1	0001	01
2	0010	02
3	0011	03
4	0100	04
5	0101	05
6	0110	06
7	0111	07
8	1000	08
9	1001	09
10	1010	0A
11	1011	0B
12	1100	0C
13	1101	0D
14	1110	0E
15	1111	0F

You can see that the decimal numbers through 15 can be represented by one hex digit, while it takes four binary digits. Similarly,

> it takes two hex digits for the numbers up to 255, while eight binary digits are required. Obviously, it's easier to remember and work with two digits than eight. Thus the utility of hex numbers.

The point is that for program data, or for ordinary binary-file data (e.g., the kind generated by a word processor), you need to have some way of making sure that the data received are exactly the same as the data transmitted. Those are really the only situations where you *need* this capability. With ordinary text, you can usually figure the message out from context.

You should realize that the susceptibility of a data transmission to error goes up with the transmission speed. Obviously, the duration of a bit at 1200 bps is considerably shorter than is the duration of a bit at 300 baud. The shorter a bit time, the more likely it is that the value of the bit can be corrupted. Thus a file that could be transmitted with relatively few errors at 300 baud might have significantly more errors at 1200 bps. Here's an example:

We have regularly transmitted document files from Long Island to an office in northern New Jersey, a distance of some 60 road miles. Such files were normally about 16,000 characters long. Typically we'd use Transend 2 in its verified file-transfer mode.

The 16,000-character file takes about sixty-three 256-character sectors on an Apple DOS 3.3 disk. Transend ships data off a sector at a time. Along with the data contained in the sector (256 characters), it also sends a checksum, which the receiving computer compares to one it calculates itself. If the checksums agree, then the sector was transmitted correctly, and the program moves to the next sector. If the checksums disagree, then the receiving computer requests a retransmission. It's interesting to note, by the way, that with this kind of error-check-and-retransmit scheme, which is popular with personal computers, the data may have gotten through without error but the checksum may have been corrupted. If either is corrupted, the data must be retransmitted.

As the program handles data transmission, it updates your screen on the number of disk sectors that have been sent and the number of sectors yet to send. The transmission is a disk-to-disk procedure. In addition, the program counts the number of transmission *tries*—the number of total transmission attempts made. Using this information, you can define a parameter, called transmission efficiency, as the number of sectors sent divided by the number of tries.

Typically, sending a 63-sector file at 300 baud will result in about 66 tries. Thus transmission efficiency at this speed will be 63/66 × 100 = 95 percent. On the other hand, transmitting at 1200 bps has required as many as 78 tries, for a transmission efficiency of 63/78 × 100 = 81 percent. That's a significant percentage drop. Now as it turns out, since transmission is 400 percent faster at 1200 bps than it is at 300 baud, a drop in transmission efficiency of that magnitude isn't anything to get worked up about. And we should caution that this little experiment has a number of uncontrolled variables in it, such as the status of the local weather and the actual routing of the telephone call, which can make the results obtained less accurate. Still, it's our observation that 1200-bps transmission is more error prone than 300-baud activity.

And that seems to mean that if you're going to be transmitting at 1200 bps, then it is a good idea to have the capability to verify the transmission.

Thus we have three situations where data-verification capability is warranted: if you're sending messages that include a lot of numerical data; if you're sending binary files, which can be programs or just ordinary text stored on disk in binary form, as opposed to ASCII text form; or if you're going to operate at speeds higher than 300 baud. How do we get verified transmission?

As we've mentioned before, a computer will always follow instructions. But you have to tell it exactly what you want done. You can't just say "Send these data with error checking and retransmission." You have to issue sets of instructions—rules—that tell the computer how to execute these functions. That's accomplished in communications software.

Using Communications Software

Communications software is the heart and soul of your communications effort. To be sure, you don't need communications software in some cases. Many modems, the so-called smart ones, have enough intelligence in their firmware to run a terminal-emulation program. Terminal emulation has the functions you'll need to dial a phone number and converse with a remote machine. But that's all you'll be able to do. If you think you might want to save something you receive on a disk, say, or print it to a printer, then you'll need some sort of communications software that will do more than just terminal emulation. And why else would you really want to communicate? Once you get information out of another computer, you want to do something with it. At the very least, you need to store it somewhere.

To store the information, print it, or, for that matter, to verify incoming data, you'll need a smart terminal. Communications software can give you smart terminal capabilities.

With your computer emulating a communications terminal with programmed intelligence, you can proceed to get some control over your communications activities. But you have to carefully consider your needs to determine exactly what you want to do when you communicate. In particular, if you have a need for data verification, then you want a communications program that can take care of the chore. It doesn't make sense to get a program that can't issue the commands necessary to make the modem shift gears.

Let's take a look first at data verification. Many terminal programs (and some are shown in Figure 6.3) don't provide for this sometimes necessary capability. Those that do usually employ the XMODEM protocol. XMODEM, as we've mentioned, is a popular error-checking protocol that was first developed for the transmission and reception of programs from CP/M bulletin boards to personal computer users and between users. It determines the occurrence of an error through the computation and verification of a checksum, and then retransmits if an error has occurred. A protocol like XMODEM is nothing more than

Figure 6.3 There is a wide variety of communications hardware and software available for computer-to-computer communications. (*Photo: Stephen Ross*)

rules for verified data communications, but the trick here is that both the computers involved in communications must understand the rules and obey them. Computers, unlike people, can't cheat.

Both computers, then, must run a program that uses the same protocol. In the case of Transend 2, for example, both computers run a proprietary protocol that checks for errors. XMODEM, in contrast, is a protocol in the public domain; more programs implement this protocol than the Transend protocol. But sender and receiver must both run compatible protocols to verify data transfers.

This can be a serious limitation. Much of the communications that goes on today is between small computers and large public bulletin boards. Though some large public boards, telecommunications carriers (like MCI Mail), and databases are beginning to experiment with error-checking protocols, the major companies still implement no protocol more complex or demanding than X-ON/X-OFF. This protocol does nothing more than make two computers understand that if a stop character comes over the line, the computer receiving the stop character (often CTRL-S, ASCII 19) should stop transmitting until it gets a start character (often CTRL-Q, ASCII 17). This means that a microcomputer communications program equipped with a good error-checking protocol won't be able to use it when communicating with the large databases. Consider a link between your computer and the Dow Jones News/Retrieval database for the latest stock quotes at 1200 bps. How do you know the information you get is correct? You don't.

There is some hope. Microcom has developed its networking protocol, which has error-checking-and-retransmission capabilities, to the point that a number of software developers, and some communications companies, such as GTE Telenet, through which we hook up to The Source, have licensed it and begun experimental implementations. And Tymnet, with its X.PC, has begun its own implementation of protocols as well. In the future, it's likely that error correcting will become a part of everyday communications life. But it isn't today, in part because no one can decide on a standard. The message is that if you absolutely need correct data transmission, you must make sure you use software and hardware that ensure error correction and end-to-end reliability.

Beyond error checking, though, communications software offers many other functions, usually accessible through software menus. The number of menus available and their utility is widely variable. For example, *Data Capture 5.0*, a program we frequently use, has four menus: Main, File, Toggle, and Options. The names are fairly suggestive of the functions of each menu. The main menu lets you wait for the phone to ring, dial the phone, and so forth. It also lets you select the other menus. The File menu lets you manipulate data files—saving, sending, and so forth. The Toggle menu lets you change some of the communications parameters. The Options menu lets you set other optional parameters in the program, like baud rate.

The theory behind *Data Capture* is to ease communications by simplifying the options. That's one data communications philosophy. The other philosophy is to try to let you do everything. Transend seems to take this approach. Transend programs have menus for everything under the sun, most of which we never use. But they're available, and using them we can even set a delay between the sending of each individual character in milliseconds. You might say that's silly. Go ahead, say it! We did. Then we started trying to use The Source's electronic-mail facility to send long files direct from disk, and it didn't work. The transmission proceeded, but then we'd start getting error messages from the receiving computer. It was obvious that the computer had interpreted some of our text as commands, and then didn't know what to do with the rest of it. What to do? We experimented, and finally found that a 1-millisecond (ms) delay between characters took the problem away. Amazing what a little extra power will do for you.

These capabilities may be accessible from menus. If they're not, the program is then said to be command-driven. *CrossTalk* is an example of a principally command-driven program. Command-driven programs are much tougher to use at the outset.

Communications Parameters

We have established that there are rules for communications called protocols, which tell the computers and modems how to interact with one another. But beyond the protocols, there are other things that have to be right before communications can proceed flawlessly. These include such things as the very structure of the data word you'll be sending or receiving. Common modems, like the Hayes Micromodem II that we use, have the ability to change the word format. Some communications programs, such as Transend, will present you with menus allowing you to send the proper information to the modem to go ahead and set these communications parameters.

The Micromodem II uses a memory location inside the Apple called the control register to control the data word length. As we've already said, there can be a wide variety of word lengths. You can use seven or eight data bits, and then one or two stop bits, and maybe even a parity bit. You tell a Micromodem II how many of each to transmit and expect to receive, by inserting values into the modem-control register. For example, if you want to have the modem send one start bit, eight data bits, and one stop bit, with no parity bit, which is its default setting, then you would stick a value of 21 in this register either using a BASIC POKE statement (POKE 2040,21) or by going into the Apple's *Monitor* program and doing the value insertion through that program's data-entry commands.

If you don't know BASIC, then that sounds a bit formidable. Using the Apple *Monitor*, where everything is really cryptic and all values are displayed in hex digits, isn't great fun either. But with the Transend communications program, it's easy. You simply select a menu option to define communications parameters, select modem format from that submenu, then select the appropriate data, stop-bit and parity-bit combination from that menu. Such a program will take away the harassment of getting into the computer, through some programming language, or something like CP/M's dynamic debugger.

We should point out that some communications programs that run under CP/M offer equivalent convenience to Transend. One in particular is *Super Term*, at least in its incarnation as provided with the Kaypro 4. The program is set to communicate with the Kaypro's built-in 300-baud modem, and also uses menus to set communications parameters, like word length, number of stop bits, character echo in full-duplex mode, and the like.

Notice that we have been mentioning specific programs here that work with specific modems. A communications program has two required areas of compatibility. First of all, obviously, it has to run on your computer. But more important, if you're going to use its capabilities to the fullest, it has to support both your modem and your serial port. Transend will support the Micromodem II, for example, but it will not support some other serial interfaces that are popular on the Apple II computers. For example, we have found through experimentation that it will not support Mountain Computer Corp.'s CPS Multifunction Card. This means it might communicate over these modems and serial interfaces, but it won't handle more sophisticated functions like switching speed, perhaps, or auto-dialing. If your communications software doesn't support your hardware, you'll have to handle these things manually. In fact, you may find that it just won't work at all.

Hooking Up a Modem

The one thing you have to do with a modem is connect it. It has to be connected twice: first, to the phone line, and second, to the computer. We've already talked about the connection to the phone company. What about the other one?

Modems connect to computers through RS-232-C ports. The usual connecting device is a large D-shaped connector called a DB-25, because it has 25 pins (male) or sockets (female) in it. You need a cable to connect the modem to the computer via RS-232-C ports, unless you have a card modem. Thankfully, most computer-to-modem connections are straightforward. Get a cable, which is available at your computer store (although it's cheaper at an electronics parts store) and plug it into both boxes. You do have to know what kind of connector is on the modem and what's on the computer. Then you need a cable that will mate with both of these connectors at the same time. Normally a cable with one DB-25 male and one DB-25 female will work. Now, plug the cable to the modem and to the computer, and you should be in business.

Transferring a File

We've assumed that the primary reason you want to use computer communications is to transfer a file from one computer to another. Most communications programs that handle unverified transfer have a device called a *capture buffer*. The capture buffer is an area of memory that's set aside to store information that either comes in during a communications session, or goes out during the session.

When you see information on a screen, it's because the information is in a screen buffer. A screen buffer is an area of the computer's memory that's reserved for the temporary storage of information to be shown on the screen. Information comes into the screen buffer and leaves it on a first-in/first-out basis. You see it as scrolling. The first information comes at the bottom of the screen, gets pushed to the top, and then disappears. What actually happens is that the information is constantly overwritten and rewritten in new locations in the screen buffer, until it's written to the top line. Then new information is written to the top line, and the information that was in the top line is gone forever—unless, as in the case of communications software at least, it was stored in the capture buffer.

A communications program with a capture buffer can save the contents of the capture buffer to disk. Usually, saving is accomplished through choosing that option on a menu. So to receive a file, you simply turn on your capture buffer at the appropriate time, and let the communications session happen. At the close of the session, you save the capture buffer to disk with a menu command.

Let's look at that step by step. Assume you're using *Super Term*, Version 5.0, as supplied with the Kaypro 4 computer. You call for that program from the disk, and, after setting the appropriate communications parameters from a menu, you go to the Receive menu. There are some choices to be made about line feeds (you can generally tell the program to add a line feed, whether you know it needs to or not) and then choose the file option. The program asks if you want to use terminal mode or verified mode (Xmodem) for transfer and you chose terminal. Then it asks if X-ON should be enabled (yes). Finally, it asks for a file name (B:RECEIVED.TXT). After you give the program that name, it creates the file on the disk in drive B:, and then waits. When you press O (to turn on the capture buffer) you're ready to go. Pressing ESC then gets you into terminal mode, ready for the other computer to send. Whatever comes in then until you go back to the Receive menu and press O again (it's an on–off toggle) is stored in memory. When you end the terminal session, the program automatically saves the capture buffer in B:RECEIVED.TXT. It's that simple. And it's that simple with other programs, too. Just read the documentation that comes with the program and follow the instructions. Then be ready to experiment.

Admittedly, we've covered a lot of ground here, and we haven't come close to touching on all the possibilities of modem communications. Often, getting communications right is a matter of experimentation. For example, we've used communications to The Source on various occasions. Every time we do, we have to go in and change the default word-length setting in the *Super Term* program from eight data bits to seven. If we don't, then the screen is incomprehensible. How did we know to do that? We just used the program's Term option on its main menu and started changing communications parameters until we found a combination that would work. Usually, you won't have to experiment that way; communications, especially with the information utilities, works very well and follows prescribed rules. But in other situations, like the Kaypro's *Super Term* program, or in direct links between two personal computers, the experimentation does come in.

Fortunately, there are some programs that try to see ahead and develop rules for special communications problems. When one is communicating with The Source—for example, sending files to someone else through the utility's mail function—it's possible to use a Transend data-transfer function to accomplish the upload. Transend's transfer options are in Figure 6.4. Although the clocks on some different computers, including computers communicating with The Source, can be going at just a different enough rate so that data coming in rapidly might be lost, dropped, or misunderstood, Transend can solve the problem of different rates of data flow. A simple rule is that if data are getting lost in transmission, then use software that can slow down the transmission by inserting a delay between each character, or a delay at the end of each transmitted line. A good data communications program will let you do that.

The way to approach this experimentation is quite simple. Get yourself Howard Hillman's *Computer Log* or a notebook, and write down the date and the time and what you're trying to accomplish. Then write

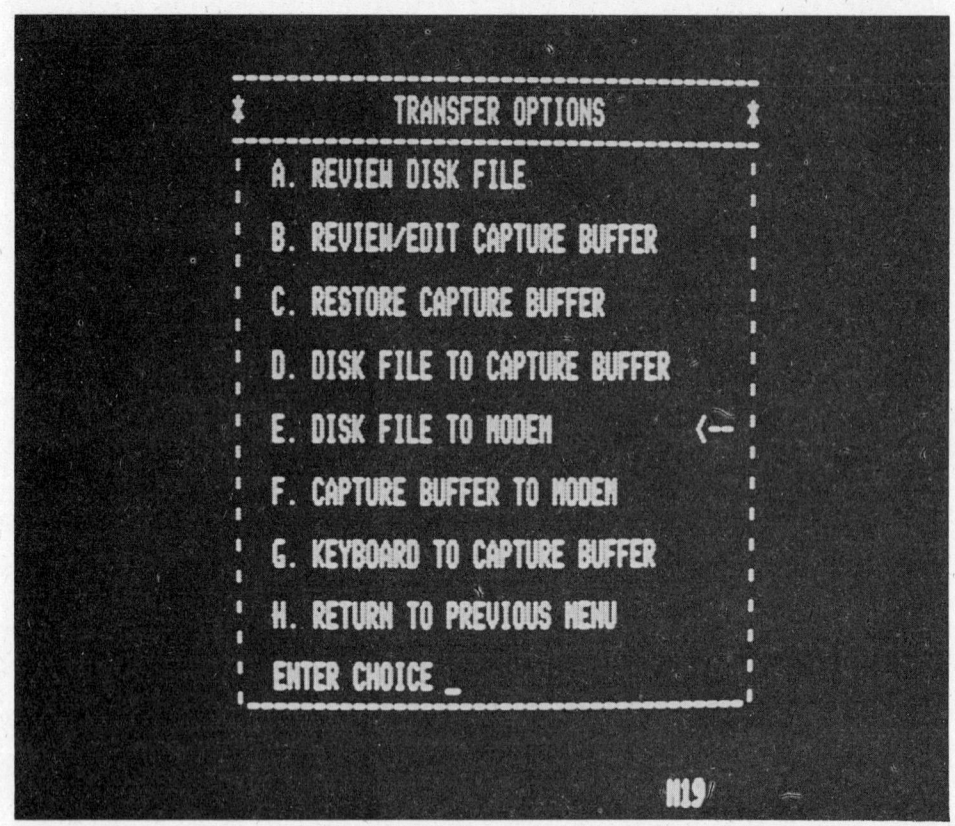

Figure 6.4 Transend's transfer-options menu. This program lets you pick a file from the capture buffer or a disk, or to send everything out the communications port that you type on the keyboard. (*Photo: Stephen Ross*)

down *exactly* what you do (put disk in computer, booted, saw main menu, etc.). Record what happens as you go along. With the Kaypro, for example, we were getting no line feeds, so letters were overwriting one another, and letters were being dropped. So we went to the documentation (finally) and found that the Term option would let us change communications parameters. Also record the page of the manual that has the information you need. Why go searching through documentation more than once? When you get communications working, then write a summary of those that will make it work. This will give you one source to go to for answers in the future.

It sounds complicated, and it's difficult at times, but it works. Unfortunately, the state of data communications today is such that experimentation is, in the final analysis, the only way you'll overcome some situations. Not all, mind you, but most. As more people begin to use communications, then more companies will implement some *de facto* standard, and more programs will come out that will make setting parameters and using protocols easier. Up to this point, though, it hasn't happened.

But at least you know enough now to get a modem and some communications software and get started. You know what you need for hardware: a modem of appropriate speed, or maybe an RS-232 card, if your computer doesn't have one. And you need communications software that will support your modem. You will probably want an error-checking protocol in software as well.

CHAPTER 7
USING A MODEM WITHOUT USING THE PHONE LINE

- The OSI Model Again • Why Get Another Telephone for Communications? • How Modem-to-Modem Works • Troubleshooting the Connection

COMMUNICATIONS BASICS

Garbage: In computer terms, any output from a computer that is incomprehensible is garbage.

Mark: A negative signal under the RS-232-C standard. Negative is from −3 to −15 volts.

Off-Hook: The condition that exists when a telephone device (or a modem) is connected to the telephone line.

Space: A positive signal under the RS-232-C standard. Positive is from +3 to +15 volts.

Transmit Data: One of the 25 signal lines associated with the RS-232-C interface. For more information, see Chapter 9.

The OSI Model Again

We've gone to a lot of trouble here to try to develop a consistent way of looking at computer communications based on the Open Systems Interconnect (OSI) model. We've done that for a very good reason: it will let you think about solutions in the same layers as the model.

As you proceed toward more difficult kinds of communications—serial direct-connect solutions and the like (see Chapters 9–11)—the model will be helpful. But the plain fact of the matter is that if you want to use a modem with your computer today, you can find manufacturers that provide a full set of virtually trouble-free communications tools.

These manufacturers provide modems, cables, and circuit cards that implement the RS-232-C port. In some cases, the modem will work with a particular set of ports, and the computer dealer who sells the modem keeps compatible cables in stock. This ensures that the physical-link layer of your communications scheme is intact and functioning properly. In addition, manufacturers provide software, in many cases, implementing the data-link layer, the session layer, the presentation layer, and the applications layer. In the final analysis, communicating with a modem is, comparatively speaking a piece of cake.

There's a caveat, though. Suppose you buy a modem to use with an Apple, CP/M microcomputer, or IBM PC for example, and the modem expects hardware handshaking and your serial card doesn't provide the correct signals? There won't be communications until you correct the problem. And certainly, you can't do any more here because we are about to hook together modems without using the telephone lines—which assumes that your modem and computer are communicating. If they are not, turn to Chapters 9 and 10 for a thorough discussion of the RS-232-C interface and how to troubleshoot it.

It's a simple matter, as we know, to get the modem communicating over phone lines with the large on-line systems like CompuServe, or even with a computer of a friend. Simply enter the commands for the modem to pick up the phone, dial the number and connect. If you have communications software that is compatible with your modem, then that software will take care of all these functions, which is equivalent to initiating all the various levels of the communications outlined in the OSI model.

Why Get Another Telephone for Communications?

Let's think for a moment about the data-link layer of OSI. When a computer is communicating over a modem, the modem converts computer signals into audio-frequency signals so they can work over the physical link. The audio signal is compatible with the phone line, which is, normally, a major component of the physical link. The data-link layer of the communications model operates on the physical link. Indeed, the data-link layer has been implemented by the modems and RS-232-C ports that drive the modems.

A simple data-link layer only needs two wires in the physical link to work. And, interestingly enough, there are two strands in the telephone wire, equipped with a modular connector you plug into the modem. You don't need telephone exchanges and switchboards and the rest of the telephone system for data communications. There is one exception: a so-called line-powered modem. Such a modem is powered from the phone system, and therefore needs to be connected to the phone system. Other modems don't.

So why connect to the phone system?

You know you can use the modem and the telephone line to swap data between any two computers that have attached modems. But suppose the two computers are sitting in the same room, maybe on the same desk. It seems a terrible waste of money to use telephones at all. And as more computers are sold with built-in modems—the Radio Shack TRS-80 Model 200 and the Kaypro 4 are now, and others almost certainly will in the not-too-distant future—it seems silly to have to configure RS-232 ports to make the computers connect directly. Since the modem is a communications device, why not make it communicate without the help of a telephone?

If you've got a modem for both computers, then it's a good bet that you can do it. Just take the phone cord that came with one modem (either one) and connect it directly from one modem to the other. Get one modem to dial a number—any number—while the other modem takes the phone off-hook.

How Modem-to-Modem Works

When an RS-232-C port is turned on, but not actively transmitting, it sends a character called a *mark*. The mark, in effect, puts a negative signal on its transmit-data line. The modem that is off-hook and connected to such a "marking" port takes the mark and turns it into a frequency it sends along the telephone line, assuming such a line is there. The modem translates the mark into an answer tone that is put out over the telephone line.

The other modem, meanwhile, dialed the simple number—a 1, say—and then "listened" with the phone off the hook, hoping to hear an answer tone from the other end of the line. Sure enough, as soon as the calling modem starts to listen, it hears the other modem's answer carrier. Since that's all it needs to establish the connection, you're in the communications business.

This method sounds simple, but it may not be. You have to make sure that the answering modem will do just what we've described, and some modems aren't equipped for it.

When you tell your modem to await a ring, that's just what it does. It "listens" for a ring. Actually, it's waiting for the ring signal, which is a 50-volt AC tone. A special component inside the modem will be activated by the ring signal when it's present. The presence of a ring signal starts a sequence of events. Just as it does when you hear the ring signal of the telephone's bell. When you hear the bell, you pick up the phone and say "Hello." When the modem determines the presence of the ring signal, it "picks up the phone" and signifies its presence by sending its answer tone along the line.

But if the modem isn't connected to the phone system, where will it get the ring signal so it can pick up the phone? Answer: it won't get the ring, so you have to make it listen to the phone line as though the ring had already happened. In this way it will hear a tone and respond by "saying hello" through its carrier.

There are a number of computer/modem combinations that can make this procedure work. We have made it work successfully with an Apple II+ as the calling computer and a Kaypro 4 as the answering computer, and with a Compaq computer as the caller and a Kaypro 4 as the answerer.

In general, to make this method work you need some way to make the modem go off-hook, that is, to close the switch that connects it to the telephone line, and turn on its transmitter. You can make some modems do this by setting values in their control registers. Some

Using a Modem Without Using the Phone Line 111

modems set these values by responding to codes sent over the serial interface; others need values set through a control program. Some won't do it at all, perhaps because they need to get a ring signal from the central telephone office, and ordinary modems don't generate ring signals. It's also possible that the modem will only go off-hook through the dialing sequence and will not connect to the line independently of the dialing sequence. The Bytcom 212AD modem is one of this type.

Troubleshooting the Connection

There's a simple way to tell if the modem is off-hook and has its transmitter on. Simply plug a telephone handset into the modular connector on the modem. It's somewhere on the modem, as shown in Figure 7.1. The handset will act like a meter for you: if the tone signal is present, the handset will convert it into an audible tone. In a similar manner, if you connect an AC voltmeter across the line, the meter will display the size of the tone, as well as its presence.

Figure 7.1 The Hayes Micromodem IIe has its own modular phone plug. You can plug a phone cord directly from this plug to the plug on another modem for easy direct connecting through back-to-back modems. (*Photo: Stephen Ross*)

If the modem is generating the tone, you'll hear it in the handset's earpiece. If you don't hear the tone, then the modem isn't transmitting. It's as simple as that.

We used the Kaypro 4 computer as the answering modem for a simple reason. The computer is supplied with the *Super Term* communications program. This is a fine package for just this kind of exercise, because it lets the built-in modem in the Kaypro 4 computer go off-hook with its transmitter on. If you happen to own a Kaypro 4, you can prove this to yourself by hooking up a telephone handset to the modem and then booting *Super Term*. You'll hear the modem tone immediately, apparently because this program initially turns the modem on. The modem starts marking right away. Select the dial mode from the main menu, and then the dial option from the dial menu, and enter a number. The modem tone will disappear and you'll hear the dialing tones instead, and then nothing. Now abort the call, and put the computer into the On-line state. In that state, you'll hear the answer tone again. The modem is marking, and any modem waiting for the answer tone will get it right away.

As we said, not all modems work in this fashion. An example is the Bytcom 212AD modem we had connected to a Compaq computer. Normally, this modem won't dial without detecting a dial tone on the telephone line. The other computer can't send a dial tone, so what to do? Fortunately, there's a switch you can set on the Bytcom modem that allows what the company calls *blind dialing*—dialing without a dial tone. Dial any number on the Compaq with the blind dialing switch set and you have a connection, Compaq-to-Kaypro, through the modems.

As it happens, *Super Term* on the Kaypro 4 has a file-transfer selection on its menu. We were running a program called *Telpac*, from U.S. Robotics, on the Compaq computer, which has a file-transfer utility also. Simply follow the file-transfer menus for each one, and a file will transfer from one computer to the other.

When should you use this modem-to-modem method? First, use it when you have two computers that have modems built in. Don't run out and spend several hundred dollars for modems. Second, use it when speed of transmission isn't critical. The fastest you'll get most popular modems to operate is 1200 baud. That's maddeningly slow compared to the 9600 bps or greater speeds you can get if you go direct-connect. Third, use the modem-to-modem direct connect if the modems allow you to. If you can't figure out a way to make them connect within an hour, don't waste any more time—unless you enjoy tinkering with your computer—but use a direct serial connection.

For real examples of how modem-to-modem direct connections

work, turn to the next chapter, where we demonstrate connection techniques and file transfers between an Apple II+, Kaypro 4, Radio Shack TRS-80 Model 100, Osborne I, and a Commodore 64 computer—all without using the telephone line. In addition, we present case studies in telecommunications—file transfers, error checking, and troubleshooting techniques for the IBM PC, Compaq Plus, Apple Macintosh, DEC PDP-11, among others. The studies will show you, step-by-step, exactly how to make your computers communicate with some of the top modems and software on the market.

CHAPTER 8
MODEM CONNECTIONS: INTRODUCTION TO THE CASE STUDIES

- Practical Considerations • Modem Connection Case Studies

COMMUNICATIONS BASICS

Comma-delimited files: Files that have their data items separated by commas.

Cyclic Redundancy Checksum (CRC): A number developed as a result of an error-checking algorithm. The checksum is generated by both transmitter and receiver. If they agree, then the data were transmitted correctly. If not, the receiver requests a retransmission.

Data Interchange Format (DIF): A special format developed by the programmers of *VisiCalc* for interchanging data files between programs with different formatting requirements.

Integer Files: Programs written in Apple's Integer BASIC.

Keyboard Macros: A sequence of commands or data that is sent by pressing one key. Used to automate log-on and other functions.

Sequential Files: Files that are written on a disk starting at the top of the file and then continuing through the data in sequence.

SYLK (Symbolic Link): Similar to a DIF file, but produced by Microsoft for use with files written by its *Multiplan* spreadsheet.

Translation Table: A table to convert the ASCII values of incoming or transmitted characters so they can be received or sent as some other character.

Virtual Files: Files that can be received format-free and written into any format that a computer requires.

Practical Considerations

There's a time to put theory aside and just get your hands dirty—and this is it. Let's summarize some practical strategies for connecting we feel will be helpful; not because they always work but because they seem to work in a startling number of cases. We begin with modem connections over ordinary dial-up phone lines.

Here are things to do first:

1. *Check your pins, protocols, and control characters, in that order.*

Before you attempt to transmit, establish a methodical way of checking your hardware, the communications protocols available for use in software, and finally, the special control codes your computer may use to perform transmission functions or formatting.

Even if standard Bell-compatible modems are used (both modems must implement the same hardware protocol, don't forget), make sure you've chosen the correct RS-232-C interface cable. Check your cable selection with a dealer and have it demonstrated before purchasing it. Otherwise you may get a garbled transmission or no transmission at all. Problems with hardware handshaking may also garble the tail end of transmission buffers (see the Radio Shack/Osborne case study.)

Communications settings in software are also paramount. Besides setting standard parameters in software (bits, baud rate, parity checking, length of data word, etc.), choose the highest level communications protocol common to sender and receiver. A high-level protocol ensures data accuracy and greater control over the transmission. Even a simple XMODEM or X-ON/X-OFF protocol is superior to none at all: these protocols give you some control over the pacing and, in the case of XMODEM, the accuracy of sent and received buffered data.

Another aspect of communications most people don't think much about—until something goes wrong—are the control characters. Used differently in different computers, these control codes let either the computer or you, the operator, control some transmission tasks and formatting. Review the list of control characters in your documentation or software menus. Learn the idiosyncracies of your communicating computers: it may be necessary to rely not only on the control codes automatically sent back and forth by the software but to enter control characters separately from the keyboard to open and close files. Some computers, such as the Radio Shack TRS-80 Model 100, use CTRL-Z characters internally to close files, so computers transmitting to it must send a second, separate CTRL-Z code to ensure that the Model 100 closes and stores a file coming from the outside. By the same token, a Radio Shack *TELCOM* program traps the CTRL-J (line feed) command when it sends data to a modem or printer, so it may be necessary to write a small program to input line feeds, or else do the inserting manually to get the Model 100 to format a file correctly.

2. *Files are best converted into as simple a format as possible when preparing transmissions between dissimilar systems.*

Start with ASCII text files and the simplest communications settings possible: 7 bits, even parity, 1 stop bit, 300 baud, for example. Ignore the parity, if necessary. Parity can confuse a sending or receiving computer, as we'll see. Avoid using an 8-bit setting because 8 bits correspond to ASCII codes above 128. These are nonstandardized, highly specialized control, formatting, and graphics characters. They are not universal. Although they are essential for programs like *WordStar*, the eighth bit is often discarded or misinterpreted by communications programs. It is a troublesome bit and should be avoided as much as possible, especially if your communicating systems or software are dissimilar.

3. *Type back and forth in "terminal mode" before beginning a file transfer.*

Once you are hooked up, access terminal mode and type a few words to test the accuracy of the data bits coming across the line. Never attempt a file transfer until you have ironed out garbles or nonmatched communications settings in your software.

4. *Choose the highest level error-checking protocol implemented in both sender and receiver communication software.*

Always try a protected or error-free protocol before you resort to straight, unprotected, buffered terminal transmission. (You can almost always do that!) Protected transfers are vital if you're sending computer programs, numerical data, or binary files. Some programs now offer a variety of error-free protocols from which to choose. Be forewarned, though: some protocols are actually subsets or reinterpretations of standard protocols (XMODEM and its subset of protocols are an example), so two dissimilar programs claiming to implement XMODEM may still be incapable of communicating. Another problem is hardware and software incompatibility. Dissimilar computers running packages implementing the same protocol may nevertheless misread incoming characters. The only way to know for sure is to experiment; you can always crank down to a simple X-ON/X-OFF, or no protocol, if the other schemes don't work.

5. *Try modem communications first; direct-connect second.*

Modem communications are almost always easier to set up and troubleshoot than a direct serial transfer. In contrast, serial and null modem cables pose the problem of hardwire connection, which is a complex question to which we devote the three chapters following this one. Take our advice—try a modem connection first. It's comparatively easy.

6. *Pay attention to parity bits, if you use them.*

A screenful of mixed garbage and legible characters often signals a discrepancy in parity checking. Make sure parity is matched before pushing the panic button. Try each parity setting methodically (even, odd, ignore, no parity) on both the sending and receiving ends, and record the results.

7. *Learn how to open and close data files on your computer using your communications software, word processor, or other applications program.*

Some telecommunications packages don't help an operator call up to the screen and survey a file that has just been transmitted. A case in point is *PC to Mac and Back!* (dilithium Press Beaverton, Oregon)— otherwise, a useful telecommunications program. Its conventions demand that you first store a file on disk, then open it up with the *MacWrite* word processing program. Some programs, however, don't tell you exactly how to save a file once it's been stored in the capture buffer, which can result in disaster the first time a file is saved in the computer's memory, but is not yet on disk. To ensure data storage, familiarize yourself with file-saving and loading operations before you attempt a transmission.

8. *Read your manuals.*

As obtuse as many manuals are, most contain troubleshooting checklists that list characteristic problems, possible causes, and corrections. Modems generally come with checklists, as do programs. Often solutions are buried in the back of the manual under "Advanced Topics."

You may also get some help by purchasing additional books geared toward your particular computer and its operating system.

9. *Experiment, where possible, with file-conversion formats made available by your applications programs.*

Some telecommunications software as well as spreadsheets, database, and word processing programs offer special file-conversion utilities that enable you to convert data files into a neutral or virtual format. These files are then suitable for transmission to other computers, and loading into specialized applications programs. For example, *VisiCalc* and *1-2-3* offer a file format called DIF (Data Interchange Format) that enables the receiving computer to read the data and reconvert them back into a form its own version of the program can use. Other telecommunications programs convert received data files into Microsoft SYLK, Lotus print files, comma-delimited files used in spreadsheets, *dBase II* files, and sequential files, among others. A program such as *PC to Mac and Back!* offers a conversion utility for transmitting data files from *WordStar* and *Multiplan* between the Macintosh and PC-DOS operating systems. And several micro-mainframe links now offer mainframe-to-PC application conversion formats for massaging data into useful forms.

10. *Transmit in half duplex when possible.*

Remember, half duplex affects local echo settings, and full-duplex settings can cause echo-back problems. Sometimes an operator may transmit to another computer in full duplex, terminal mode, finding that his own words, entered from the keyboard or from a disk file, don't appear on his own screen. The remedy is almost invariably a switch to half-duplex setting. Half duplex echoes characters both to the screen and the communications line; full duplex sends characters out the communications line, then waits for the receiving computer to echo back the characters. In some cases, though, the echoed characters are filtered or screened automatically from local view, or they are misinterpreted as a control code.

11. *If your files are overtyped, add line feeds to reformat the document and make it readable.*

Some communications programs don't send line feeds after carriage returns, for example, although the option is available in most programs. Some computers' own screen controller (a hardware device) will send line feeds; others, like the Radio Shack Model 100, will screen out or trap the ASCII codes indicating line feed, so that the type is overwritten on the receiving end. However, the ASCII codes for line feeds may be stored, along with text, in the receiving computer's memory. Off-line, the receiver's own word processing program or other application may be able to read these codes and execute the instructions accordingly, or provide line feeds automatically. If that fails, you may need to write a BASIC program to insert line feeds in the transmitted text when needed.

These are the basic observations we've made. Now let's proceed to the case studies and isolate problems by type and machine.

Modem Connection Case Studies

- Apple II+ to Apple IIe
- Apple IIe to Macintosh
- Apple IIe to IBM PC
- IBM PC to Apple IIe
- Apple IIe to Compaq Plus
- Kaypro 4 to Apple IIe
- Apple IIe to ATEX TLM (DEC PDP-11) system
- Radio Shack TRS-80 Model 100 to Apple IIe
- Radio Shack TRS-80 Model 100 to Compaq Plus
- Radio Shack TRS-80 Model 100 to Osborne I
- Commodore 64 to Apple II+
- Commodore 64 to Apple II+ (Direct Connection, Modem to Modem)
- Sanyo MBC 555 to Compaq Plus (2400 BPS)
- Compaq Plus to Apple IIe (2400 BPS)

Apple II+ to Apple IIe (Step-by-Step Modem Connection

Equipment:

Apple IIe (64K)
Computer with two disk drives
D.C. Hayes Micromodem IIe (300 baud)
   (printed circuit board modem)
Modular phone connector
Telephone cord

Apple II+ (48K)
Computer with two disk drives
Hayes Micromodem II
   (printed circuit board modem)

Communications Software:
Transend 2 (Transend Corp., San Jose, California)   Transend 2

General: A connection between Apple II series computers using the same communications software enables the sender and receiver to transfer files using a high-level error-checking protocol. Transend's proprietary Apple-to-Apple verified file transfer protocol is known as a disk-to-disk protocol because it is capable of sending and receiving directly from disk files instead of from the Apple's capture buffer.

Verified File Transfer Mode is accessible through choices in the Transend master menu. It allows you to specify a list of files to send by individual file name and type (binary, ASCII text, Applesoft BASIC files, Integer files, among other types). An entire diskful of files may be sent during a single transmission. The program lets you catalogue your disk, delete files, lock and unlock files, and check the amount of sector space available for received files. It works with Apple-to-Apple transfers only. It will work with Pascal, ProDOS, OS, Microsoft CP/M (installed in the Apple), or ALS CP/M format.

Procedure: The first step in the transmission is to configure the Transend (or other Apple communications) software to your hardware device. A typical communications configuration could be specified as follows on a Transend menu:

1. Printer: Slot #1: Other
2. Modem: Slot #2
   D.C. Hayes Micromodem IIe (as shown in Figure 8.1)
3. Screen Display (auxiliary slot): Apple IIe 80 column board
4. Number of Drives in System: 2 [6,2,0.]

Having configured the system, now choose the best protocol for sending files. If you select the Verified File Transfer Mode option (letter B) on the Transend master menu, software parameters are automatically set. They include the following:

8 data bits + 1 stop bit + no parity
Half Duplex Mode
Default Parameter Set loaded

In Verified File Transfer Mode, the computers always transmit in half duplex. Decide, off-line, which computer will send first and which will receive.

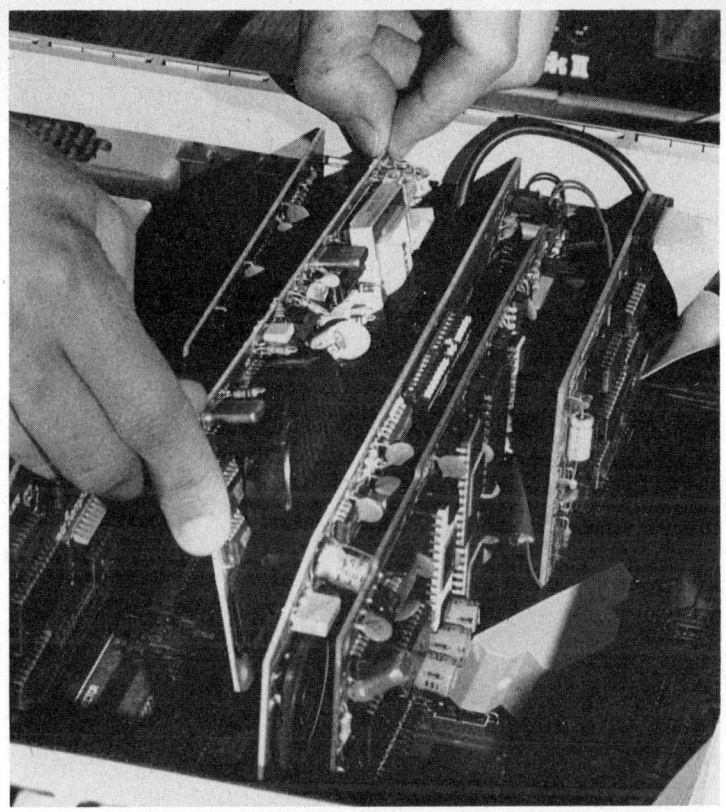

Figure 8.1 The Micromodem IIe is connected by a cable, shown at the rear, to the modular phone socket. (*Photo: Stephen Ross*)

Sending Files: Once you have selected the Verified File Transfer Menu option, select the Choose Files to Send suboption, and respond to computer prompts allowing you to name the files you wish to send. Having specified these to Transend, return to the 'Terminal Mode' option to establish the connection. Choose the 'Place Call' option in terminal mode. At the prompt, type in a phone number and the modem will automatically dial.

When the connection is established the computer beeps and the screen flashes a message telling the computer's current status. The remainder of the screen will be blank. Type back and forth to establish the accuracy of the transmission. Then press two control commands CTRL-A, CTRL-X, which tell the program to drop out of Terminal Mode and return to the Verified File Transfer Mode Menu.

Press the Send Files option, respond to prompts, which remind you to insert a data disk in drive B. Once you've done this, press the RETURN key. When the connection is synchronized, the program will show the file name, type, total sectors to transfer, sectors already transferred, and sectors remaining. The screen will update as transmission proceeds.

On the other end, pick Receive Files in place of Send Files. Disk status will be monitored as specified above.

Comments and Discussion: A session layer protocol in Transend's Verified File Transfer Mode enables an operator to send single or multiple files during transmission directly to a receiver's disk. The menu for this transmission mode is shown in Figure 8.2. The protocol verifies binary data using the cyclic redundancy checksum (CRC) method, so that transmissions are highly accurate and complete. The protocol follows some of the layering conventions of the OSI model.

A disk-to-disk protocol that offers a CRC error checking is ideal for high-volume data transfer. It contrasts with a lower level buffer-to-buffer protocol. (XMODEM is a prime example) that uses a less rigorous form of error checking and is capable only of lower volume data transfer directly from the sender's capture buffer.

Moreover, the transmission path to verified mode is direct. The user needs to do the following:

1. Install modem
2. Configure Transend's software to the hardware selected by following menu options
3. Choose a ready-made parameter set (verified Apple-to-Apple transfer)
4. Set the computer to auto-answer or auto-dial
5. Establish physical connection
6. Type in Terminal Mode
7. Use a CTRL-A, CTRL-X sequence to switch to transfer options menu
8. Select Choose Files to Send
9. Name Files to Send
10. Send files
11. End transmission by pressing CTRL-A, CTRL-Z keystroke sequence

Notice the importance of a few selected control characters in Transend. Control codes must be learned by consulting the documentation or a menu listing. Transend also adheres to standard X-ON/X-OFF (CTRL-Q/CTRL-S) control codes, among several other formatting codes, which permits the user to start and stop transmission on-line.

Figure 8.2 This socket, mounted on the rear panel of the Apple IIe, provides grounding protection for the modem, and carries the data signals into and out of the computer. (*Photo: Stephen Ross*)

Two State-of-the-Art File Transfers

1. Apple IIe to MacIntosh (Step-by-Step Modem Connection)
2. IBM PC to Apple IIe (Step-by-Step Modem Connection)

General: If you want to transfer error-free files between dissimilar computers and operating systems, you need communications equipment with muscle: a state-of-the-art protocol. One such protocol is MNP (Microcom Networking Protocol), based on the layered architecture of the OSI model, and licensed now by more than 80 communications software, hardware, and network vendors. MNP's primary advantage over other systems is that it resolves file incompatibilities. In addition, the software produced by Microcom Corporation, called *ERA 2,* offers special user functions—keyboard macros—to automate communications through the modem.

We begin with the Apple IIe-to-Macintosh step-by-step connection. (*Note:* This represents a more complete description of the case study illustrated in Chapter 2, page 000)

Equipment:

Macintosh Personal Computer Computer with one microfloppy disk drive and 128K memory

MacModem and *ERA 2* software (Microcom, Inc.)

Modular phone cord
Modular jack

Apple IIe Computer with two disk drives and 64K memory DOS 3.3

ERA 2 Modem and software for the Apple IIe with telephone jack (Figure 8.3)

Modular phone cord

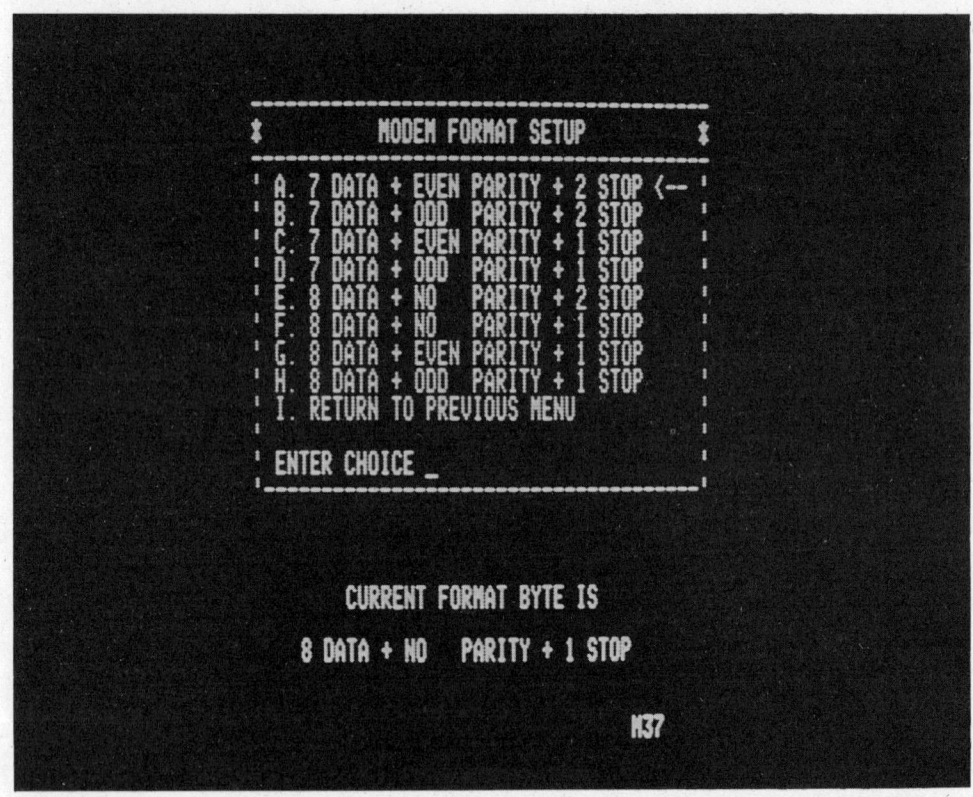

Figure 8.3 A Transend set-up menu. The software allows for a multitude of data formats. (*Photo: Stephen Ross*)

Procedure: Install *ERA 2* (or Hayes-compatible) modem in an available slot inside the Apple IIe.

Install MacModem by plugging one end of the connecting cable into the Macintosh phone socket and the other end into the MacModem socket. Attach phone cord from MacModem phone socket to the telephone wall jack.

Boot *ERA 2* in the Apple IIe, and the MacModem software disk in the Macintosh. Double click on the MacModem icon. Choose the Display/Change Configuration option on the first menu you see on the Apple IIe. On the Macintosh, choose Setup, then drag down the menu that appears and move the cursor to Communications, and then release the button on the mouse. You see the Communications Settings dialogue box. Select speed, and set it; then parity, and set it. When done, click on OK box, which will take you back to the main menu.

On the Apple IIe, after initial boot, press RETURN, and the program will ask you to specify your modem slot number, dialing default (a tone or pulse), and the number and location of disk controller cards, clock cards, and the like. Answer the questions, press ESCAPE when finished, and return to the main menu. Your configuration will be automatically written to a disk file.

You now have two options to send or receive error-free text or binary files.

Option 1: See Case Study, Chapter 2, page 000, for details of operating procedure. In this option you specify your own communications settings, enter Interactive Mode, and choose the menu option that lets you dial up the remote computer—Open Apple D—or set your modem to auto-answer—Open Apple A. This establishes the connection and then lets you choose the reliable MNP file-transfer mode, Open Apple F on the Interactive Mode menu, or reliable link, Open Apple L Mode.

Option 2: Designate, off-line, a special user function keyboard macro that contains all the instructions your computer needs to dial and communicate with a remote system, sending your files automatically at 1200 bps.

To create a user function, select the Display/Change Terminal Set-Up option on the main menu, then choose the option called Create/Edit User Function. You'll see a display with numbers 0–9. For your first user function, select 0 and press RETURN. The system will ask you to specify a name for the function. Then it will present you with options to create an automated file.

Scan these options, then decide what you need to do. If you want your computer to dial a remote system and send a file, then press the dial option, Open Apple D, and type in the phone number. Press the auto-answer function to receive. Now press the MNP file-transfer option Open Apple F. Once again, the system will ask you whether you are sending or receiving. In send mode, type your file name, the type of file, the disk drive you'll be sending from, and the name of the file as recorded on the remote system. In receive mode, you'd simply type R. *ERA 2* will wait for the remote computer to begin sending the file, and it will store it automatically.

Save your user function by pressing CTRL-F, then exit to the main menu and select option 4, Save Terminal Setup. A default file name will appear in the brackets on the display; you can use it by pressing RETURN, or specify a new name by typing it in. You are now ready to enter Interactive Mode and begin transmission.

Notes of caution: You may delete and edit user functions with available commands (CTRL-C), cursors, and delete keys while off-line. Be sure to keep your CAP lock down at all times on the Apple while creating a user function. The FILE NAME AND DISK DRIVE NUMBER MUST BE TYPED IDENTICALLY ON BOTH SYSTEMS; otherwise, *ERA 2* will get confused and abort the transfer.

Connection and File Transfer: Once in Interactive Mode, press the appropriate user function key, Open Apple 0, in this example. The system automatically accesses your stored user function, then dials, logs-on, and establishes a reliable link, session, and file transfer. A status line showing the progression from physical connection all the way up to file transfer flashes on the screen. You do nothing now but watch. In reliable MNP file transfer mode, the system automatically sets the communication parameters and does the file translation necessary to accommodate dissimilar operating systems. You don't have to specify parameters in advance. All files are automatically checked for accuracy.

Apple IIe to IBM PC (Step-by-Step Modem Connection)

Equipment:

Apple IIe equipped with *ERA 2* Modem and Software detailed above. [Any Hayes-compatible modem will work with certain restrictions (see Comment)]

IBM PC with 128K, one dual-sided disk drive (minimum), DOS 2.1 Hayes Smartmodem (300 or 1200 bps) or compatible

> Alternately: Microcom Series RX/1000 modems or Series PC/2000
> *IBM Personal Communications Manager* (Microcom, Inc.)

Procedure: Install modems and boot software in the manner outlined above. On the PC, you'll need to make a working diskette from the *IBM Personal Communications Manager* master diskette. This involves copying parts of the diskette and configuring the system to your specific disk drive setup. The system automatically starts a Set-up program to help you. After typing date and time, you'll see that the screen clears. A new screen describing the available configurations for running the program now appears. Designate hardware parameters (disk drives, screen display, column width, etc.), then follow prompts on the screen to copy files from the master diskette onto the work diskette. You will have to answer additional configuration questions (such as your name, the computer's phone number, and information about your modem) the first time before the program will let you get started.

Getting Started: The *IBM Personal Communications Manager*, a communications program, implements most of the essential elements of MNP. However, it has less capability than *ERA 2*. *ERA 2* modems and software are available for the IBM PC and XT, and they follow the same programming conventions as the Apple II *ERA 2* system.

The Terminal Mode menu provides most of the same functions of the *ERA 2* menu, including the Interactive Mode, Saving and Loading Terminal Set-ups, Display/Change Communications Settings, and Create/Edit User functions. With this menu it's possible to communicate with remote computers by setting communications parameters manually and then entering interactive mode to dial up, or else by invoking specific user functions that automatically access The Source, *CompuServe*, and Dow Jones News/Retrieval. These functions can be edited using codes similar, but not identical to the codes used in the *ERA 2* version.

Sending and receiving files are accomplished in two modes. First, nonverified or normal mode, by pressing either Alt-S (Send File Control) or Alt R (Receive File Control). The system will ask you to specify a file name and press RETURN. It will immediately send your file to the remote computer. The Alt-R command stores incoming data on a disk file. If the file specified for storage of incoming data already exists, you can either append the incoming information to it or overwrite the existing file with the new information. You can pause or abort the transmission in midstream by pressing P (for pause) or E (for end).

A true, error-free MNP file transfer must be accomplished by selecting Option #2 of the main menu, Electronic Mail, and then choosing the Send/Receive file options. This sets the IBM PC to communicate with any other computer implementing MNP protocols, and will work in both attended and unattended modes. The system checks the modem's status, then sets communications parameters accordingly. Specify the Send Files option or the Receive Files option, and the program will provide prompts asking you to specify the names of the files, the subject, and the time of day they are to be sent or received. The system will then automatically check an Outgoing Mail Log or an Incoming Mail Log to find the files or space to store incoming files. Status messages will flash informing the operator that the program is AWAITING LINK, SENDING, or RECEIVING.

The Apple setup for sending and receiving files is the same as the procedure outlined in the Apple IIe to Macintosh connection detailed above and in Chapter 2.

Caution: When sending a file from the *IBM Personal Communications Manager* to *ERA 2*, make sure to enter something in the subject field. What's entered as a subject becomes the name for the file received on the *ERA 2* system. A transfer can't take place without it!

Notes and Comment: MNP is an exciting protocol because it's sophisticated, easy-to-use, and offers a communications architecture that follows closely the layered services of OSI. MNP handles session and presentation/applications functions, can create virtual file formats capable of accommodating data transfer between dissimilar hardware and operating systems—PC-DOS, Apple DOS, TRS-DOS, to name a few. Software packages implementing MNP also provide preset functions to access the major databases—Dow Jones News/Retrieval, The Source, CompuServe, MCI Mail, Western Union EasyLink, and RCA Global Communications. Some products, like *ERA 2*, for example, are also equipped to emulate popular terminals, among them, the DEC VT100, DEC VT52, and IBM 3101. These features expand the range of communications beyond ASCII file transfer and make MNP an excellent candidate for broad-based support in the communications industry.

At present the MNP, as implemented in *ERA 2*, features two kinds of error-checking functions: a reliable link and MNP file transfer mode. This means that sender and receiver can swap verified messages in both terminal mode (interactive link) and in file transfer mode, a dual capability few other communications packages can claim. The file transfer component enables computers to swap binary, Applesoft BASIC, and other programming files, text files with control codes included, or message files, which are ASCII files without control codes. A sophisticated sessions protocol allows communicating systems to swap pertinent systems information and to determine whether special and automatic file and data translation procedures are needed. The protocol can be used with both asynchronous and synchronous communications.

Quick Connection Techniques

General: Sometimes your connection needs are quick and dirty. You've got Apples and IBM PCs, or compatibles, a portable Radio Shack TRS-80 Model 100, or CP/M computers, and you need to transfer rough drafts of documents between them and a document-editing system on a minicomputer.

Most likely, your Apple or CP/M computers are at home, while the IBM PC is at the office. Your portable computer may be in your briefcase. Each computer is equipped with a modem, word processing software, and nonmatching telecommunications programs offering no more in common than a buffered terminal mode and a straight X-ON/X-OFF communications protocol. Can you make a successful file transfer? Chances are you can, by converting text files on each end to binary files, and then editing them with your word processor with proper indentation and line spacing.

In these brief studies we summarize experiments with an Apple IIe, Compaq Plus (an IBM PC XT-compatible), Kaypro 4, and a DEC PDP-11 (ATEX COMM TLM) minicomputer and document-editing system. All of the computers are routinely used by information workers.

Apple IIe to Compaq Plus (Step-by-Step Connection)

Equipment:

<u>Apple IIe</u>
Computer with two disk
   drives and 64K memory
DOS 3.3

<u>Compaq Plus</u>
Computer with two
   disk drives (one
   hard disk and

Apple IIe
Hayes Micromodem IIe (or
  any of several Apple-
  compatible modems)
Modular phone cord
Modular jack

Compaq Plus
  one floppy),
  256K memory
Bytcom 212AD
  Modem
IBM Asynchronous
  communications
  adaptor
RS-232-C cable
Modular phone
  cord

Software
Transend 2

Telpac (U.S. Robot-
  ics, Chicago)

Procedure: Install the modems and attach them to modular phone cords as outlined in the previous case studies. The external Bytcom 212AD modem should be connected to an RS-232-C cable, which will then plug into the IBM Asynchronous Communications Adaptor card. You should install the card in whichever free slot is available inside your computer. (On the Compaq Plus, two I/O slots are available for modems, asynch adaptors, and other communications equipment.) Your communication software may ask you, in the hardware configuration setup, to designate each port as "COM1:" or "COM2:".

Prepare your hardware setup and configure the communications software to the proper requirements. Any of dozens of modems designed to work with the Apple IIe and Compaq Plus are acceptable. Just make sure your communications software is designed to drive your modem and offers the standard communications menus as well as a buffered terminal mode capable of sending and receiving standard ASCII text files.

Boot your Transend or other telecommunications program on the Apple and do the same for the Compaq, IBM PC, or operationally compatible machine. Remember: this is a straight text file transfer in terminal mode. In most cases, you won't be using protocols beyond the simple X-ON/X-OFF flow control. If you are planning to transfer graphics or special formatting characters, you may need to establish a translation table in your software to convert special characters into ASCII codes the other computer can store and interpret. A translation or look-up table is merely a device that changes one ASCII value to another. For example, if a receiving computer can't accept a CTRL-Z

(ASCII 26), a translation table would translate 26 to 00, or some other harmless code.

Choose the Define Parameter Set option on Transend, and, if using *Telpac*, use the DEF command as the first operation after booting. DEF allows you to set communications parameters. Specify these minimum requirements:

8 bits, no parity, 1 stop bit; or
7 bits, no parity, 1 stop bit (as shown in Figure 8.4)
300 baud
Half duplex
Output line feeds after carriage returns, if possible
Capture buffer on
X-ON/X-OFF enabled

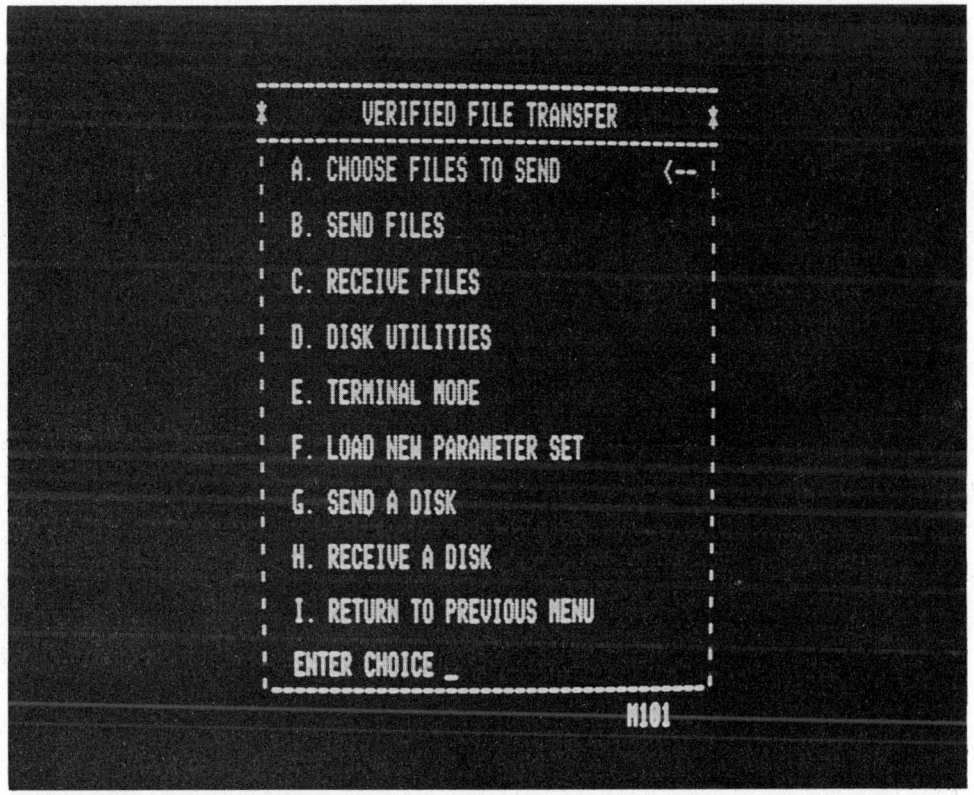

Figure 8.4 Transend's verified file transfer menu. Error-checking protocols are used for this kind of transfer, and operation is transparent to the user. (*Photo: Stephen Ross*)

Save these rules on a disk and choose the Buffered Terminal Mode option in your program, the term capture buffer, or TERM. In the *Telpac* program, type TERM, and enter terminal mode. Decide who will send, receive, and dial. If your IBM PC at the office has an automatic timing device with which to send transmissions, and also has an auto-answer and electronic-mail capture and storage feature, you can set it to receive. Access terminal mode on your Apple, place the call, and watch the screen go blank. If you are dialing into a system controlled by a human operator, type back and forth in terminal mode.

Note: We made this connection using Transend/*Telpac* in an 8-bit, no parity, 1 stop bit mode. The transmission was fine. Our only problem at first was that we were in full duplex and thus couldn't see our typing echoed locally on the computer screens. Switching to half duplex solved that problem, and our characters were echoed both locally and out the modem port to the remote computer, so we could carry out a dialogue in terminal mode on the screen.

Once you've assured yourself that parameters are matched, prepare for file transfer. Make sure both of your files are in text format. Avoid sending graphics or control codes unless you've created and verified a common ASCII translation table. Normally, Apple has a different way of handling the eighth, high-order bit. It's set to one in the Apple and zero in the IBM PC. If you send graphics or formatting codes requiring the high bit, they will be garbled. You must stick to "plain vanilla" and, where possible, a 7-bit data word. Specify your file name both on the sending and receiving ends, and initiate transfer by accessing your Transfer options menu. Normally, you'll send from a disk file to the receiver's memory buffer.

You may find that each computer's system may either fail to send or acknowledge line feeds. The Apple screen controller, however, will provide line feeds when the incoming data exceed the maximum width of the screen. On an IBM or a Compaq, though, a file may appear to be overwritten. You should save the file nonetheless and reboot it with a word processor; line feeds will then appear, and the file will be legible.

Kaypro 4 to Apple IIe (Step-by-Step Direct Connection)

Equipment:

Kaypro 4 computer with two floppy disk drives 64K	Apple IIe equipped exactly as in the last case study

      memory, built-in 300-baud
        modem
Modular phone cord
<u>Software</u>
SuperTerm (supplied with the   Transend 2
    Kaypro 4)

Procedure: Connect the modular phone cord directly from one modem to the other. Boot the communications software on both computers. Choose your parameter-set menus, and define your parameters as follows:

Kaypro	Apple
8 bits, no parity, 1 stop bit	8 bits, no parity, 1 stop bit
the *Super Term* program has no special feature to set the 8th bit condition	8th bit condition for modem output set on "low"
Capture buffer on	Full duplex
	Capture buffer on

    Alternately, try a 7-bit, even-parity, one stop bit setting on both computers. Then you won't need to consider the eighth bit condition.
    On the Kaypro 4, choose Dial from the main menu, then on-line. The computer turns on its carrier signal and waits to get a carrier from the modem. On the Apple, enter Terminal Mode, then input any number (1 will do). The modem will dial, thinking it's hooked to a telephone system. The Kaypro will wait for the carrier, and once it gets it from the Apple, it will send its own. You cannot reverse the dial procedure (Kaypro to Apple) easily, as the Hayes modem needs a ringing signal; it won't go off-hook without it. So you must dial from Apple to Kaypro, and proceed with file transfer from there.
    Once you get a connection, type back and forth in Terminal Mode. You should get clear characters on both ends. If you get garbage going from the Apple to the Kaypro, it means that your eighth bit is coming through, with distortion. The Kaypro will turn any eighth bit from Apple DOS into a funny graphics character. Recheck your settings. Either suppress the eighth bit with an eighth bit low option on your Transend menu or change all your settings to match a 7-bit protocol and try the connection again. In our experiments, we found that transmission was clear going both ways only when the eighth bit was suppressed on the Apple side. The Apple, however, had no problem handling the eighth bit protocol from the Kaypro.

You can initiate file transfer as soon as you've established the matching of protocols. Follow procedures outlined above. You should find that ASCII files transferred from the Apple to the Kaypro will be legible. However, you may get a graphics + sign on certain lines; this indicates that certain codes are being distorted. The Kaypro will send a file back to the Apple, but with a few extra errors. Use the 7-bit format to see whether that improves matters. Then save the files and edit them using your word processing packages.

Apple IIe to ATEX TLM (DEC PDP-11) System (Step-by-Step Connection)

Equipment:

Apple IIe as equipped above
Transend or other communications software equipped for buffered terminal transmission, half duplex

ATEX COMM TLM (a DEC PDP-11-based minicomputer equipped with 8 cpu, Control Data hard disk drives, and terminals)
Equipped with A500 remote modem unit, disk drive, and communications software (able to transfer files and respond to ATEX system commands). Allows modem transmission from other ATEX systems or microcomputers that have open-formatted ASCII files

General: This is a modem connection between a reporter's microcomputer and a fair-size, DEC PDP-11 minicomputer system. The steps taken here apply to any variety of personal computers linking remotely to the ATEX text editor system using modems and ordinary dial-up line.

ATEX has long been the granddad of newspaper video display terminal systems. Equipped with an asynchronous modem and a remote communications unit containing a disk drive and software ATEX accepts files from computers on the outside. The trick is simply to format the document correctly, using acceptable control characters, and also to set bit protocol to the safe 7-bit level. These controls allow for standard text file transfer.

Specific Features/Problems: Attempts at initiating file transfer in full-duplex mode failed using the Apple system described above. Only a half-duplex setting will work.

In full duplex, the Apple disk drive stops dead after sending a single character. On the screen, one or two characters of a file will be echoed back, and if you press the space bar, the screen "unfreezes" and more data are sent along the line. Pressing the space bar is an unsatisfactory remedy for sending long files, however; half duplex clears the problem by eliminating the echo-back feature. If a program is set in full duplex, it waits to receive an echoed character before it sends the next one. If the character is not echoed back, or is misinterpreted for some reason, the computer stops transmitting.

Frozen screens can be a problem when two different personal computers are communicating. While sending files from Transend on the Apple to *Crosstalk* on the IBM PC, we encountered the frozen screen. But again, the problem was cleared immediately by switching to a half-duplex setting. Whenever possible, unless stated otherwise in connection directions, transmit in half-duplex to other minicomputer and microcomputer systems until you are certain the connection will go through.

Procedure: Prepare, off-line, a text file on the Apple for transfer. Strike out all header and formatting codes, such as dot commands, indentations, control characters, and the like. Switch to single-space. Eliminate all spaces between paragraphs. At the top of the file, insert the necessary header information, which must be provided by the minicomputer operator that will allow the minicomputer to recognize the file as legitimate. In our case, the ID and header codes appeared as follows:

```
{ID NAME OF FILE{QUCHIEF-COMPANY NAME{by EMMETT{BT
```

This was followed immediately by text formatted to the specifications of the ATEX system.

A reporter's document would thus look like this:

```
{ID TRANSEND2{QU CHIEF-NAL{By EMMETT{BT
                    ¦
              Text follows
                    ¦
```

What do these codes mean? They are simply the formatting codes that the ATEX minicomputer system needs to accept and format text properly on the dedicated terminals connected to the system.

Once you've formatted your document correctly, resave it as a text file. Boot your Transend or other communications package. Set your parameters to these minimal requirements:

7 bits, 1 stop bit, no parity (even parity will work also)
Half duplex
300 baud
Capture buffer on
Output line feeds off
(include a default phone number if your software allows it)
X-ON/X-OFF enabled

Now save the parameters, access terminal mode, and dial into the minicomputer system. Once your screen goes blank, and you've established the connection, exit terminal mode with CTRL-A, CTRL-X keystrokes on the Apple and choose your transfer option, Disk File to Modem. Specify your file name(s). Use voice phone transmission with an operator of the minicomputer system to confirm that your file arrived safely.

A procedure such as this one offers no error checking. However text files will be transmitted with a good amount of reliability. Check with your minicomputer operator to ascertain the exact access codes and procedures for the particular system you want to enter. Most minis and mainframe supporting asynchronous, ASCII communications will specify a protocol and type of file formatting that will let you get in and communicate.

Radio Shack TRS-80 Model 100 to Apple IIe, Compaq Plus, Osborne I

General: The Radio Shack TRS-80 Model 100 is a versatile portable computer and telecommunications device. Equipped with a 300-baud modem and a separate RS-232-C serial port, the Model 100 offers a program, called *TELCOM*, which handles communications rules: baud, data word lengths, parity settings, as well as auto-dial/auto-answer and X-ON/X-OFF flow-control protocol. In this set of experiments, we used a Model 100 to exchange data files back and forth with the Apple IIe, Compaq Plus, and Osborne I computers.

Special Features/Problems: While the Radio Shack offers the advantages of portability and friendly communications procedures, it does have a couple of drawbacks. Aside from limited memory, which restricts the length of files being transferred, Model 100, like other Radio Shack computers, doesn't send line feeds after carriage returns when transmitting data. This means that the receiving computer must provide the line feeds to prevent a file from being overwritten on the screen display or in memory. Though some telecommunications programs either automatically insert line feeds or provide menu choices to do so, other communications programs do not. In that case, you have to find some way of inserting line feeds in the transmitted or received text.

One method, as we've already mentioned, is to save the file and then boot up an applications package like a word processor that provides line feeds automatically. You may also insert line feed commands manually as you enter text on the Radio Shack—CTRL-J is the line feed character—as long as the command does not immediately follow a carriage return. The Radio Shack computer will strip it out in that case. Another option is to write a small BASIC program on the Radio Shack computer—or send for one—that does the job for you. You won't need to do that, however, unless you're planning to communicate with a recalcitrant computer, like the Osborne I.

Here's a program, courtesy of George Heidenrich, that handles the line feed insertion. It runs on the TRS-80 Model 100.

```
5  CLS:PRINT "WELCOME TO 300 BAUD TRANSFER OF"
10 PRINT "TRS-80 MODEL 100 TEXT TO OSBORNE CP/M"
20 MAXFILES -2
30 EF$-CHR$(26)
40 INPUT "FILE TO SEND!";FI$
45 OPEN FI$ FOR INPUT AS 1
50 INPUT "TO RS232C OR PRINTER (R/P)";O$
55 IF O$="R" OR R$="r" THEN FO$-"COM 38N1D":
   PRINT "RECEIVING
   CUMPUTER: STAT RDR:-PTR:
   then PIP (filename.typ)-RDR:
   [E:INPUT "READY";AN$:GOTO 60
57 IF O$="P" OR O$="p" THEN FO$=LPT:
   INPUT "PRINTER READY";
   AN$:GOTO 60
60 OPEN FO$ FOR OUTPUT AS 2
70 IF O$="P" OR O$="p" THEN GOTO 200
```

```
100 A$=INPUT$(1,1)
110 PRINT #2,A$
120 IF EOF(1) THEN GOTO 1000
130 GOTO 100
200 A$=INPUT(1,1)
210 PRINT #2,A$
220 IF EOF(1) THEN GOTO 1000
230 GOTO 200
1000 IF O$="R" OR O$="r" THEN PRINT #S,EF$
1005 IF O$="P" OR O$="p" THEN CLOSE 2
1010 BEEP: PRINT "RECEIVING COMPUTER: STAT RDR:-TTY"
   :FOR X=1 TO
      2000: NEXT:MENU
```

The other major difficulty is the way the computer handles the eighth, or high bit when it receives information from computers outside the Tandy family. The Model 100 can't read the bit properly. *TELCOM* has no programming to interpret and translate high bits—usually formatting or special graphics bits—into characters it recognizes. When it receives data from computers running *WordStar*, for example, which requires the eighth bit to format end of words and end of lines, it appears to turn the bit into a funny graphics character. Sometimes it misreads an eighth bit as a parity bit, so if you're using computers to send certain specialized data files to the Radio Shack requiring the high bit, prepare for interface hassle. The solution, whenever possible, is to go "plain vanilla"—convert your binary and BASIC files to text files that have no special graphics or eighth bit formats, and transmit using a 7-bit protocol.

Equipment:

Radio Shack Model 100	Apple IIe
Radio Shack TRS-80 Model 100, 24K RAM, Proprietary operating system, built-in modem modular telephone cable	Apple IIe Computer with 64K RAM and two disk drives, 64K, DOS 3.3 Hayes MicroModem IIe (300 baud) modular telephone cable
Modular phone jack	Modular jack

Procedure: On the Model 100, plug the silver-colored branch of the phone cable into the wall phone jack, and attach the amber end to the modular jack on your telephone. Now plug in the adaptor end of the phone cable into the Radio Shack modem socket located at the back

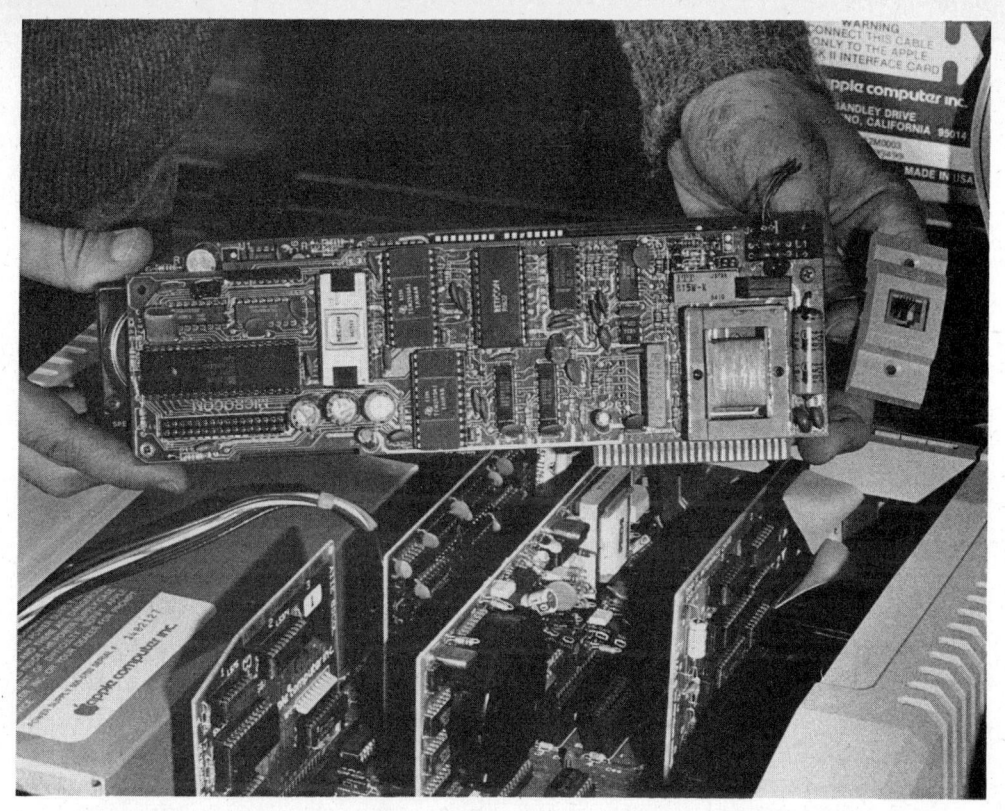

Figure 8.5 The *ERA 2* modem for the Apple II is also a card modem that installs in one of the I/O slots. It has its own modular phone socket. (*Photo: Stephen Ross*)

panel of the computer. You will now have a three-point cable connection. The amber attachment to your telephone will allow you to pick up the handset to get a dial tone. This may be necessary if you are dialing through switched telephone systems that have a slow dial-tone pick-up.

Install the Hayes Micromodem IIe in an available slot in the Apple. As an alternate, use any other Bell 103- or 212-compatible modem as long as you have the proper serial card and adapter cable to go with it. The Era II modem for the Apple is in Figure 8.5. Plug a phone cord into the Hayes modular connector, and attach the other end to the telephone wall jack. Boot your communications software. In this particular connection, we used Transend 2, which offers great flexibility in its control of communications settings. But other packages for the

Apple, featuring adjustable settings, X-ON/X-OFF, and standard ASCII transfer in a buffered terminal mode, will work also.

Find and toggle the switch on the side of the Model 100 to originate or answer. Turn on the Radio Shack and, using the arrow keys, move the cursor across the screen until you reach the *TELCOM* program. Press your STATUS function key F3, and making use of the standard Radio Shack codes (see explanation below), set your parameters as follows:

> Modem (M); Full Duplex; 300 baud, seven bits, No Parity, One Stop Bit, X-ON/X-OFF protocol enabled.

This translates into the following Model 100 code: M7N1E, which you should type in at the status line.

NOTE: The newer Radio Shack Model 200 displays minor operational differences from the Model 100, although both TELCOM software programs function in virtually the same way and both RS-232-C serial interfaces are identical, according to Tandy Corp.

In the portable Model 200, however, the STATUS line of TELCOM is longer and requires users to set additional parameters, among them control-character filtering and line feeds. The user first inputs the standard TELCOM communications rules (M for modem, for example, then codes for baud rate, word length, parity, stop bits and X-ON/X-OFF), then adds an "N" or an "I" for control character filtering, which tells the Model 200 either to allow control characters through "normally" or ignore the control codes (with the exception of carriage returns and line feeds; these come through automatically). The user then sets an "N" or an "I" for added line feeds. "N" means don't add extra line feeds and "I" means add them. Finally, the new 200 STATUS line allows the user to specify pulse or tone dialing. (Tone is indicated by a "T"; pulse dialing is indicated by specifying the numbers 10 or 20, indicating pulses per second.)

Unlike the Model 100, the commands for Originate a call ("O") or Answer a call ("A") are input directly from the keyboard. In the Model 100, they are set as a hardware toggle. The Model 200 also offers a 16-line screen as opposed to Model 100's 8 line screen. But other communications functions are identical.

{Note on Tandy's Model 600: A still newer Tandy computer, the portable Model 600, uses a different operating system and offers a much higher level of functionality, according to Tandy Corp. The Model 600 has a version of TELCOM, but otherwise offers much more by way of sophisticated features: 80 columns, one quarter megabyte storage, a disk drive, and XMODEM protocol.

Explanation: The "M" tells the computer to look to its modem port for input/output. The "7" number is bit setting, "N" indicates no parity, "1" indicates 1 stop bit, and the final letter indicates X-ON/ protocol is Enabled. (E-Enabled; D Disabled.) Baud and parity settings are designated as follows for the Model 100.

300 baud = 3 600 baud = 4
1200 baud = 5 2400 baud = 6
4800 baud = 7 9600 baud = 8
Parity Settings: E = Even, O = Odd, I = Ignore Parity
X-ON/X-OFF Enabled = E X-On/X-OFF Disabled = D

Some sample settings on your Radio Shack would look like the following: 2400 baud, 8 bits, no parity, 1 stop bit, X-ON disenabled = 68N1D; 1200 baud, 7 bits, even parity, 1 stop bit, X-ON enabled = 57E1E. (*Note:* when you use the RS-232-C serial port, which is capable of transmitting from 300 to 9600 baud, you eliminate the "M" from the initial sequence of commands. "M" is only used for the modem setting, which runs at 300 baud automatically.)

The full- and half-duplex toggle appears on the STATUS screen. It can be switched back and forth by pressing the appropriate function key.

Now access your telecommunications program on the Apple and adjust the menu parameters to match your Model 100. Note that if you are using Transend or a similarly designed program, which offers a number of bit/parity and stop-bit combinations, but no specific "7 bits, No parity, 1 stop bit" combination, you will be able to set your parameters as "8 bits, no parity, one stop bit," with an eighth bit *preserved* setting, and maintain the Radio Shack settings (seven bits, no parity, 1 stop bit) as before. A preserved setting means that the telecommunications program will allow the eighth bit to go through no matter if it's low (a 0-bit setting) or high (a 1-bit setting). In the case of a straight Apple ASCII text file, the essential data are sent in 7-bit data words. Radio Shack strips out the eighth bit anyway, so the effect is as though the Apple were set at 7 bits, no parity, 1 stop bit. When we tried these settings, they worked quite well, and text was transferred back and forth between the Apple and Radio Shack clearly.

In addition, there are some supplementary settings to make on the Apple software program. Make sure that the Capture buffer is on.

Adjust the settings for your print buffer. In our particular setup, the Transend default settings appeared as follows:

    FULL DUPLEX
    PRINT BUFFER OFF
    CAPTURE BUFFER IS ON
    PRINTER LF (LINEFEED) AFTER CR (CARRIAGE RETURN)
      IS ON
    OUTPUT LF AFTER CR IS OFF
    PRINT BUFFER 256 BYTES
    CAPTURE BUFFER 13568 BYTES

We ignored the print settings as we were focusing on a buffer-to-buffer data transfer. If you want to output data to your printer, turn the print buffer on and adjust the line feeds accordingly.

You're now ready to begin your connection.

To dial from the Apple, load your Radio Shack parameter set, access Buffered Terminal Mode on the main menu, then Terminal Mode, and choose the Place Call option. The menu will ask you to type in the phone number. If you were using another program, like *ERA 2*, you'd go through a different menu, as in Figure 8.6. Figure 8.7 (page 148) shows another *ERA 2* menu that will allow you to complete calls automatically. Set your Radio Shack Model 100 to answer. After setting your status, pick up the phone handset to make sure you have a dial tone. In areas with slow dial-tone recovery, the Radio Shack may have trouble dialing and receiving successfully, so it's important that you ascertain whether a dial tone exists.

Now press the RETURN key and let the Apple execute its dialing function. As the phone rings at the other end, press F4, Terminal Mode, on the Model 100. Terminal Mode lets both computers swap handshaking signals. Once clearance to send data is complete, the Apple will beep and its screen will go blank. Type back and forth on the Apple and Model 100 to determine whether all communications settings are matched.

If you get a mixture of garbage and legible characters on your Model 100 or Apple, check your parity setting. Switch on both ends to 7 bits, even parity, 1 stop bit, and then recheck the connection. If you can, avoid 8-bit settings entirely. If you get duplicate letters, recheck your duplex settings. You can easily toggle to half duplex.

If you fail to get a connection, check dial tone again and redial from the Apple. Check the Carrier Detect LEDs on your Hayes modem; the LED will monitor the status of the carrier signal from the remote modem, and light when it detects it. Remember: as soon as you hear a ring, press F4 on the Model 100. The Radio Shack will not send a

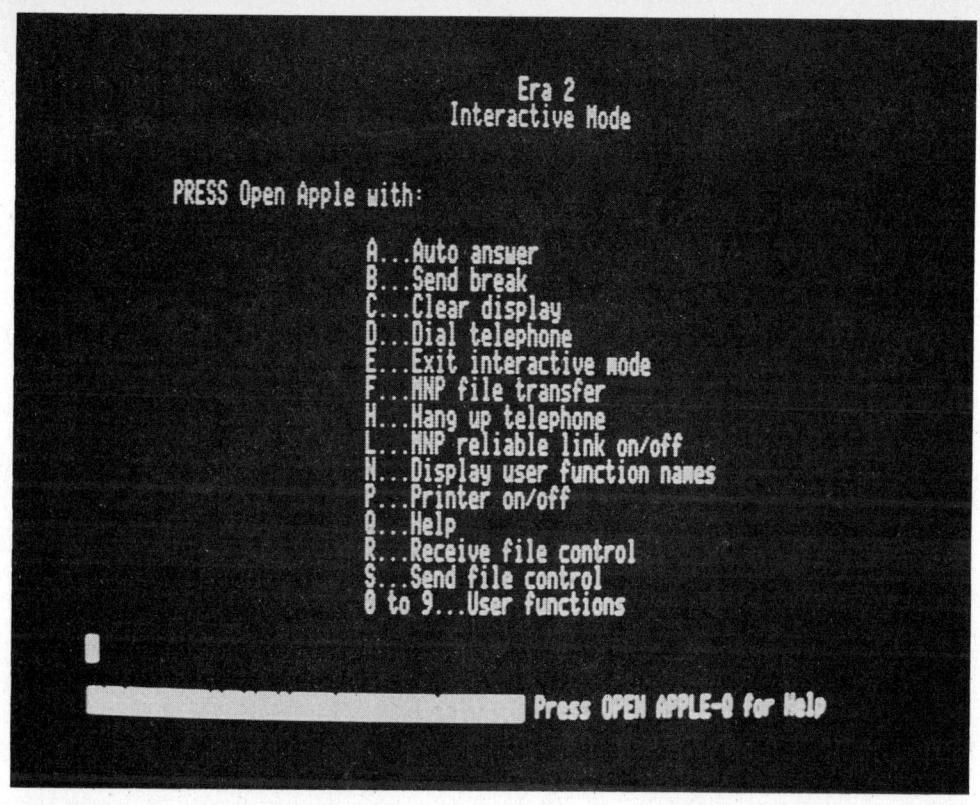

```
                    Era 2
                Interactive Mode

      PRESS Open Apple with:

                  A...Auto answer
                  B...Send break
                  C...Clear display
                  D...Dial telephone
                  E...Exit interactive mode
                  F...MNP file transfer
                  H...Hang up telephone
                  L...MNP reliable link on/off
                  N...Display user function names
                  P...Printer on/off
                  Q...Help
                  R...Receive file control
                  S...Send file control
                  0 to 9...User functions



                                 Press OPEN APPLE-Q for Help
```

Figure 8.6 *ERA 2*'s interactive mode allows a number of user-selectable capabilities. (*Photo: Stephen Ross*)

carrier signal unless you're in Terminal Mode. If you press F4 before you hear a ring, you're liable to get a high-pitched squawking sound from the Model 100, which is highly unpleasant.

To initiate file transfer from Transend to *TELCOM*, press the exit terminal mode keystroke combination on the Apple CTRL-A, CTRL-X, in sequence, and choose the Transfer Options selection on the first menu you see, and then choose your mode of file transfer on the submenu. Most likely, your file will be stored on disk, so you'll choose the Disk File to Modem option. You could also choose a Buffer to Modem option, sending files first by loading them into memory.

On the Model 100 side, press the F2 function key, a command that will prepare the computer for downloading. Responding to a prompt, you'll specify a name under which the incoming Apple file is automatically stored. Hit the RETURN key once, and downloading will begin. You'll see text very quickly scrolling across your Model 100 screen.

The Model 100 will remain in the downloading mode until it

receives a special end-of-file command—CTRL-Z—from the Apple. Enter CTRL-Z manually from the Apple keyboard after file transfer is complete and you've returned to Terminal Mode. Pressing F8 will terminate the connection on the Model 100. CTRL-A, CTRL-Z will hang up the modem on the Apple.

(*Note:* you may find that some of the text is overwritten on the Radio Shack. However, line feeds are recorded in memory, so that when you reload your text in an edit mode, you'll find it's readable and complete.)

To send files from the Model 100 to the Apple, first set the Model 100 to originate a call. Then pick up your phone handset and check for the dial tone. Enter the *TELCOM* program, set your status indicators, and, at the prompt, enter the number of the remote system manually, or load it from a file in Radio Shack memory. On the Apple end, enter Terminal Mode and press the option allowing your modem to auto-answer, or Wait for Phone to Ring. Your Model 100 will now dial the Apple. Once the connection is established, type back and forth in Terminal Mode before you begin file transfer. Press the File UPLOAD function on the Radio Shack, specify your file name and width. (Sixty-five is a comfortable column width if you're hard-pressed to guess; otherwise, press RETURN and leave it blank. This tells the Model 100 to send carriage returns only where they are discovered in the text.) A RETURN keystroke will start the upload.

Once the file is stored in Apple memory, exit Terminal Mode, choose the Buffer Options menu, and save the capture buffer to a disk file. If your software has an auto-buffer-save option, choose it before you begin the file transfer. It will tell your computer to automatically start writing the contents of the buffer to a disk file. If you use the auto-buffer-save option, don't forget to enable the X-ON/X-OFF protocol on the Model 100. Flow control will be needed to halt the data transmission temporarily while the Apple writes its buffer to the disk. Apple suspends all receiving functions during disk access.

Radio Shack TRS-80 Model 100 to Compaq Plus (Step-by-Step Connection)

Equipment:

| Radio Shack Model 100 equipped with modem cable, 24K | Compaq Plus computer Computer with two disk drives, 64K RAM |

RAM, as specified above
Modular wall jack

Bytcom modem (Bell 212-AD compatible)
IBM Asynchronous Communications Adaptor (RS-232-C interface port)
RS-232-C cable

Software
TELCOM (built-into Model 100)

Telpac (U.S. Robotics)

Procedure: Install communications equipment as outlined above. On the Compaq, boot the *Telpac* software program. Choose, as starting communications parameters, 300 baud, 7 bits, no parity, one stop bit, at half duplex. Set the program to auto-answer and save the capture buffer. On the Model 100, access the *TELCOM* menu and match the parameters as specified in the procedures above. Disable X-ON/X-OFF.

Using the Model 100, dial up the remote system and type back and forth in terminal mode. If you switch to a full-duplex setting, you won't see your own characters echoed to the screen. In half duplex, your characters are both echoed to your own screen and sent out over the modem port. It's easier to correct a connection if you can see what's being printed on both ends.

Now prepare to upload or download a file, following the procedures specified above.

Specify a name for the file and execute. On the Compaq side, prepare to receive a file. As you do, text will scroll across the screen. If the text is longer than 80 columns, the Compaq screen controller will provide a carriage return and line feeds; otherwise, the incoming text from the Radio Shack may overtype itself. The Radio Shack, again, has stripped out the line feeds. Nonetheless, save the received file on Compaq to a disk, and then review the file using a text editor or other applications package. You will find that the document was stored adequately in memory; the word-processing package will input line feeds and the document will now appear formatted and legible on your Compaq computer screen.

Reversing the direction, from Compaq to Radio Shack, you'll find that received files on Radio Shack aren't overwritten because Radio Shack's display controller provides line feeds and carriage returns. It's all downright quirky, but that's the way these systems were designed. Because there's a way to provide line feeds on both ends, you can transfer and edit files between the computers without a problem.

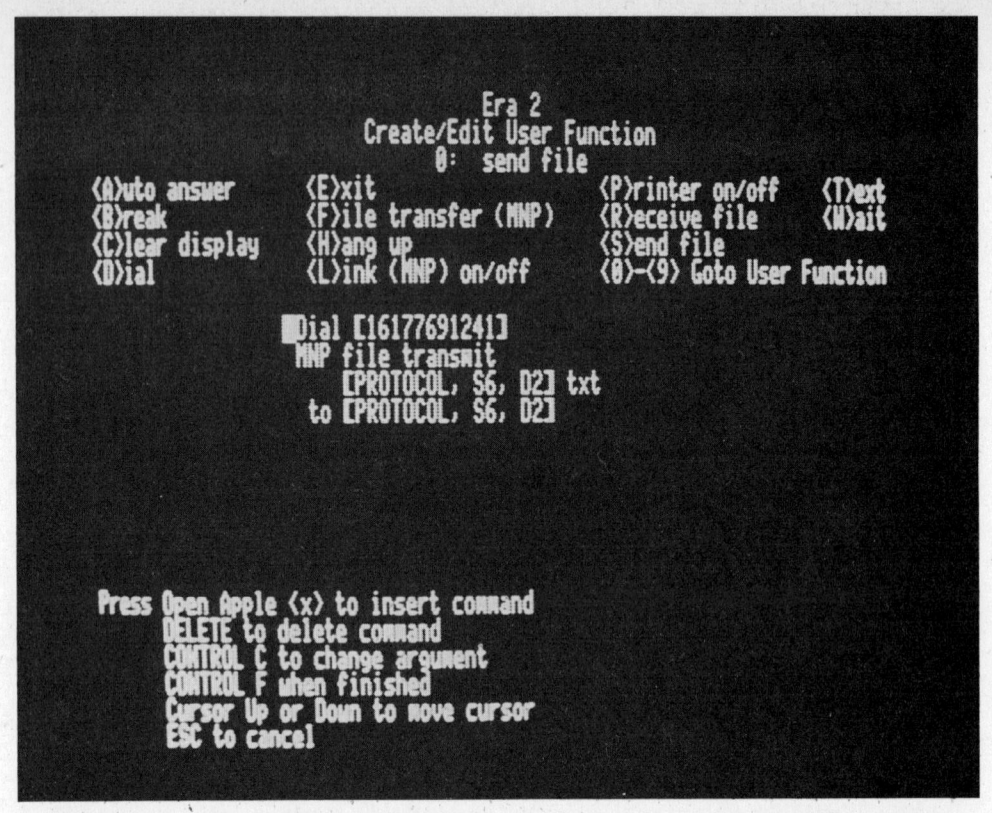

Figure 8.7 With *ERA 2*'s user-function menu, you can create functions that are essentially macro instructions. You can make a whole series of functions happen automatically. (*Photo: Stephen Ross*)

Radio Shack TRS-80 Model 100 to Osborne I (Step-by-Step Connection)

Equipment:

Radio Shack Model 100 as equipped above with *TELCOM* communications Model 100 telephone cable

Osborne I with its own modem *AMCALL* (Auto Micro-Call Communications program MicroCall Services 2.06)

Procedure: There are two possible ways to proceed: either use the phone lines, or direct-connect a phone cable from one modem socket to the other. We will review the direct-connect technique first, since the other follows the standard techniques we've outlined above.

First, plug the Radio Shack beige phone cable into the Osborne I modular modem socket, attach the other end directly to the Model 100, set the Model 100 to answer, then access *TELCOM* in the manner described above. On the Osborne I, boot the *AMCALL* telecommunications program, and choose a parameter setting as follows:

FULL DUPLEX
300 BAUD
PROTOCOL: X/ON (ENABLED)
7 BITS, EVEN PARITY, 1 STOP BIT
FILE NAME (SPECIFY, eg. B:RSXFROS.RST)
CONTROL CHARACTER SCREEN ON
ORIGINATE MODE

These options are presented in turn on the *AMCALL* menu. A default configuration will appear first. You may change the configuration, escape to CP/M, or use the defaults. You select a letter on the menu to make a change. U, for example, refers to UART data bits specification (e.g., 7 or 8 data bits, parity bit, stop bits, etc.). When you press U the operator accesses the bits menu and makes a selection that will change the UART settings. Ditto for all the other parameters. A control-character screen, as the name implies, filters the screen of control codes so the captured or sent text is in straight ASCII.

Set the same communications parameters on the Model 100. You are still in the M = Modem mode. Even though this is a direct connection, your computers must look for data through the modem port.

On the *AMCALL* menu, press O for originate, then the @ key, and then RETURN. This tells *AMCALL* to use the telephone dialer and to send out a carrier signal. The Model 100, recognizing the signal as a phone call, will buzz. At that sound, press F4 for Terminal Mode. The Osborne will flash a message saying Connection Established, Begin Communications. Now type back and forth in Terminal Mode to ensure that your parameters are matched.

To transfer a file from the Model 100 to the Osborne, execute the following: on the Osborne, press an ESC R, which prepares it to receive a file. On the Radio Shack, press F3, File to Upload, and specify a file name, a width, and press RETURN. The Radio Shack upload light will turn on. Your Osborne will not automatically save the file on the disk, however, so you must enter a separate CTRL-Z command from the Radio Shack keyboard. That closes the file and now writes it, as specified, on your Osborne disk drive. It will probably be necessary to input separate CTRL-J commands in the Model 100 text to insert line feeds. Alternately, you can print out your file, and let your printer provide the line feeds. Otherwise, they must be added through a BASIC program like the one above, or by using a Search-and-Replace option in an Osborne applications program.

To transfer files the other way, you will still have to use the Osborne phone dialer; the Model 100 can't dial in the same manner. Configure parameters as before. The difference now is that you'll press an ESC-T on the Osborne to begin transferring a specified file. On the Model 100 you'll press the F2, File to Download option, then specify the file name, and hit RETURN. If the file does not transfer properly, you may have to enter CTRL-Q (X-ON) commands on the Osborne keyboard to send line by line. If the file is short, that is satisfactory; otherwise, another program must be written to input separate CTRL-Q commands into the text.

Notes of Caution: We don't know why, exactly, but when we used the direct modem connection, sending files from Osborne to Radio Shack, we needed to input separate CTRL-Qs to send line-by-line. We surmise this may have been a problem with both software and hardware; some handshaking signal is missing. The Osborne will accept a CTRL-Q command from the keyboard as it thinks it's coming from the Model 100. We haven't solved this problem yet.

Comments: Our extensive experience with the Model 100 tells us that both hardware and software handshaking—some options are shown in Figure 8.8—are vital for accurate file transfer. From our work with the Osborne I—drawing heavily from the experience of George Heidenrich, who worked closely with us on the research—we can conclude that the Osborne handles some aspects of handshaking differently from other computers. For example, it apparently does not always raise or lower control signals when communicating with the Model 100. An alternate explanation, provided by Heidenrich, is that the Radio Shack may be at fault, failing to provide either a handshaking signal or an X-ON control code.

Whatever the explanation, the result is that transmission is quirky and intermittent: you have a situation in which files can be transferred in one direction (Model 100 to Osborne) with relative ease, but with difficulty in the other.

Our studies also showed that just about any 8-bit protocol used in conjunction with a Model 100 will cause grief and uncertain results. Just how much grief depends on the type of file being sent. ASCII

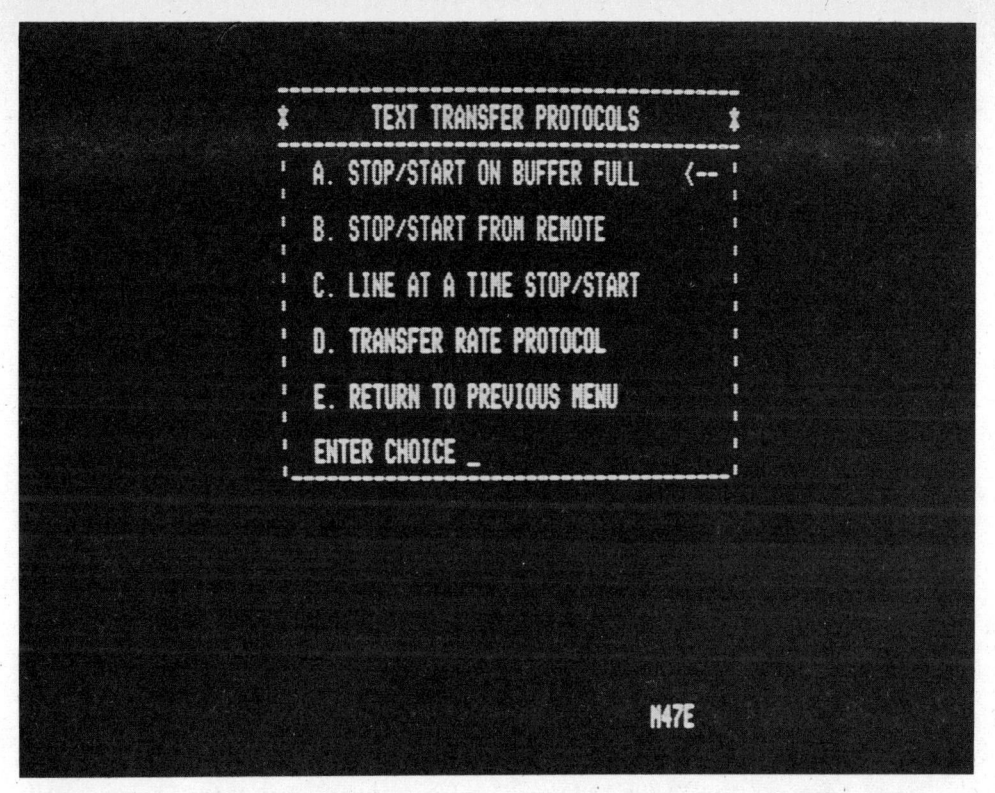

Figure 8.8 Transend offers numerous flow-control protocols as options for unverified communications, with no error checking in effect. (*Photo: Stephen Ross*)

files are generally no problem. Files containing special high bits for formatting and graphics are another matter. The Osborne dropped or even spliced characters and failed to close a file when transferring in the 8-bit mode. *WordStar* files were particularly troublesome. In fact, people have gone to enormous lengths to figure out ways to transfer and reformat Model 100 to *WordStar* documents, although all the methods we have reviewed thus far are cumbersome and require both programming skill and a large number of steps.

By contrast, 7-bit transfer through a modem is easier and much more reliable. We found that settings of 7 bits, no parity, one stop bit, or 7 bits, even parity, one stop bit produced the best results. The only exception was communicating with the Apple, a case requiring that we trick the Model 100 into thinking the settings were identical.

We are looking forward to more experiments with the Radio Shack in Chapter 11.

Commodore 64 to Apple II+ (Step-by-Step Connection)

Equipment:

Apple II Plus	Commodore 64
Apple II+ computer	Commodore 64 computer
64K RAM	One disk drive
Two disk drives	Commodore Automodem
Hayes Micromodem II	Model 1650
Data Capture 5.0	*Easycom 64*
Communications software	Communications software
Modular phone cord	Modular phone cord
	BW television set for monitor

Procedure: Boot the Apple computer with *Data Capture 5.0* software. This software supports the Hayes Micromodem II or IIe, and has been configured for that modem, at 300 baud, with 7 data bits, one stop bit, and no parity bits. After booting, use the program's Toggle menu to toggle the state of the duplex flag to FULL (to give local screen character echo) and the line feed flag to YES (to output a line feed after a carriage return). Also toggle the drive selector to DRIVE 2.

When the software boots, you are given the choice of moving DOS to the upper 16K of RAM, or of running the program. Moving DOS allows more buffer space.

Press ESC to access the main menu, and then enter D, for Dial the Phone. Enter the phone number to dial, then press RETURN to dial the number.

On the Commodore 64 (see Figure 8.9), switch the modem's Answer/Originate switch to Answer, the Duplex switch to Full, and the Talk/Data switch to Data. Insert the communications software disk into the drive and type LOAD "*",8. The computer responds "SEARCHING FOR *," and then LOADING. When load is complete, enter RUN, and you are presented with a title screen. Pressing the Commodore Meta key (the key with the Commodore symbol at the extreme lower left of the keyboard) along with an M, gets the main menu, from which the Meta key and @ gets you to the Modem menu. Enter 2 for auto-answer.

When the phone rings, the modem will answer, and the computers will connect. On the Apple, the connect message reads "YOU ARE IN ENTER/RECEIVE MODE." On the Commodore, the message reads, "TERMINAL MODE, REMOTE CARRIER PRESENT."

Type at both keyboards to make sure everything works correctly. Be

Figure 8.9 An Apple IIe and a Commodore 64 prepare to swap data files with one another. (*Photo: Stephen Ross*)

particularly careful of local echo, so that you get one strike of a keyed character on the monitor, but not two. If no character image appears, change DUPLEX on the Apple by pressing ESC to access the main menu. T for Toggle menu, and D for Duplex. On the Commodore, press the Meta key, then Q for Query/Status menu, then 1 for Duplex, then H or F for Half or Full, whichever you need. Also, test the transmission on both computers by pressing the RETURN key on both. If line feed doesn't get through, adjust line feed on the Apple with the Toggle menu; adjust line feed on the Commodore with the Query/Status menu.

To transfer a file from the Apple to the Commodore, press ESC, then F, for File menu. Enter M for Merge file into capture buffer. Respond when the program prompts for a file name. After the file is merged, press ESC, then S for send text. The program will prompt for the extent of buffer to transmit. Respond, and the file will be sent to the Commodore.

Before transmission, open the capture buffer on the Commodore by pressing Meta-key-O, so the incoming file will be saved into memory. Save the file on the Commodore by pressing Meta-key-M, for main menu, then Meta key-U for unedited save. Provide the file name when asked.

(The Commodore uses variations on ASCII code to allow it to use certain graphic characters. If you receive a file from another computer using normal ASCII, then perform an unedited save. This will save the characters as they are.)

To reverse the procedure, and send the file from the Commodore to the Apple II+, boot and adjust the software as before. On the Commodore, open the buffer with Meta-key-O, then Meta-key-K for Load ASCII file. Respond to the prompt with the proper file name.

On the Apple, make sure the capture buffer is open by pressing ESC, then T for Toggle menu, then B to open the capture buffer.

On the Commodore, press Meta-key-V for transit. The buffer will be transmitted to the Apple.

When transmission is complete on the Apple, press ESC, F for File menu, S for Save. Respond when prompted for the file name. The Apple will save the file under Apple DOS.

Commodore 64 to Apple II+ (Direct Connection, Modem-to-Modem)

Commodore *Easycom 64* software has the capability to take a modem off-hook manually. Press Meta-key-@ for the Modem menu, then press 3 for Off-hook.

Connect the modular phone cord between the Micromodem II and the Automodem. Switch the Originate/Answer switch on the Automodem to Answer. On the Apple, press ESC, then D for dialing, input the number 1, and then press RETURN. The Micromodem will dial 1, and then turn on the Originate tone. When Automodem hears MicroModem II's tone, it will turn on its Answer tone, and the connection is established. Transfer files as indicated for connection through the telephone.

Sanyo MBC 555 to Compaq Plus (Step-by-Step 2400 bps Connection)

General: The following connection with the Hayes Smartmodem 2400 represents a state-of-the-art transfer at 2400 bps over ordinary dial-up phone lines. Both the Sanyo MBC 555 and the Compaq Plus are MS-DOS machines.

The Hayes Smartmodem 2400 is distinguished from earlier Hayes modems (such as the Smartmodem 1200) in that it uses software commands from the computer rather than hardware switches to control modem settings (e.g., auto-dial/auto-answer and ring signal). Documentation for many software programs still assumes that hardware switches are in effect; moreover, some manuals (such as the Sanycom Telecommunications Package manual) tell how to set hardware switch settings for the 300 and 1200 baud Smartmodems, but neglect to describe the function of each of the switches. This can cause major problems in getting both modems to communicate and to exchange the proper handshaking signals. The way around the problem is to change settings in the software, toggling functions like auto-answer until the modems are set correctly. We found that the Hayes Smartmodem 2400 auto-answer feature is turned off as a factory default; you must turn it on through software to make a connection work.

Equipment:

Sanyo MBC 555
Microcomputer with two disk drives and 128K memory
Hayes Smartmodem 2400
RS-232-C standard serial cable
MBC-232-C serial card

Compaq Plus
Computer with two disk drives (one hard disk and one floppy), 256K memory
Hayes Smartmodem 2400
RS-232-C standard serial cable
IBM Asynchronous Communications Adaptor

Software
Sanycom telecommunications (Sanyo Business Systems Corp.)
DOS 2.11

Telpac (U.S. Robotics) Version 2.1
DOS 2.1

Procedure: Attach one end of the RS-232-C standard cable to the serial card installed in each computer. Attach the other end of the cable to the Hayes Smartmodem 2400. Cables are standard RS-232-C male-to-female cables. Then plug one end of the phone cord into each Hayes modem and the other end into a modular phone connector.

On the Compaq Plus (or IBM PC-compatible), boot the *Telpac* communications software package. Use the DEF command as the first operation after booting. DEF allows you to set communications parameters. Specify the following requirements:

2400 baud
Half duplex
Touch-tone dialing
7 bits
No parity

On the Sanyo MBC 555, boot DOS in drive A. Enter the date and time, get A⟩ prompt, then remove the MS-DOS diskette. Insert the *Sanycom* telecommunications program in drive A, and at the A⟩, type MODINSTL, which will bring up the configuration setup for the *Sanycom* program. Once you've installed the configuration, you can get immediately into the telecommunications program by typing SANYCOM, but the first time you must go through the install routine.

You'll now respond to prompts in the *Sanycom* program asking you to change parameters vis-à-vis carrier detect, touch-tone dialing, and baud. Set the baud option to 2400. Set parameters at 7 bits, parity disabled, 1 stop bit, the auto-line feed switch off, and transmission at half duplex. The program will return you automatically to DOS.

Now prepare for connection. On the Compaq, type TERM, which puts the *Telpac* Program into Terminal Mode. Enter AT SO = 1 to get auto-answer on the first ring. On the Sanyo, at the A⟩ prompt, type SANYCOM, and you will see a menu of communications options. Choose the CALL option; the program will prompt you for a number. Type the phone number, press RETURN. The Compaq, set to receive the call, will answer. Press "T" on the Sanyo to enter Terminal Mode. Now type back and forth between the computers to verify the connection.

To prepare for file transfer from the Compaq to the Sanyo, press ESC-T on the Compaq. You will see prompts for a file name. Enter the file name and respond to prompts for flow control (X-ON/X-OFF). On the Sanyo, Type "T" (filename). This creates a terminal mode with the capture buffer on. The Sanyo will await file transfer. Once transfer is complete, type WRT to save the capture buffer.

To transfer files from the Sanyo MBC to the Compaq, enter "T" (for Terminal Mode) on the Sanyo, then CTRL-T, which prompts for a file name. Enter the file name, and the Sanyo will send the file. On the Compaq, enter TERM and specify a file name. After the file is sent, enter ESC-W to write the file to disk.

Compaq Plus to Apple IIe (Using *Crosstalk XVI* and Smartmodem 2400)

General: This connection demonstrates the compatibility of the latest generation of consumer communications equipment—2400-bps modems—to communicate with the older types. These new modems can run at 2400 bps, but they are also compatible with the Bell-212A standard, so they can communicate with slower modems.

As in the study directly preceding this one, we found that software companies are not prepared for this latest modem generation. All instructions in the *Crosstalk* manual referred to the switch settings for the Hayes Smartmodem. But the Smartmodem 2400 has no switches; parameters are to be set by commands from the terminal mode of the communications program.

Smartmodem 2400s are sent from the factory set to ignore handshaking signals (DTE, RTS—more about them in Chapters 9 and 10). *Crosstalk* uses these signals, with the result that when *Crosstalk* was running, the signals told it that the modem was connected when, in fact, it was not. *Crosstalk*'s documentation is unclear about how to send codes to the modem. We booted *Telpac* from U.S. Robotics to set up the modem properly, and then rebooted *Crosstalk XVI*, set its parameters, and then completed the modem connection, at 300 baud, to the Apple IIe.

Equipment:

Apple IIe	Compaq Plus
64K main memory	Two floppy disk drives
Two disk drives	One 10-Mbyte disk
Micromodem IIe (Hayes)	IBM Asynchronous communications adaptor
	Smartmodem 2400 (Hayes)

Software	
Transend	*Crosstalk XVI*

Procedure: First, make a working copy of the *Crosstalk* software to use. Then boot the software by entering XTALK and run the set-up script file by entering SETUP that prompts for the communications settings you will use. If the *Crosstalk* program shows you a status of ON-LINE on the top right corner of the screen with no connection being made by the modem, then you have to reset the modem parameters. Hayes documentation is very good for setting these parameters. Every one is set with an AT & (command suffix) command. After setting the parameters to enable DTE and RTS, enter AT &W to save the new settings in nonvolatile memory inside the modem. Then, press ESC on the Compaq to get into *Crosstalk's* command mode. Enter NU for entering a number, and then the telephone number to call. Enter GO to make *Crosstalk* dial. When the connection is accomplished, type in Terminal Mode to make sure that the parameters are set properly. Follow the menu choices to send a file. Press ESC, then enter SE, and the program asks for a file name. Enter the file name, and the file is sent. To receive a file, merely stay in Terminal mode, and the file is received. Use menu commands to save the file.

To use the Apple IIe in the connection, follow the procedures already described.

CHAPTER 9
THE DIRECT CONNECTION

- The EIA Serial Interface • How to Make RS-232-C Work • The General Solution • The UART

COMMUNICATIONS BASICS

Asynchronous Communications: Communications that occur with no end-to-end synchronization of the data transmission and reception. Data pacing is controlled by reception of the data rather than by separate control signals.

Asserted Control Line: A control line in the RS-232-C interface is said to be asserted when the UART controlling the communications port has placed a high voltage (between +3 and +15 volts, usually +12 volts) onto the line.

Control Signals: Those signals defined in the RS-232-C specification that control the transmission of data.

Data Signals: The signals defined in the RS-232-C interface specification that transmit actual information.

DCE: Data communications equipment, the term in the RS-232-C specification that is used to refer to modems.

DTE: Data terminal equipment, the term RS-232-C uses to refer to communicating terminals, which connect to modems for remote communications.

Synchronous Communications: Communications that are paced through the use of separate timing signals external to the data transmitted.

We've now seen two ways that the links between computers can be accomplished: through the use of modems and telephone lines, and through the use of modems connected one to the other. In both of these cases, we've pointed out how the various layers of communications come into play—how the data-link layer and the "higher" layers act to control the link itself as well as the machines connected to one another through the link. Now we'll get to the most fundamental of data-communications connections, the direct connection.

Direct connections require a physical link, a data link to control the flow of data on the physical link, and various higher layers to select the data to be sent and then manipulated by the receiver. In actual practice, a good communications software package may be able to provide the data-link control. A 25-line ribbon-cable (Figure 9.1) connected to meet the requirements of the RS-232-C standard implementations in the two computers provides the physical link, and does away with some of the otherwise necessary data-link control. So all we need do is connect a ribbon cable for serial communications from one computer to the other, and we'll be in business, right?

Wrong! That's the idea, but it won't work without further interfacing.

So how do we go about bringing all these things together into a functioning computer-communications system? First, we have to understand RS-232-C and its derivatives, including the current standard, EIA-232-D.

The EIA Serial Interface

The Electronic Industries Association has traditionally defined its recommended standard, RS-232-C, as the way in which data should be sent to and from terminals and modems in serial mode. Serial data transmission means that the bits in a byte of data are sent one at a time, while parallel transmission means bits are sent eight or more at a

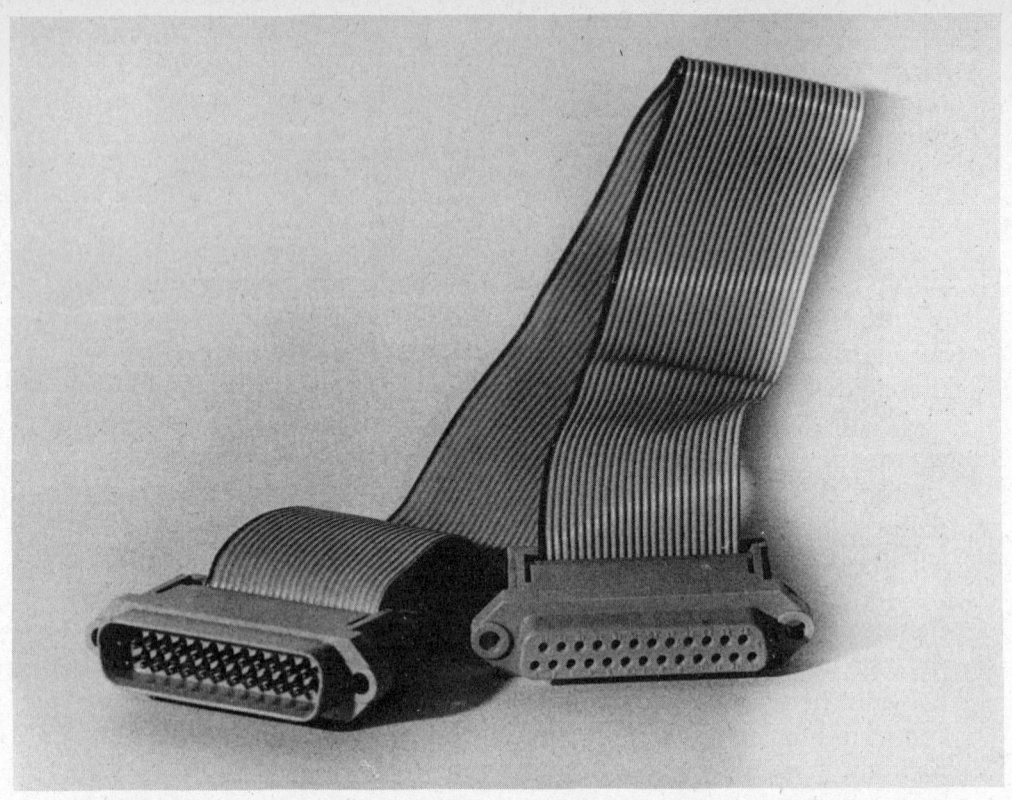

Figure 9.1 A ribbon cable used to connect RS-232-C ports together. The connectors are a DB-25 male (left) and a DB-25 female (right). These connectors are used almost universally for serial data transmission. (*Photo: Stephen Ross*)

time, over several wires in parallel. RS-232-C defines the parameters and methods of serial transmission. The revised EIA standard, EIA-232-D, maintains most of the parameters of the RS-232-C, but provides more explicit diagrams of physical interface connectors, adds three new specifications for interface leads, and rekeys circuit definitions to broaden the applicability of the standard to current equipment requirements, including data circuit terminating equipment in digital services.

The prevailing standard for most personal computers on the marketplace today remains the RS-232-C, the earlier standard. Recommended in its original form by the EIA back in 1969, and then revised, the RS-232-C was promulgated to solve the problem of how computer terminals, printing terminals, and so-called "glass Teletypes" (CRT screens that acted like teletypewriters, printing character by character rather than by line or screen) were going to be connected to modems. So that was what the standard addressed—how to connect terminals to modems—and nothing more. Unfortunately, subsets of the standard have been incorporated into a number of products other than terminals and modems. One of the most pervasive uses of RS-232-C has been its incorporation into serial printers, printers that incorporate serial data interfaces. Printers are not modems, and printers are not thought of these days as terminals, but many of them use the RS-232-C standard, or parts thereof, to receive their data from a computer. In fact, there is a class of data terminal called a receive-only terminal, a data terminal that acts as if it were a printer, and the RS-232-C standard is used in this device. The standard and all the subparts of its definition pertain to terminals and modems.

First of all, a terminal, in the language of the standard, is called Data Terminal Equipment (DTE). A modem is called Data Communications Equipment (DCE). Everything in the standard is defined in terms of these two pieces of hardware.

The RS-232-C standard defines the signal condition of 20 different signal lines. (EIA has since added three additional lines to its EIA-232-D standard: local loopback, remote loopback, and test mode, which are used in signal testing.) In both the older and newer EIA interface standards, the lines on the interface are grouped according to function: either data, control, timing, secondary data, secondary control, or ground. The signal lines are given names and numbers that are defined in the standard. Interestingly enough, the physical connector that provides the terminating points of the lines and the connection capability is not defined in RS-232-C. It is, however, defined in EIA-232-D, and EIA is actually looking into ways of offering a limited number of connector specifications to give manufacturers some flexibility in choosing the most appropriate connector for their needs.

At present, though, manufacturers can, and often do use any off-the-wall connector to implement the RS-232-C serial interface. Still, a type of connector called the 25-pin subminiature D connector seems to be the one that is in most favor. (Figure 9.2 shows two of them, connected back-to-back.) EIA-232-D has defined this connector and included diagrams in its standards document. The connector has 25 pins (male connector) or 25 sockets (female connector), so there are five extra lines in the connector that could be used for something. Sometimes they are, but not usually.

When we communicate with other computers over the telephone lines, we use a form of communications called asynchronous communications. This kind of communication doesn't require any timing signals, so the timing lines aren't used at all in asynchronous communi-

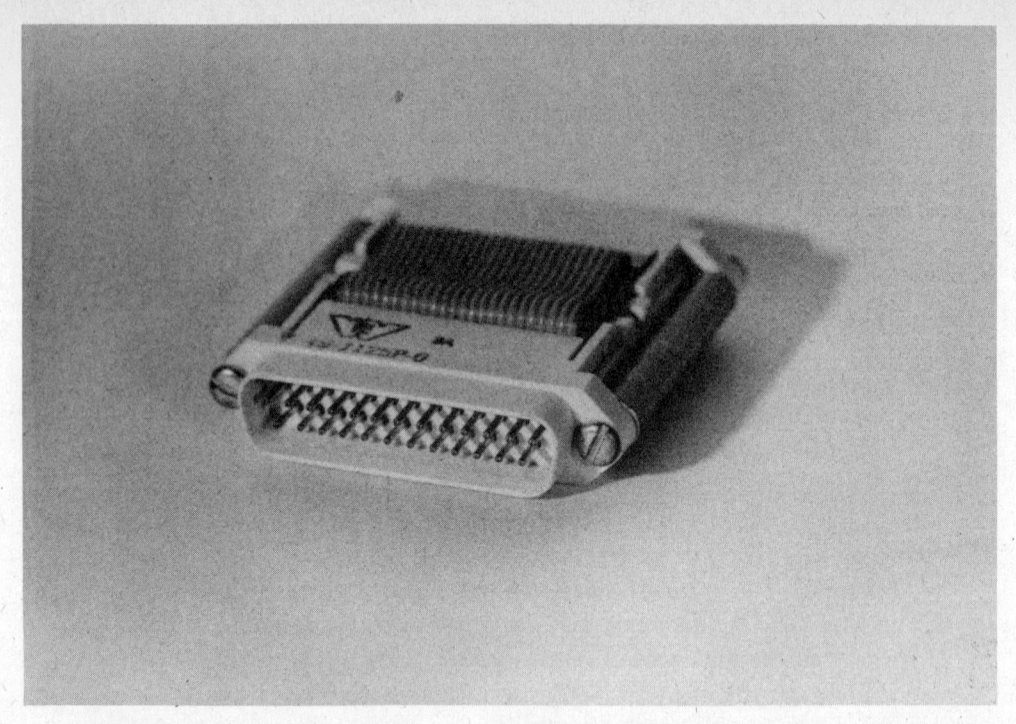

Figure 9.2 A gender changer for RS-232-C circuits. This device is really two male connectors back-to-back. (*Photo: Stephen Ross*)

cations. The control signals are used, though, and these signals cause many of the problems people encounter when they try to make a computer communicate with a printer or another computer.

Notice that the signals are not the same as the connecting wires. We too often tend to think of the wire as the signal, and that's incorrect. Confusing the two can get us into trouble, since the signals are designated for the *pins* of the interface, not for the wires that connect the interfaces together. Thus we can have a control signal on one serial interface that we attach to a different control-signal pin on another interface. If we do this in a way that satisfies the rules of serial communications, then the connection will work. The problem is that for computers to communicate with one another, we can't just connect all the pins to their opposite number on the other computer, or we'll have data lines in the wrong place and control lines that can't control anything. So we have one clear task: decide which control lines are important, and where they should be connected. That's going to take a bit of explaining, but first, there is one problem that's easy to solve: the data signal line connection.

The table on page 167 shows the assignment of each of the lines connected to the RS-232-C interface, as well as the signal direction with respect to the DCE (to or from the DCE, in other words). This notation is in accordance with the specification itself. Notice that pin 2 is assigned for transmitted data, and pin 3 is assigned to receive data. That works just fine if you're talking about connecting a modem, a DCE, to a terminal, a DTE. In that case, a modem will expect to receive data coming into its RS-232-C port on line 2, and will send data over line 3 to the computer or terminal directly attached to it. The modem will take data captured from the local terminal or computer and then convert it into signals compatible with phone-line transmission. That works fine. But consider the situation we have: we have RS-232-C ports that are both installed in personal computers. These ports usually, but not always, are configured as DTE, which means they will transmit data on pin 2 and look for received data on pin 3. Both of the ports, the one in an Apple computer, say, and the one in an IBM computer, will want to transmit data on their pin 2, so neither of them will monitor that line for incoming data. Rather, each of them will monitor pin 3 for incoming data, which won't be there, because each of the computers will be transmitting their data on pin 2.

How to Make RS-232-C Work

There's an obvious solution for this problem. Simply reverse the leads connected to pin 2 and 3, so that the line connected to pin 2 on one computer will be connected to pin 3 on the other computer. Figure 9.3 will help you visualize the crossover.

We'll use this kind of a diagram for all the connections we make between DB-25 connectors (the subminiature D connectors) to make computers communicate. This simple diagram shows that the data lines have to be crossed to get one computer receiving on the same line as the one on which the other computer is transmitting.

This will take care of the data lines in those situations where both devices are configured as DTE. Interestingly enough, not all personal computers are DTE, some are configured to look like modems (DCE). By the same token, the ports on printers may be either DCE or DTE. Since many printers are descended from earlier printing terminals that were configured as DTE, the aforementioned R/O terminals, they hold that identity, and are now configured as DTE also. They transmit on pin 2 and receive on pin 3 of their interface. It is, therefore, not at all

```
       --------              --------
          ¦                     ¦
          ¦                     ¦
      2 +__    ____+ 2
          ¦  \  /     ¦
          ¦   \/      ¦
          ¦   /\      ¦
      3 +__/    \____+ 3
                          •
                          •
                          •
                          •
                          •
          ¦                     ¦
          ¦                     ¦
     20 +                    + 20
          ¦                     ¦
          ¦                     ¦
       --------              --------
```

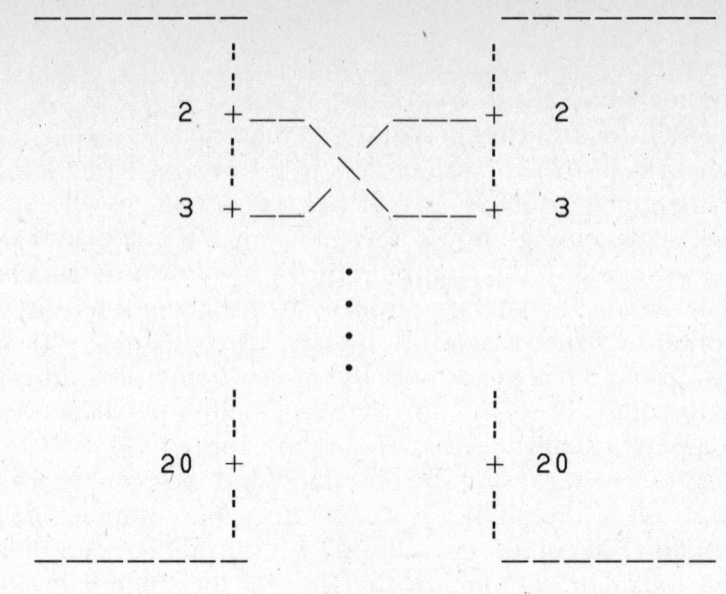

Figure 9.3

unusual to have to exchange the data lines between a serial printer and a personal computer.

That takes care of the data. What about those control signals?

We need to be aware of five of these signals. They are found on pins 4, 5, 6, 8, and 20. Referring to the table, we find that pin 4 carries the Request to Send signal (RTS) that travels to the DCE from the DTE. Pin 5 carries Clear to Send (CTS) from the DCE to the DTE. When a DTE wants to transmit a character, then it raises (brings positive) pin 4, RTS, telling a DCE, if that's what's connected to the port, that the DTE would like to send a character. If DCE accepts the request to send, then it raises pin 5, CTS, to tell the terminal that the way is clear for transmission. CTS cannot be active unless DSR (Data Set Ready) is active. DSR is carried on pin 6, and signifies that the DCE is connected to the phone line, but isn't dialing, and has completed whatever actions needed to answer the phone or dial another number.

Interestingly enough, DSR won't be active unless Data Terminal Ready (DTR), carried on pin 20, is active. DTR says that the port in the terminal is active and can transmit and receive, alerting the DCE to be prepared to connect to the communications channel. In the case of an auto-answer modem, for example, when DTR goes high, it can tell the modem to monitor the phone line for a ring signal. Then when the modem hears a ring, it will go off-hook, send its answer tone, and wait for an originate tone from the other end. After that happens, it will raise DSR, telling the terminal that it's connected. That frees the terminal to raise RTS, telling the modem it wants to transmit. If all is OK, the DCE will raise CTS, and transmission can proceed.

When the originate tone appears, the DCE will also, quite often, raise pin 8, popularly called Data Carrier Detect (DCD). If this pin isn't asserted, then according to the RS-232-C standard, the received data pin will be held in a high state, effectively prohibiting the reception of any data. Many modems use DCD to signal a loss of carrier, which makes the modem release the line and drop the signal on DSR. (This stops the transmission as well.) Thus DCD, the signal on pin 8, has to be asserted for communications to happen.

RS-232-C Pin Assignments

Pin Number	Circuit	Description	Direction
1	AA	Protective Ground	None
2	BA	Transmitted Data	To DCE
3	BB	Received Data	From DCE
4	CA	Request to Send	To DCE
5	CB	Clear to Send	From DCE
6	CC	Data Set Ready	From DCE
7	AB	Signal Ground	None
8	CF	Received Line Detect	From DCE
9	—	For Testing	
10	—	For Testing	
11		Unassigned	
12	SCF	Second Received Line Detector	From DCE
13	SCB	Second Clear to Send	From DCE
14	SBA	Second Transmit Data	To DCE
15	DB	Transmitted Signal Timing	From DCE
16	SBB	Second Received Data	From DCE
17	DD	Received Signal Timing	From DCE
18		Unassigned	
19	SCA	Second Request to Send	To DCE
20	DC	Data Terminal Ready	To DCE
21	CG	Signal Quality Detector	From DCE
22	CE	Ring Indicator	From DCE
23	CH	Rate Detector	To DCE
24	DA	Transmitted Signal Timing	To DCE
25		Unassigned	

The general rules that are incorporated into the standard are fine for modem-to-terminal communication, but they fall down when you try to make two computers—two DTEs—talk to one another. You can't change the rules, because the rules are incorporated into the hardware inside the RS-232-C interface. What's the solution? Provide control signals such that the sensing circuitry inside the RS-232-C hardware will find the way clear for communications to begin. Make it appear that the rules are being followed. And you can do that simply by the way you connect the RS-232-C ports to one another.

Connecting the RS-232-C ports so that they sense the presence of all the necessary signals is complicated by the fact that different computer manufacturers implement their ports differently. RS means, as we've already pointed out, recommended standard, and people follow the recommendation as far as their sensibilities and budgets allow. So first you have to figure out how the port is working before you can decide how to connect it to another port. There is no universal solution to the problem of connecting computers together, despite the fact that there are a number of so-called "universal solutions." None of them works all of the time.

Nevertheless, we have hit upon a solution that has worked in all the cases of direct connections we've tried so far. Since we've tested a wide variety of computers, we call it a "general" direct-connect solution. It applies to personal computers, but not necessarily to other types of connections, such as computers to printers, or computers to Koala Pad, for example.

The pin-out diagram in Figure 9.4 shows the general solution. Notice that it includes everything we've talked about so far. Pins 4 and 5 are connected together on each side of the interface. Then pin 20 on each side is used to raise pins 6 and 8 on the other side. In other words, as soon as one computer is ready to transmit, then it tells the other that it (the other computer) is ready to receive.

The General Solution

To figure out how to come up with a general computer-to-computer connection, you need to think about how RS-232-C control signals work. And you have to think about how data signals are handled. Let's take care of the data signals first.

It's a good bet that computers are set up as DTE, which means they expect to transmit data on pin 2 of the interface, and receive data on

```
   ----------                        ----------
       !                                  !
       !                                  !
    2  +____      ____+  2
       !     \    /     !
       !      \  /      !
       !       \/       !
       !       /\       !
    3  +____  /  \  ____+  3
       !                                  !
    4  +____            ____+  4
       !     !        !     !
       !     !        !     !
       !     !        !     !
    5  +__   !        !   __+  5
       !                                  !
       !                                  !
       !                                  !
    7  +_____+  7
       !                                  !
   .6  +____            ____+  6
       !     !        !     !
       !     !        !     !
    8  !     !        !     !  8
       +____ ! \  / ! ____+
       !       \/       !
       !       /\       !
   20  +____  /  \  ____+  20
       !                                  !
       !                                  !
   ----------                        ----------
```

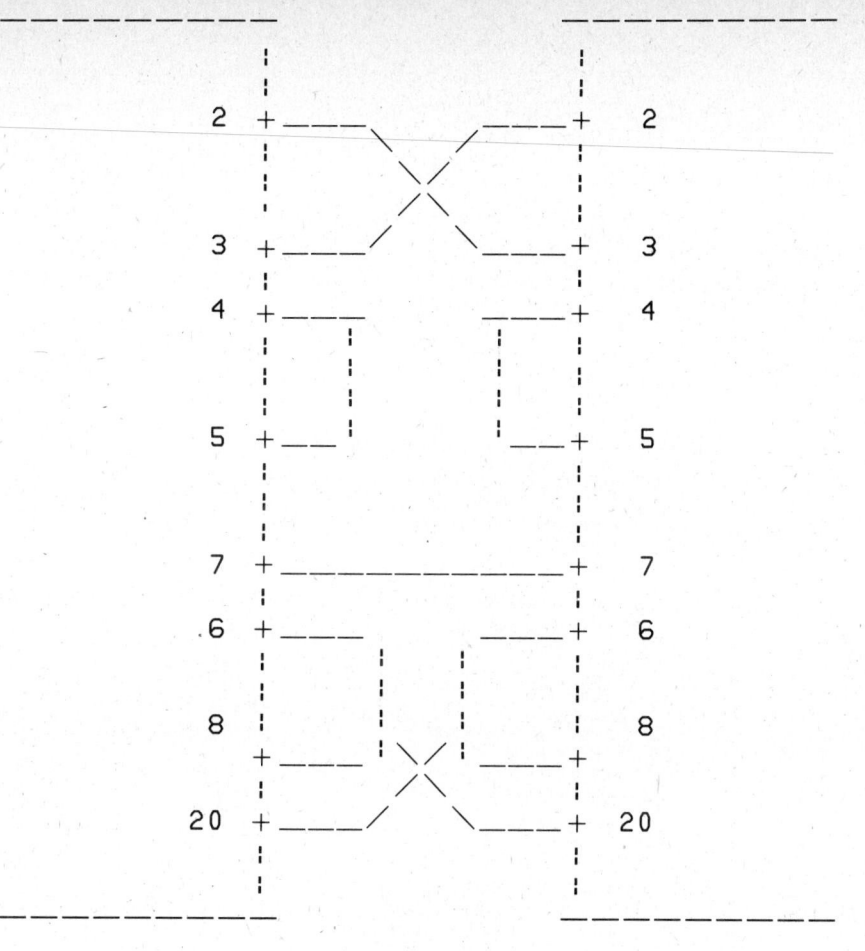

Figure 9.4

pin 3. That would be fine if we were connecting them to modems, which are DCE. Received data comes into the DCE from the phone line, and is sent to the DTE over pin 3, the received-data pin. In the reverse direction, a DTE transmits data to a connected DCE on pin 2, so the DCE receives data on its pin 2. But if you connect two DTEs together, they'll both try to receive and to send on the same lines. Therefore, we have to switch the lines connecting transmit and receive, so that one can hear what the other is saying. Figure 9.4 shows this connection.

It bears repeating that no law requires that manufacturers configure the serial port in their computer as DTE. You can tell, however, if the port is or is not so configured. (See Chapter 10 for more details.)

But just because the data lines are properly swapped doesn't mean anything will happen. Data will not begin flowing from one computer to the other unless the control signals are properly hooked up.

The control signals we care about are those that cross pins 4, 5, 6, 8, and 20. These pins, along with pin 2, Transmitted Data (TD), pin 3, Received Data (RD), and pin 7, Signal Ground (SG) are what have been called the "big 8" signals for making communications happen. These signals are the important subset of the RS-232-C signals that make most computer-to-computer (and computer-to-anything-else serial) communications work.

The following table shows what the signals in this important subset do.

Pin No.	Signal Name	Direction	Comment
2	TD	To DCE	Transmitted data
3	RD	From DCE	Received data
4	RTS	To DCE	Terminal asks, "Can I transmit?"
5	CTS	From DCE	Modem responds, "Go ahead, transmit."
6	DSR	From DCE	Modem connected and ready to communicate
7	GND	N/A	Completes all signal circuits
8	DCD	From DCE	Modem declares, "I am connected to another modem."
20	DTR	From DTE	Terminal tells modem, "Get ready for data communications."

If you look at the table for a minute, you can see the way this is supposed to work. When a terminal comes on line, it raises the DTR signal, telling the modem (the DCE) that the terminal is in proper condition for communications. The modem then signals back that it is on the line and ready to communicate by raising its DSR signal (Data Set Ready); this is done after the modem has completed its dialing and switching activities. Now the terminal is ready to communicate, and the modem is ready, also. The next thing that happens is the reception of a signal from the DCE on the other end of the line. When it gets that, the DCE raises its DCD (Data Carrier Detect) signal to inform the DTE that there's another modem on the other end of the line. Now there are two control signals to the DTE that have been raised: DSR and DCD. These give the terminal the go-ahead to transmit.

There's more, though. The modem may be busy receiving data, so the terminal, when it has some information to transmit, raises the signal line called RTS. This signal tells the DCE that the DTE has information to send onto the communications line. If the line is clear, then the DCE will reply by raising CTS (Clear to Send). At this point, there are three signal lines that have been raised by the modem: DSR, DCD, and CTS, pins 6, 8, and 5, respectively. All these signals have to be high before a DTE will transmit the first character out pin 2.

The UART

Inside every RS-232-C port is an integrated circuit that can be called, generically, a UART, which stands for Universal Asynchronous Receiver Transmitter. This is the device that raises the signal lines, responding to the raising and/or dropping of signal lines in the other device on the communications channel.

UARTs have many other connections than just the "big eight" signals we've described here. At the same time, they may not have all the connections we've talked about. Or, if the inputs and outputs we've mentioned here are present, they may not be connected to the UART itself. Unless we happen to take the time to study the documentation of the interface, we won't know which lines are connected where, and what they do. Most people don't have the technical competence to decipher a circuit schematic. Even if you do have that competence, it's likely that you won't want to bother with it. So we have to find an easier way to handle all these control signals—often called "handshaking lines," lines and signals often being used interchangeably—so that everything works.

There are actually two ways to go about this. First, you can use our general solution for connecting computers together. Second, you can use a simple, external diagnostic procedure that will follow our general solution, figuring out for yourself what each serial port is doing, and configuring your connection accordingly.

First, let's look at what we've called the general connection. This is a connection that seems to work with personal-computer-to-personal-computer hookups. The reason it works is simple: the connection provides all the signals that an RS-232-C transmitter must detect before it can transmit. Neither transmitter depends on the other transmitter to signal anything. Both transmitters are "fooled" into thinking that they are connected to a modem, and that the mythical modem is connected to another modem on the other end of a (mythical) telephone line.

The connection is diagrammed in Figure 9.4. Note that the first requirement is the swapping of the data lines. The transmitter pin (TXD) of one RS-232-C interface must be connected to the receiver pin (RXD) of the other, as we've already explained. Then, there must be a way to fool the interfaces into thinking all is in readiness for data transmission. Now think about the way the interface checks to make sure everything is working as it should. First of all, the terminal (in this case, a personal computer) asserts (brings to a high voltage) its ready line, DTR on pin 20 of the interface. An asserted DTR means the terminal is ready to go on-line if the modem (DCE) will cooperate.

The DCE signifies it's prepared to cooperate by asserting its Data Set Ready signal (DSR) on pin 6. Then, when the DCE is connected on the other end of the phone line and detects the other modem's data carrier signal, it asserts Data Carrier Detect (DCD) on pin 8. After DSR and DCD are asserted, the transmitter, according to the interface specification, can assert its request to send (RTS) on pin 4. RTS and CTS are used in half-duplex modems, by the way, to change the direction of transmission. The DCE, seeing RTS, asserts CTS (clear to send), and transmission starts.

The general solution takes care of all these signal requirements. First of all, we've connected DTR, pin 20, on each side of the interface to both DCD (pin 8) and DSR (pin 6) on the other side of the interface. What does this accomplish? It says that whenever a computer signifies that it wishes to transmit, it tells the other computer at the same time that there is a communications device connected to the second computer's communications port (the port is thus hooked to a remote device via a telephone line. In other words, either computer in this connection tells its partner that it has data to transmit—and that the partner can transmit as well, simply by asserting DTR. When both computers are ready to transmit, then each of them is also aware of the presence of the other through the control-signal lines.

Finally, a DTE has to ascertain whether it's all right to transmit. It does this by asserting RTS, a query to the DCE. The DCE is expected to answer, but we don't have a DCE. So we've connected pins 4 and 5 together on each side of the interface; therefore, when one computer requests clearance to send information, it is also telling itself that it's cleared to send. The same thing occurs on both sides of the interface. We had to cross from one side of the connection to the other in the case of pins 6, 8, and 20 because DTEs look for inputs on pins 6 and 8. There's no logical place other than pin 20 to connect them to tell a computer that another is on line. We could have connected pin 20 of one computer to pins 6 and 8 of the same computer, just as we connected pins 4 and 5 together on the same side of the connection. But the problem with that arrangement is that neither computer can then tell whether something is on the other side of its interface or not. So, we've devised a "fail-safe" for our setup: if pin 20 isn't wired to the 6/8 combination, the transmitter won't work, and you'll know something's wrong right away.

We have made two very large assumptions to develop this general cabling solution. First, we assumed that both computers' RS-232-C interfaces were configured as DTE. They don't have to be. On the contrary, it's possible that one of them, or even both of them, is a DCE. If both are, we still may be in business, but if only one is a DCE, then we have to unflip the data lines so that 2 connects to 2 and 3 to 3.

The second assumption is that the interfaces work the way RS-232-C says they'll work. As the song goes, "It ain't necessarily so." Remember that no one has to implement the standard correctly; therefore, you may find that the general solution works for one set of computers, and not for others. What is the problem then? Is it the data lines? Is it the control-signal lines? Is it . . . ?

For some diagnostic strategies, see the next chapter.

CHAPTER 10
A DIRECT-CONNECT METHODOLOGY

- The Physical Link • Diagnostic Strategies: Getting Physical • Quick and Easy Solutions • The Higher Levels of Communications

COMMUNICATIONS BASICS

Asserted Control Signal: A control signal in the RS-232-C interface that has a high value (greater than +3 volts).

The Big 8: The eight signals in the RS-232-C interface that are required for data communications. They are:

TXD/RXD: Transmitted and Received data.

RTS/CTS: Request to Send/Clear to Send—control signals that clear the way for data to be sent from the port of the DTE.

DTR/DSR: Data Terminal Ready/Data Set Ready—control signals that signify the presence of a data terminal and a modem on the communications channel.

DCD: A control signal that signifies the presence of a data carrier being sent from a remote modem.

Protective Ground: Neither data nor control, this line in the RS-232-C interface provides a complete path for each of the circuits in the interface. It must be in place at all times.

We sandbagged you in the last chapter. It wasn't fair, but we did it anyway. We went through all the details of the RS-232-C port, including its control and data lines, as though once the ports are correctly wired, there will be no more problem communicating. This is not at all true; in particular cases we may not get a connection at all. In fact, we gave you only one general solution for establishing the physical-link layer of data communications. We talked about a solution that seems to work in the cases we've tried for direct connecting one computer to another.

There are actually two potential problems with what we've done, however. First, as we've said, there's no assurance that the physical link has been established in both computers; in other words, the RS-232-C "standard" may not be implemented in each port in the ways we expect. Second, in focusing on the physical link only, we haven't taken other factors into account. Remember the OSI model: the physical link is only the first in the chain of many links needed to make our communications attempts successful.

Since there are two problems with what we've done, there must be a solution that can be undertaken in two stages. Indeed, the first stage is in understanding, and fixing, the physical link when the general solution presented in the last chapter doesn't work. The second is in making sure that the higher level links work in conjunction with the physical connection.

The Physical Link

If the general solution we derived in the last chapter doesn't work, then what? It could be that the physical link hasn't been properly established. What then? You can watch for certain kinds of signals and messages the computer uses to tell you the physical link isn't there. In some cases, the hardware will tell you immediately with an error message.

In the next chapter, for example, we describe a direct connection between a Compaq Plus and an Apple II+. That was something of a seminal connection, because it tested much of our theoretical knowledge. When we began the experiment, unsuccessfully at first, we knew right away the physical link wasn't working. The Compaq computer told us by flashing an error message on the screen.

In the experiment, we had started out by initializing a serial port under MS-DOS on the Compaq by invoking the operating system's MODE command. In our case, we'd type MODE COM1: 12,N,7,1 to tell the computer to set up the port for 1200-baud communications (as fast as our Apple can handle), no parity checking, 7 data bits, and one stop bit. These are the parameters the communications port needs for proper operation of the physical-link layer. Then, to read a file coming in from another computer, we told the computer to copy the file from COM1 to a disk. Simple. But if the computer doesn't have a good connection on the port—if the physical link isn't intact—then a Read Fault Error message is issued by the Compaq. We knew there was something wrong, and that we had to find it.

Programmers of other computer operating systems were not so courteous as to provide an error message in this situation. The operating system built into Applesoft BASIC, for instance, simply stops running.

Different computers may handle physical-link problems even less competently than the Apple. A CP/M computer, for example, may deceive the user: it appears to go ahead and respond to your commands with a system prompt when, in fact, it is doing nothing. That's the result we got with a Kaypro 4, a CP/M-based machine.

The message here is that if the physical link isn't operating properly, then there will be an indication that something is wrong. Either the system gives you an error message, or "hangs up" (not like hanging up the phone, but hanging up in the sense of completely ceasing operations), or what you thought would happen doesn't happen. In these cases, the first priority is making the physical-link layer work.

Though this book isn't intended to make you an expert on diagnosing the physical link, we outline below a simple set of strategies to get the physical link operating. If you're interested in delving still further into the RS-232-C interface, consult the bibliography for a list of reference materials that outline in detail the signal connection problem and electronic diagnostic procedures.

Diagnostic Strategies: Getting Physical

First of all, you need some way to make measurements on the interface connections. The best tool for this purpose is an RS-232-C breakout box. A breakout box, as the name implies, breaks the signal lines out of the cable between two devices so you can look at the signals present. We arrived at the general communications solution in the last chapter by using a breakout box.

Our box is made by Carrol Touch Technologies, and costs about $175 retail (see Figure 10-1). That's expensive, but then these tools cost money. The box we used has, first of all, 20 switches that can be opened or closed. Each switch is in the path of one signal line, like TXD or RXD. You can allow the signal line to pass through the breakout box uninterrupted, or open the switch and the line. On either side of the 20 switches are double rows of pins. These pins are connected to the signal lines inside the breakout box, so that a signal that appears

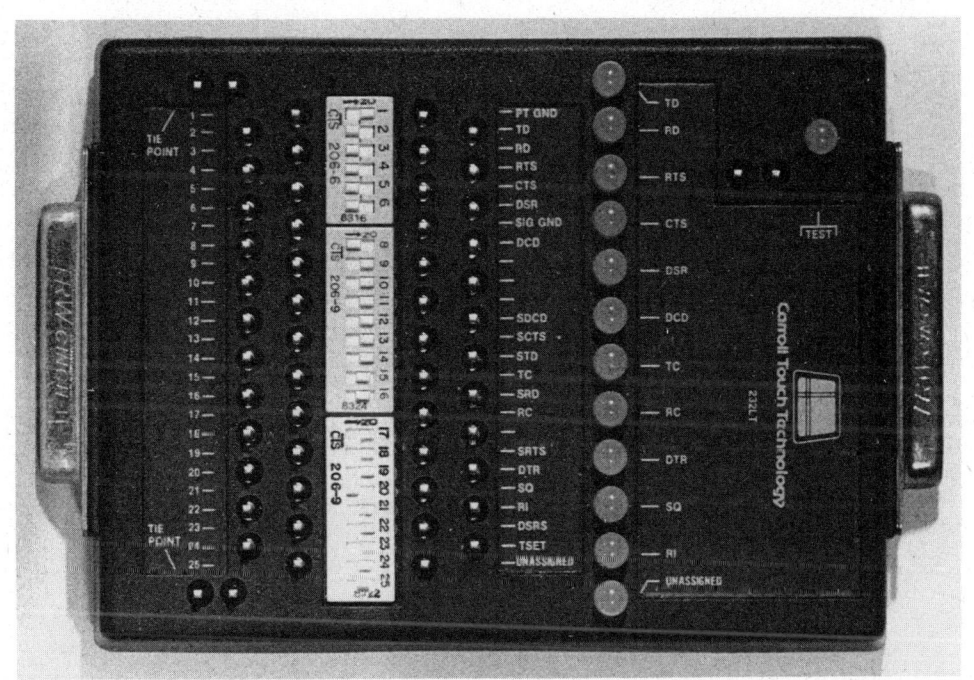

Figure 10.1 Our RS-232-C breakout box. The small globes are two-color (red/green) LEDs. The pins are connected to each of the data and control circuits. The row of switches is used to open any of the lines, and this allows you to check the condition of any line, jumper lines together, and cross lines using this device. (*Photo: Stephen Ross*)

A Direct-Connect Methodology

on one of the lines appears on the pins as well. You can make a connection to one of the pins for the purpose of measurement, or for connecting a signal or control line to another line.

For example, in the last chapter, we said that we needed to swap the TXD and RXD signal lines. Accomplishing this with a breakout box is simple: open the switches on lines two and three, and then use the jumper wires (supplied with the breakout box) to connect line 2 on one side of the switches to line 3 on the other side. You have to accomplish the opposite connection as well, of course, and, in effect, you wind up with an "X" of wires from one side of the switch bank to the other side of the bank, from line 2 to line 3, and then from line 2 to 3 going the other way.

You can accomplish the other connections for the general communications solution in a similar manner. Thus you can use a breakout box as a handy "universal" RS-232-C connection system. But that's not its real utility. The whole point of a breakout box is its diagnostic capability.

Alongside the rows of pins on one side of the box is a row of light-emitting diodes (LEDs). These devices emit light when they have a voltage properly connected to them; that is, if one side of the diode is put at a positive voltage with respect to the other side, then the diode lights. If it were a regular light bulb, then it wouldn't make any difference which side was positive. But LEDs are one-way devices. If you make one side positive, then the LED will light. Make the other side positive, and the lamp won't light. Since that's the way a LED works, then this simple device can be used to tell not only the presence of a voltage signal, but its polarity as well.

As it happens, that's exactly what we need with an RS-232-C interface, because the signals that travel over that interface can be either positive or negative. A positive signal on a data line—that is, a signal greater than +3 volts—is called a *space*, and is known as a logic 0. A voltage less than −3 volts is called a *mark*, and is known as a logic 1. It's just the reverse of what you'd expect.

But the point is that the signals can have either polarity; that is, they can be positive or negative with respect to the zero level, or ground. The breakout box takes care of these possible signal polarities by having two LEDs connected with each signal line, one red and one green. The green LED on each line is connected so that it will light if the line has a positive voltage on it with respect to ground, and the red LED is connected so that it will light if the line is negative with respect to ground. If there is no signal, or if the signal is between −3 and +3 volts, which are the thresholds defined for RS-232-C-compatible signals, then neither LED lights.

You can use the breakout box right away by simply plugging it into the port and looking at the LED connected to pin 2, TXD, or transmitted data. The serial transmission standard requires that a port configured as DTE hold this signal in the marking condition (-3 volts to -12 volts) whenever data are not being transmitted. This means that if your port is a DTE, and you connect a breakout box to this port, the red LED will light for line 2 (TXD). On the other hand, the standard also requires that a port configured as a DCE must mark on pin 3 whenever the data are not being transmitted. This means that if your port is a DCE, and you connect a breakout box to this port the red LED will light for line 3 (RXD).

If you have a DTE connected to a DTE, then you need to swap the data lines, 2 and 3. But if you have one computer configured as DCE, and one configured as DTE, then no switching is needed. That's the importance of this little exercise. By simply plugging a breakout box into the port, you've determined the configuration of the port, what some writers call the "sex" of the equipment. You have to know the sex of the equipment before you can do anything with RS-232-C ports.

This one simple test will help you start connecting two computers that might otherwise seem to defy communications. Then while the breakout box is connected, take a look at the LEDs connected to other pins. Are any of them lit? What do they mean?

For example, the Apple II+, upon which this is being written, has a card plugged into slot 5 called a CPS Multifunction Card. (Mountain Computer Corp, Scotts Valley, California). The exact terminology isn't important. What is important is that the card has a serial port on it, and the serial port can be accessed with Apple's familiar IN# and PR# statements, which assign input (IN) and output (PR) to various I/O slots.

Connecting the breakout box to the serial port on the CPS Card and issuing the PR#5 command makes the following LEDs light up:

1. Red on pin 2 (TXD)
2. Green on pin 4 (RTS)
3. Green on pin 20 (DTR)

That's not all that happens. In addition to these LEDs lighting up, the cursor on the Apple screen disappears—the computer hangs. What do we know from this experience?

We know, first of all, that this serial port is a DTE, because it is marking on pin 2, which is TXD—the transmitter pin, which is the pin a DTE uses to transmit data. We also know that the DTE is required to mark on pin 2 when it is not sending data according to the RS-232-C standard. So we've determined that this is a DTE port. Good.

We also know that something is very wrong, because the computer's just sitting there, as if it were waiting for something to happen. Indeed, that's what's going on—it's waiting to have one or more of its hardware handshaking signals properly satisfied. The problem is, you don't know which one(s), so you have to think about what the breakout box is telling you.

You see that the positive control lines are those connected to pin 4 and pin 20. Pin 20 is DTR, which signifies, when it's asserted, that the terminal is powered up and ready for communications. A modem, a DCE, sensing that this signal is asserted (positive) knows that it has a terminal connected that is prepared to communicate. When the modem connects to the phone line, and has gone through its auto-dialing routine, it will reply to DTR by asserting its DSR (Data Set Ready) lead to tell DTE it's connected. That's the way it will work, at least, if everything's following RS-232-C. If not, DSR may be the modem's way of merely signaling its presence with no qualifiers about the condition of a phone line.

At any rate, the DTE may want to see a positive voltage on pin 6 (DSR). It may not—DSR may not be connected inside the DTE's RS-232-C port. If you don't have any written documentation on the port, a not uncommon occurrence, or if the documentation is so badly written as to be incomprehensible (even more common), then the only way to find out whether the port wants a high input on pin 6 is to put it there.

It's fortunate that the framers of the RS-232-C standard and its derivatives set it up so that you can connect any line of the interface to any other line without making the interface suffer physical damage. Though connecting lines willy-nilly won't often make the interface communicate, it won't harm it either (as long as the connection comes close to meeting the standard). So you can use any high control line to connect to any other control line that should also be asserted. The high line will pull up the line that should be high, so that they will both carry a voltage higher (more positive) than +3 volts.

Now let's look at the Apple II+ again: the cursor is still missing! The breakout box shows a mark on line 2, indicating that this is a

DTE. Control lines 6 (DSR) and 20 (DTR) are asserted; that is, they have a positive voltage on them. It seems a good bet that since the port has asserted RTS, it's looking for CTS. If that's all it wants, then connecting CTS to RTS should make the cursor appear again. So we try that, using one of the jumpers supplied with the breakout box.

No good. Everything stays the same, except now there's a green light on the CTS line as well as the RTS line, since we've pulled up that line. Clearly, we haven't solved the problem yet; we have to keep trying.

If you go back to the last chapter, you'll see that the RTS/CTS pair of signals is the last that talks to each other. Before that pair talks to itself, as it were, the DTR/DSR signals are exchanged, and then after dialing is complete and another data set answers, the DCD line is asserted by the data communications equipment. So our starting with the RTS/CTS pair may have been backwards. No matter, since signal lines can be connected to one another, we can leave RTS and CTS joined, and look elsewhere. Leaving these two connected will not cause a problem later on, because the CTS signal must be high before this port can communicate anyway. Leaving the pins connected ensures that CTS will be high.

If we now connect a jumper between DTR and DSR, DSR's LED turns on green, as we would expect, since DSR is now at +12 volts. But still the cursor doesn't appear on the screen. If this isn't a totally unpredictable interface (and we hope it isn't), then there's only one more line to pull up—DCD (Data Carrier Detect). Some interfaces monitor this line to detect the presence of another modem's signal on the line. If it isn't there, then they terminate communications. Perhaps this is one that looks for DCD. Jumpering that line to DTR makes the DCD LED light up green, and lo and behold, the cursor appears on the screen. We have just enabled that particular RS-232-C port for transmission and reception of data.

The connection looks like Figure 10.2. Notice that there's only one side with connections, because we've only looked at one serial port.

We just went through a simple diagnostic procedure to get that RS-232-C port operating. First determining the sex of the equipment, we found it was a DTE. Then we looked for handshaking lines that were able to control the transmission of information. It turned out that all the control lines, 4, 5, 6, 8, and 20 were important here. We used 4 to pull up 5, and we used 20 to pull up 6 and 8. Notice that the connections we wound up with were very similar to the general solution for computer-to-computer communications we had before.

```
        _____              _____
            ¦                         ¦
            ¦                         ¦
         2  +                      +  2
            ¦                         ¦
            ¦                         ¦
            ¦                         ¦
         3  +                      +  3
            ¦                         ¦
            ¦                         ¦
            ¦          ¦              ¦
         4  +----------+           +  4
            ¦          ¦              ¦
            ¦          ¦              ¦
            ¦          ¦              ¦
         5  +----------+           +  5
            ¦                         ¦
            ¦                         ¦
            ¦                         ¦
         7  +                      +  7
            ¦                         ¦
            ¦                         ¦
         6  +----------+           +  6
            ¦          ¦              ¦
            ¦          ¦              ¦
            ¦          ¦              ¦
         8  +----------+           +  8
            ¦          ¦              ¦
            ¦          ¦              ¦
            ¦          ¦              ¦
        20  +----------+           + 20
            ¦                         ¦
            ¦                         ¦
        _____              _____
```

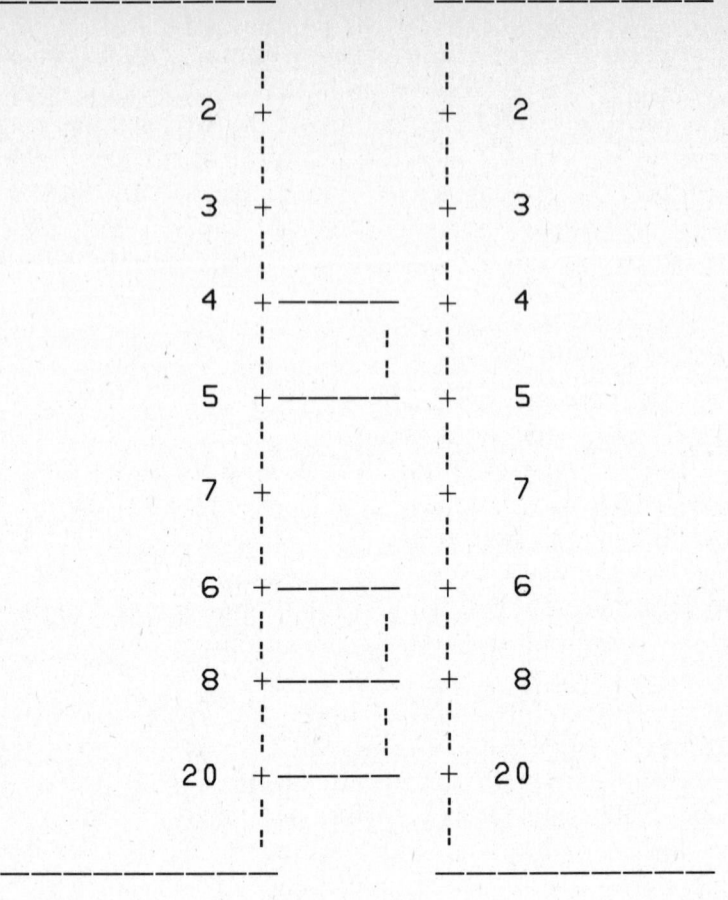

Figure 10.2

Diagnosing A Second Computer

Can this procedure work with another computer? Here's what happens to a Compaq Plus (IBM PC XT-compatible) equipped with an IBM Asynchronous Communications Adaptor. Plugging the breakout box onto the adaptor makes LEDs light up like this:

1. Red on pin 2 (TXD)
2. Red on pin 20 (DTR)
3. Red on pin 4 (RTS)

This is not at all what you might expect, but never mind. Under normal conditions, you'd expect the mark on pin 2, because you expect that this interface is configured as a DTE. You also expect to see an asserted DTR, and maybe an asserted RTS. But the control lines are negative. If you execute the MODE command, which is the command in MS-DOS (you have to boot DOS) that initializes the communications adaptor, the computer screen will say the resident portion of MODE is loaded, and that the port is set. Nothing changes as far as the LEDs on the breakout box are concerned. This is somewhat surprising, because you'd think that when the port is initialized it should announce its presence to the world with an asserted DTR. It doesn't, however.

The next thing to try is to send some text out the port, even though it isn't connected to another piece of hardware. If text moves, then you can figure out what is happening at the interface. If text doesn't move, then you can start connecting control lines to one another as in the case of the Apple's serial port. So we used the DOS COPY command to copy any file (we had one called TEST.TXT on the disk) to COM1:. As soon as the command is executed, the LEDs on lines 20 and 4 turn green. They are finally asserted! Then the LED on TXD will begin to change quickly from red to green and back again, showing that data are actually being sent out the port, but with no signals to tell the port to go ahead.

Then why are the control lines there at all? Why is RTS asserted? Why is DTR asserted? In the case of the Apple, we had asserted, by pulling up, the handshaking lines, one by one, until the cursor came back. When it did, we had an interface that would transmit. In this case, pulling up the control lines has no effect. Text keeps going, as you can tell by the flashing TXD LED. So try the reverse—apply a negative voltage to the control lines. If bringing a control line positive doesn't change anything, then try the opposite. Sure enough, tying any of the input control lines 5, 6, or 8 negative (using the negative voltage on the TXD line) causes the transmission of data from the copy command to be inhibited. And the screen gives an error message: "Write fault error writing device COM1:."

Now try this. Disconnect the negative voltages from the control leads, and try the copy operation again. Another error message appears. Once the lines have been pulled negative, the transmitter will not transmit until they have been pulled back up to a level more (positive) than -3 volts, the threshold for negative control signals. Pulling each of the lines up, momentarily, makes the port transmit again.

This suggests why these handshaking, or control lines are there. If there is a need to make the transmitter stop transmitting for some reason, then bringing one of those lines down below -3 volts will make that happen. You might need to stop transmission in a case where there's a serial interface on a slow mechanical device, like a printer. When the buffer, the temporary data-storage memory in the printer, fills up, then the printer should have some way of telling the computer to stop sending until the buffer empties out. Then the printer can signal the computer to send again.

This is the purpose of hardware handshaking, which is implemented in the control lines of the RS-232-C interface. In our particular case, computer-to-computer communications, there really is no need for handshaking, because both the communicating devices are computers, and they can store information much faster than reading from, or writing to a port.

Indeed, RS-232-C is slow when compared to memory-transfer speeds. It's unlikely that one computer will ever have to signal the other to stop transmitting, providing that certain conditions are met. You have to ensure, for example, that the file you're sending is smaller than the available memory in the receiving computer. Both computers should also be operating at a speed close enough so that the transmitter won't overrun the receiver. Beyond that, there is really no need for the hardware handshaking at all.

You could implement hardware handshaking, of course. But if you did, then you'd need to write a program that could control the UART chip inside the serial port, but, such a program is beyond the scope of this book. Rest assured, though, that you're not going to need hardware handshaking. Just remember the two rules we listed, and your data transfer will work without problems.

Figure 10.3 shows the way that the Compaq Plus can be wired to make it transmit. If we want to ensure that none of the handshaking lines will go negative, thus stopping transmission, we can connect a jumper from pin 20 (DTR) to pins 6 and 8, to hold them up.

Now that the Apple and the Compaq have been tested, we can think about connecting them. Notice that even though the ports are different, they can be connected in the same way for communications. In fact, we could use the DTR signal of the Apple to assert the DSR and DCD signals of the Compaq. And we could use the Compaq's DTR to assert the DSR and DCD of the Apple. If we did that, then the connection diagram would look like the one in Figure 10.4 which is, you will recall, the general solution we presented in the last chapter.

We've gone through the diagnostic exercise here to show how it would be done if the general solution didn't work. But try the general solution first. It really works in most cases.

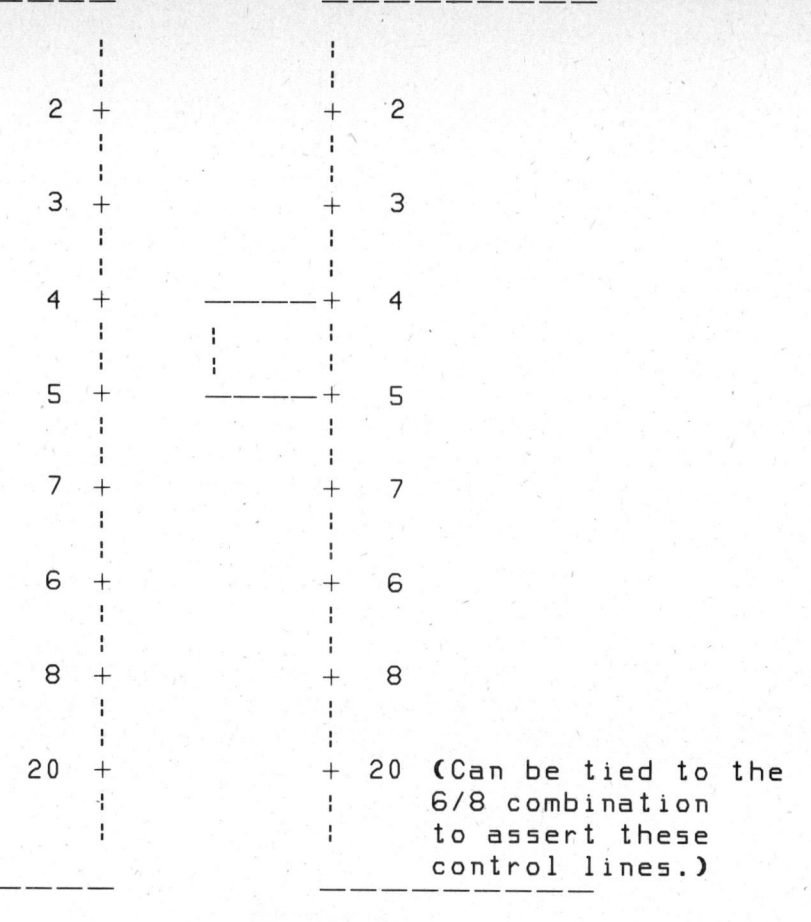

```
  ----------              ----------
      :                       :
      :                       :
   2  +                   +   2
      :                       :
      :                       :
   3  +                   +   3
      :                       :
      :                       :
   4  +         ------+   4
      :            :      :
      :            :      :
   5  +         ------+   5
      :                       :
      :                       :
   7  +                   +   7
      :                       :
      :                       :
   6  +                   +   6
      :                       :
      :                       :
   8  +                   +   8
      :                       :
      :                       :
  20  +                   +  20  (Can be tied to the
      :                       :      6/8 combination
      :                       :      to assert these
                                     control lines.)
  ----------              ----------
```

Figure 10.3

Quick and Easy Solutions

We should mention at this time that there is a much easier route to direct connections between dissimilar computers.

A company called Micro-Module Systems Inc., in San Diego, makes a device it calls EZ-232. Four or five EZ-232 adaptors handle the interfacing chore for most personal computers and printers on the market today. The EZ-232 is actually a hybrid connector, with a DB-25 connector on one side and a modular phone connector on the other. You get the device designed for your particular brand of computer— Micro-Module publishes a list of computer brand and the appropriate

A Direct-Connect Methodology   187

```
         _ _ _ _ _ _ _ _             _ _ _ _ _ _ _ _
              :                           :
              :                           :
           2  +---\       /-----+  2
              :    \     /      :
              :     \   /       :
              :      \ /        :
              :       X         :
              :      / \        :
           3  +---- /   \ ------+  3
              :                           :
              :                           :
           4  +----:         :----+  4
              :    :         :    :
              :    :         :    :
           5  +----:         :----+  5
              :                           :
              :                           :
           7  +------------------+  7
              :                           :
              :                           :
           6  +----:         :----+  6
              :    :         :    :
              :    :         :    :
           8  +----:         :----+  8
              :       X         :
              :      / \        :
          20  +----/     \------+  20
              :                           :
              :                           :
         _ _ _ _ _ _ _ _             _ _ _ _ _ _ _ _
```

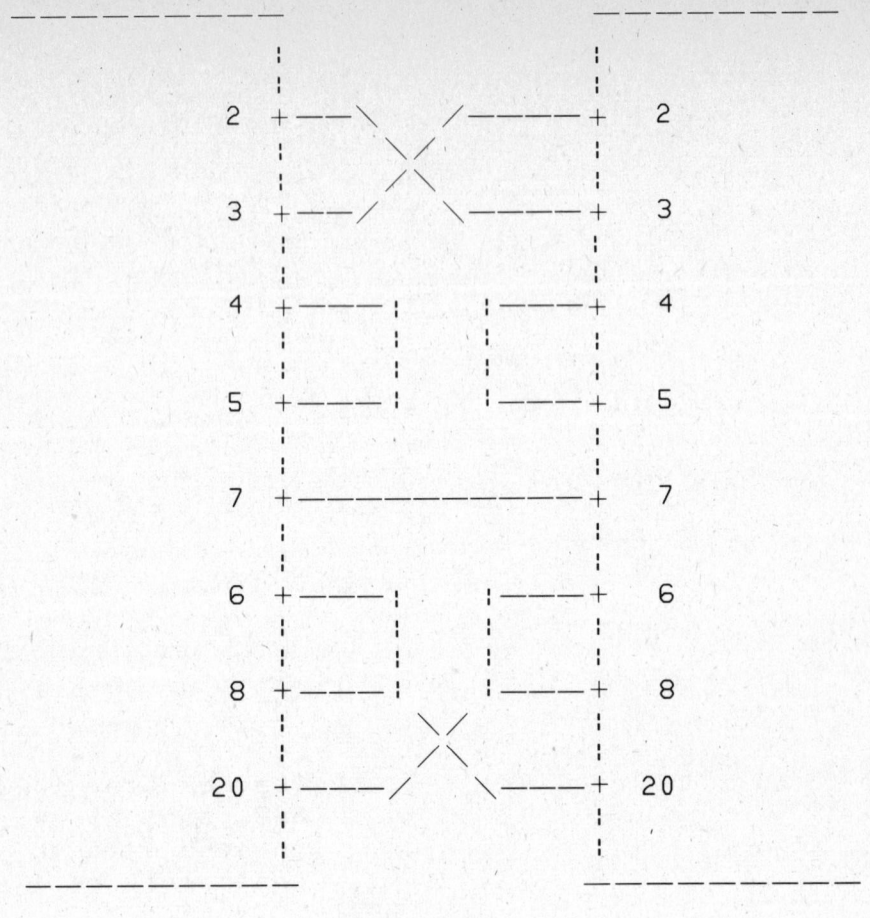

Figure 10.4

"color-by-number" connector—and then you plug the DB-25 into your RS-232-C port. Connect two computers together using two EZ-232 adaptors, run a phone cord between them (the phone cord snaps into the back of each connector), and the physical link is established. You can easily buy the EZ-232 connectors from MISCO, the catalog seller of computer supplies, or from Micro-Module Systems directly.

Inside the EZ-232 adaptor, incidentally, the manufacturer has connected the pins of the serial interface in such a way that handshaking is defeated and the data lines of the two computers are consistent with one another. This is a really quick-and-dirty way to make one computer talk directly to another.

The Higher Levels of Communications

So far, all our discussion has centered on the physical-link layer of data communications. In the direct-connect case, this has to be a primary area of concern. Manufacturers don't provide the physical link for such direct computer connections as they do for modem-to-computer connections. Nor is there a convenient public data link (as there is, say, in modem-to-modem communications, in which both modems rely on the public phone network).

But now you should have enough information to implement a physical link, from the first step of determining the configuration of the equipment to the final step of connecting control lines to one another. This is the first priority in a connection.

Still, you have yet another task. You want to make data flow usefully across the physical link, but you need software to control the flow.

As it happens, there are a number of communications programs that will work off-the-shelf to control the flow of data over the connection. Remember that we completely disarmed the handshaking lines that control data flow across the data-link layer.

This means there is no automatic cessation of the flow of data on a full buffer, for example. The handshaking signals are all tied high by virtue of connecting them to the DTR of the other computer. Consequently, you need a piece of communications software that will not read the handshaking signals provided by a modem to a serial port. Some programs do read these handshaking lines, and that has unfortunate results. If you don't have a modem on a computer running communications software that looks for handshaking lines, then the software may not even switch into Terminal Mode, a necessity if communications are to occur.

The answer to the problem comes in two flavors. First, you could find a communications package that doesn't look for handshaking signals. *Telpac* software from U.S. Robotics is one such. In general, software for Hayes Smartmodems doesn't look for handshaking signals, but controls the communications link by imbedding commands into the data stream. When you type {AT} to a Hayes modem or compatible, for example, the modem looks for a command to follow.

The second solution is self-programming. You can write a simple program to read a text file from a disk and send it out the communications port. By the same token, it isn't too hard to write a program to read a text file and save it to disk. Such a program for an Apple II+ is shown in Figure 10.5.

```
7    ONERR GOTO 170
10   D$ = CHR$ (4)
20   PRINT "THIS PROGRAM READS A TEXT FILE"
30   PRINT "FROM DISK AND SENDS IT OUT THE"
40   PRINT "COMMUNICATIONS PORT IN SLOT 5"
45   PRINT : PRINT
50   INPUT "FILENAME ";NM$: REM PROMPT FOR FILE NAME
60   IF NM$ = "" THEN 50
70   INPUT "DRIVE# ? ";S$: REM DRIVE WHERE FILE IS
80   INPUT "NUMBER OF CHARACTERS? ";NC :
     REM HOW BIG IS FILE
85   HOME : VTAB 10: HTAB 10
86   FOR I = 0 to NC: POKE 24577 + I,0
90   PRINT "READING FILE INTO MEMORY"
100  PRINT D$;"OPEN";NM$;",D";S$
110  PRINT D$;"READ";NM$
120  FOR I = 1 TO NC
130  GET A$
140  IF A$ < > "" THEN POKE 19456 + I, ASC (A$)
150  M = I: REM STORE FILE IN MEMORY
160  NEXT
170  HOME : VTAB 10: HTAB 10
180  PRINT "TRANSMITTING FILE"
190  PRINT D$;"CLOSE"
200  PRINT D$;"PR#5": REM OPEN COMMUNICATIONS PORT
210  FOR I = 0 TO M
220  A = PEEK (19456 + I) :REM GET A CHARACTER
221  IF A = 13 THEN PRINT CHR$ (10); CHR$ (A);: GOTO 230
222  REM ADD LINE FEEDS AFTER CARRIAGE RETURNS
225  IF A > 31 THEN PRINT CHR$ (A);:
     REM SCREENS CONTROL CHARS
230  NEXT : PRINT
240  PRINT CHR$ (26): REM CLOSE FILE ON COMPAQ
245  PRINT D$;" PR# 0" : REM CLOSE COMMUNICATIONS PORT
250  INPUT "ANOTHER FILE? ";Y$
260  IF Y$ = "Y" THEN 50
270  END
```

Figure 10.5 This program reads a file from disk and sends it to a communications port in I/O slot number 5 on an Apple II+ or IIe computer.

We'd like to give you more generic programming information, but we can't, since you must adapt this BASIC program to the conventions required by your own computer.

The program we cite, however, does exactly what the remarks indicate: it shuttles a data file directly from an Apple disk to a serial port in a particular I/O slot number. The program you'd write could look very much like this, or it might look different, depending on your computer and your particular dialect of BASIC.

You should note, by the way, that you may not need a program. CP/M computers have a command called PIP in the operating system that copies files. Most people familiar with CP/M know how to use PIP to make copies from one disk to another, but the most important part of PIP is that it can copy data from disk to any logical device inside the computer such as LST:, the currently logged list device. (Remember: a logical device denotes a general function of a microcomputer, as opposed to a physical device, which is the specific piece of hardware used to perform that function.)

LST: can be assigned to devices like LPT: a line printer, or to TTY: which is a communications port. Then, let's assume you had a file on the disk in drive A called TEST.TXT. You'd simply type PIP LST:=A:TEST.TXT, and the file is called from the disk and sent to the peripheral to which LST: was assigned.

In the case of a computer running MS-DOS, you can use the COPY command. There are preliminary steps to take, of course. You first have to initialize the communications port, for which you use the MODE command. Then you simply use the COPY command, by typing COPY A:TEST.TXT COM1. If the physical link is working, then the file will be read from the disk to the COM1 communications port. If everything's working on the other end, then there will be no communications problems at all.

That "if" is a big one, though. We have to say again that we took away all the handshaking: that's the key to our solution. If there's an error, then there's no way to recover. You must monitor the communications carefully, and perhaps adjust the timing of the transmission/reception to make the data come out intact. Some of the direct-connect case studies in Chapter 3 and in the following chapter show what happens if timing isn't right, or if some funny control characters get into the data stream when they shouldn't be there. In some cases running MS-DOS, the operating system's COPY command just doesn't work reliably. It will stop copying and write an incomplete file to disk before transmission is done. There is no apparent explanation for such aberrant behavior. During our experiments, we used a terminal emulator program with DOS, and the communications proceed reliably with it.

Timing is a particularly important factor to consider. As a computer user, you have no way to measure how fast data are moving inside your computers or on the data lines connected to each machine. You don't even known when timing's a problem until something goes wrong. We found timing problems can happen any time two computers are communicating asynchronously. The faster the communications are proceeding, the more likely it is that something will go wrong. Therefore, communicating at 300 baud is usually the safest bet.

Of course, we've seen timing problems when transmitting long files from personal computers to The Source. The problems were cured by inserting delays after each line, effectively giving the other computer the chance to catch up with the sender's data rate.

You can detect timing problems by observing the transmission process. Using The Source, for example, we had timing difficulties when trying to use Source Mail with a long file. After the file was transmitted, we started getting funny messages from the Source computer indicating that it had lost track of the information coming in. In some other circumstances, you might see that characters just don't make it through. For example, one or two characters might be lost when you compare the transmitted text with the received text. If that happens, the simplest thing to do is slow down the transmitter, by inserting delay loops into the transmit program. Figure 10-5 is an example of a transmit program for an Apple II+ or IIe, while Figure 10-6 is a receiver program. If you are using a terminal program that was purchased off-the-shelf, then you should be able to tell the program to add a delay at the end of a line.

Notice that there's nothing here about the speed of the transmission, just as there was nothing in the first program we listed for sending data. As it turns out, with an Apple II, sending data can go as fast as the receiver can accept the information reliably. But the Apple has a problem receiving data—a big problem. It has certain activities it must perform, such as writing characters to the screen and translating the next line in its BASIC program. What happens if the Apple is busy doing some screen updating and a character is about shoved out of the input buffer by the next character from the sending computer? What happens is simple—a character gets lost. It might have been in the Apple's input buffer, but before the Apple could read it, the character was shoved out again.

This, you might recall, was the problem that Ernie Mau encountered (see Chapter 3). His solution was to slow down the Morrow computer he had by inserting delays at the end of each line the computer sent. That's one of a number of possible solutions. Another is to slow the speed. We used this technique when connecting the Apple II+ to a Compaq Plus computer. At 1200 bps, a not-unreasonable speed for something as fast as a computer, the Apple II+ lost most of the characters coming in. We just slowed down the communications port to

```
10   D$ = CHR$ (4)
20   PRINT D$;"IN#5": REM INPUT FROM SERIAL PORT
50   GET A$: REM GET CHARACTER FROM SERIAL CARD
60   I = I + 1: REM ADVANCE CHARACTER COUNTER
70   IF A$< >CHR$ (19) THEN POKE (19456 + I), ASC (A$):
     GOTO 50
80   REM LINE 70 CHECKS FOR AN EOF CHARACTER TO
     DROP FROM LOOP IF CHARACTER IS NOT CTRL-S THEN STORES
     CHARACTER IN MEMORY
90   PRINT: PRINT D$;"IN#0": REM TURN OFF SERIAL CARD
100  INPUT "NAME TO SAVE FILE?" ;F$
110  PRINT D$;"OPEN";F$
120  PRINT D$;"WRITE";F$
130  FOR J = 0 to I: REM WRITE FILE TO DISK
140  PRINT   CHR$ ( PEEK (19456 + J));
150  NEXT
160  PRINT: PRINT D$;"CLOSE"
170  INPUT "UPLOAD ANOTHER?";U$
180  IF U$ = "Y" THEN 20
190  END
```

Figure 10.6 This BASIC program for an Apple II+ or IIe computer will receive a file from a serial card installed in slot number 5 and save it to disk, after prompting for a file name.

300 baud. The Apple was quite content with this solution, and happily took every character we gave it.

Other possible solutions include adding a delay after writing each character to the port, or even writing a program in assembly language that won't make the computer go through the agony of BASIC translations to read every character. If you want to do something like that, then you might as well go on and make yourself a program that is interrupt-driven. Interrupts will do just what the name implies: they'll interrupt the processor when they find that a character is ready to be read from the serial port. The interrupt makes the computer stop everything except one interrupt-service routine, until that routine is over. Then normal processing can continue. Programming with interrupts is beyond the scope of this book, though; it can be done with enough time and effort, with the help of references on assembly-language programming. Basically, you'd write a program that would check for the presence of a character in the serial port, interrupt, get and store the character, and resume normal processing, the first task of which would be to check for a character in the serial port.

But assembly-language programming, interrupt-driven processes, and the like are somewhat difficult. Anyone with programming expertise can do it if forced to, but most people just don't have the time or the inclination. If you don't, then how can you make sure that computer-to-computer direct connections will work?

Follow the methodology we've outlined here. Step-by-step, it works like this:

1. *Establish the physical link layer of communications.* This means using some trick RS-232-C connections that we reviewed to make each computer think it's connected to a modem. The "general solution" connection we discussed should work. If it doesn't, then you have to analyze the interface with the help of a breakout box. You can buy a breakout box at a local electronics store. The other *easy alternative* is to buy prefabricated RS-232-C connectors (like the EZ-232 system from Micro-Module Systems, Inc.) that someone with expertise has configured and tested to fit your computer. That saves a great deal of time and trouble.

2. *Establish the data-link layer of data communications.* This means get some software running that knows how to handle the communications port. Since we've turned off, effectively, all the handshaking lines, then the software must send and receive characters without recourse to those lines. Otherwise, it might just ignore the fact that there is a connection present, or it might look for a modem that isn't there. You can, in some cases, establish the data-link layer with the operating system, as in the case of the CP/M PIP command, (PIP AUX:=A:filename), or in the case of MS-DOS (COPY A:filename COM1:). The latter is chancy, however, from our experience and from anecdotal evidence from others, while PIP seems to be quite reliable. You can write a BASIC program to handle the communications, or you can use a commercially available terminal program.

Once the physical-link layer of communications is established and the data-link layer is firmly in hand, then communications should happen with no real difficulty. You may even be able to use software protocols to handle flow control and error checking. The only real problem that you might still encounter, which really resides in the data-link layer, too, is timing. If you are dropping characters in the receiver, then try slowing down your transmission speed. That should work.

CHAPTER 11
DIRECT-CONNECT CASE STUDIES

- Radio Shack TRS-80 Model 100 to Apple II+ • Tandy 2000 (or Compaq Plus/IBM PC XT-Compatible) as Host; Radio Shack TRS-80 Model 100 as Terminal • IBM PC to Apple Macintosh (Including a *WordStar* File Transfer) • Cable Requirements for the Macintosh and IBM PC • Apple Macintosh to Radio Shack TRS-80 Model 100 • Compaq Plus to Apple II+

COMMUNICATIONS BASICS

AUX: The MS-DOS designation of the auxiliary communications port logical device.

CON: The MS-DOS designation of the console logical device.

Function Keys: Keys on a keyboard that perform some task with a single keystroke. In the Model 100 *Telcom* program, function keys put you into terminal mode, and upload and download files.

In the past two chapters, we discussed a general solution to the problem of a simple, hardwired direct connection between the serial ports of two different kinds of computers. We said that our solution didn't work in every case, and that other direct-connection approaches are sometimes required. In this chapter, we outline these alternate techniques in a series of direct-connect case studies. All the studies outlined use interfacing through the RS-232-C serial port.

Radio Shack TRS-80 Model 100 to Apple II+

Step-by-Step Direct Connection

General: You can achieve a simple and reliable hardwired connection between these two computers by crossing data pins 2 and 3 and tying "high" four basic handshaking signals specified in Figure 11.1. On the software side, the Radio Shack Model 100 provides the *TELCOM* program, which can be used to control direct serial communications; on the Apple side, a terminal emulator program or the Apple file sending and receiving programs (which we demonstrated in the last chapter) will control the data-link layer and let the Apple swap files across the port.

Problems: Once again, the Model 100 strips out line feeds when it sends its data out through the serial port. Fortunately, the screen controller on the Apple II+ provides a line feed, so you will get intelligible copy. The Model 100, in turn, doesn't register Apple's line feeds, but its own screen controller will provide them when each line of copy reaches its maximum width.

Equipment Needed:
Radio Shack TRS-80 Model 100
25-wire serial cable, wired as specified below

Apple II+ (or other Apple-computer: II, IIe, IIc)
CPS Multifunction Card (Mountain Computer Corp.)

```
1————————1

2————————3

3————————2

4         4
:         :
5         5

6
:————————20
8
          6
20————————:
          8

7————————7
```

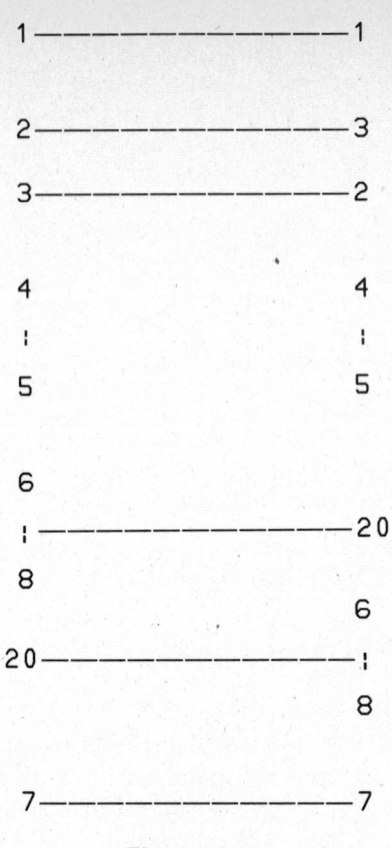

Figure 11.1

PIN Connections: Using wire and solder, or jumpers with alligator clips (small clips that look like alligator jaws that will clip onto an electrical contact), cross pins 2 and 3 (the transmit and receive data pins) on each interface connector. Pins 4 and 5 (RTS and CTS) are shorted on each side. Tie pin 20 (Data Terminal Ready) on the one side to pin 6 (DSR) and 8 (DCD) on the other. The diagram is shown in Figure 11.1:

Communications Settings:

Model 100	Apple II+
Type: 67N1E, which translates into 2400 baud, 7 bits, No parity, 1 stop bit, X-ON/X-OFF enabled	SAME
Full or half duplex	SAME

Note: When the Apple is receiving data it may not be able to operate at high speed, depending on the communications program that you're running. The Receive program from the last chapter will lose characters at any speed over 300 baud. The Transmit program works fine at 1200 baud. If you have a speed problem, you can speed up transmission by writing an assembly-language patch for the reception program.

Procedure: Once you've completed the wiring, set communications parameters on the Apple. Run Mountain Computer's Setup program, and follow the menu choices to set parameters in the serial-control option of the menu. Also set the serial output and serial input portions of the parameters. Then run the transfer program (send or receive) on the Apple.

Set your parameters under the STATUS option on the Model 100 *TELCOM* program and enter Terminal Mode by pressing the F4 function key. Now type back and forth between the Apple and Model 100 to verify the accuracy of the transmission. If you get funny characters, recheck your communications settings, and switch to even parity on both sides.

To transfer a file from the Apple II+ to the Model 100, run the transmit program from the last chapter, or use a terminal emulator package and follow that package's instructions. On the Model 100, press F2, the Download function. Type a name for the file to be stored (e.g., TEST.DO) Specify full or half duplex (F4 function key). Remember: a half-duplex signal will allow you to see the characters echoed locally to the computer screen. In full duplex, your characters will echo only on the remote computer screen. Press ENTER. When the transmission is finished, press CTRL-Z on the Apple keyboard. The Model 100 will then save the file. Choose the F8 key to disconnect.

To transfer a file from the Model 100, type F4 (Terminal Mode), and then F3, for Upload. Type in the name of the file, press ENTER, then specify a width at the prompt (any number from 10 to 132 will do). On the Apple, prepare for file transfer by running the receiver program. When you're ready, press the ENTER key on the Model 100 and watch the Upload light come on, indicating the file is being transferred. Enter a CTRL-Z at the end of the transmission. When it is completed, press F8 to disconnect. You may then call it up on your word processing package to edit and reshape the file. Each screen controller will provide its own line feeds.

From Model 100 BASIC: The setup is the same as that just discussed. On the Apple, run the Receiver program. On the Model 100, choose the Text Mode, then a file to edit, and insert any necessary formatting characters (control characters) in the text. If you wish to transfer the text to the Apple, press the F3 function key (still in Text Mode)—the "SAVE" key on the Model 100—and, at the SAVE TO: prompt, type COM:67N1E. This sends the current BASIC program still in ASCII format out the RS-232-C port. Of course, what you have in memory isn't a program, it's an ASCII text file. But the Model 100 doesn't know or care. This function is useful if you have embedded commands you wish to send directly to the other computer or a serial printer. Going in the other direction, a file can be transmitted from the Apple and loaded and run directly on the Model 100 by typing LOAD COM:67n1e. You will need to run the transmit program on the Apple.

Discussion: The Model 100 to Apple II+ connection (and other Apple II series computers using the CPS Multifunction Card) requires an RS-232-C pin-out configuration that follows the "universal" recipe we specified in Chapter 9. Since both computers' RS-232-C serial interfaces are configured as DTE, it's necessary first to swap the transmitter and receiver pins on each connector. In addition, pin 20 (Data Terminal Ready), which is active on the Model 100 and Apple II+, is tied to the 6 and 8 pair on the opposite computer. (*Note:* pin 8, or DCD, is inactive on the Model 100.) This configuration lets each side know that the other is ready to communicate. When Pin 20 (DTR) is asserted, so are DCD and DSR; thus the Model 100 tells the Apple that it's on line, ready to transmit, and ready to receive transmissions from the Apple.

In addition to these lines, pins 4 and 5, (RTS) and (CTS), respectively, are tied together so that each computer tells itself it's okay to send data. These simple signals are the only ones required to make the Model 100 talk directly to the Apple II+ using a standard CPS Multifunction Card. Other serial cards implementing the same RS-232-C configuration will also function this way.

Tandy 2000 (or Compaq Plus/IBM PC XT-Compatible) as Host; Radio Shack TRS-80 Model 100 as Terminal

Step-by-Step Direct Connection

General: Here is an ingenious way to connect IBM compatibles with the Radio Shack Model 100. It was originally developed as a method for connecting the MS-DOS-based Tandy 2000 computer with the Model 100, but we found it works perfectly on the Compaq Plus and other IBM clones as well. The trick is to make sure the hardware and pin connections link correctly; the software connection will then work, permitting file transfer and terminal/host communications. The entire system is based on the communications capability of the MS-DOS operating system; a separate communications software package isn't needed.

Specific Features: The system outlined here employs some simple MS-DOS operating system commands and a cookbook knowledge of BASIC language, meaning you can manage simply by copying the recipes below. Just remember that quotation marks and other seemingly superfluous bits of punctuation are essential to the connection. You will find that this link will temporarily disable the MS-DOS computer keyboard (but not its CPU), thus turning the Model 100 into a complete terminal. You can type on the Model 100 and execute file transfers back and forth; the MS-DOS operating system will do the work for you and your Tandy 2000, Compaq, or other compatible will act as host. This is a particularly useful connection for field workers who need to dump the contents of their portables into a main MS-DOS system, which in turn can be linked to a mainframe or minicomputer host.

The hardware interfacing required for this connection is made easy by the "color-by-number" EZ-232 direct-connect adaptors (Micro-Module Systems, Inc.) we mentioned in the last chapter (see Figure 11.2). The adaptors provide an instantaneous hardware handshaking solution—no null modems or specially configured cables are required. Four or five adaptors, each of which are numbered and coded to particular kinds of personal computers, will handle up to 85 percent of the computers and serial printers on the market. The adaptors cost less than $20 apiece.

Equipment:
Tandy 2000 (MS-DOS computer)   Radio Shack TRS-80 Model 100
128K RAM, two disk drives   RS-232-C cable and null modem
An RS-232-C serial port

Instead of the RS-232-C cable and null modem, the following adapters may be used:

EZ-232 #102 adaptor with   EZ-232 #102 adaptor
   modular phone cord

Note: If you use a Compaq, IBM PC, or other IBM-compatible,

Direct-Connect Case Studies   201

Figure 11.2 EZ-232 connectors. These devices plug onto an RS-232-C port and convert the connection to modular-phone jacks. The connectors take care of the required handshaking and data lines. (Photo courtesy Micro-Module Systems, Inc.)

instead of the Tandy 2000, you may require a different EZ-232 adaptor. A number 202 adaptor, for example, works with the Compaq and IBM PC; Columbia Data requires a 102 or 104, depending on the make, and a Corona PC requires a 104. All Radio Shack TRS-80 and Tandy 2000 computers require a 104.

Null Modem Pin-out:
If you make your own null modem, which consists of two DB-25 connectors with certain lines crossed between them to simulate a modem between the connectors, you should cross-connect pins 2 to 3, 4 to 5, and 6 and 20 to 8, as specified in the pin-out guide in Figure 11.3. This type of null modem satisfies the requirements of most computers with the standard RS-232-C port, including the Radio Shack Model 100.

In the EZ-232 interconnect system, data transmission is accomplished with a modular telephone connector. Serial data are always sent on pin 4 of that connector, called "I Send," and always received on pin 3, called "You Send." Handshaking is accomplished using pin 1

```
2----------------------------3
3----------------------------2
4-------    -----5
        :  :
5-------    -----4
8--------------------------6
                          :
                         20
6--------------------------8
```
Figure 11.3

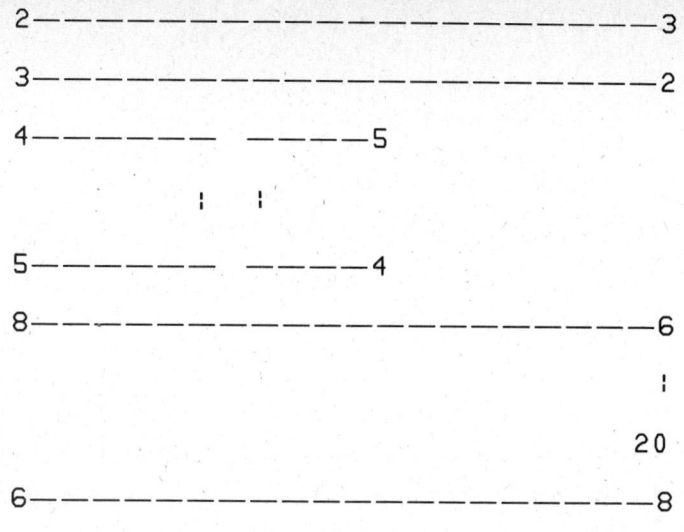

(You May Send), which allows the other end to send, and pin 6 (May I Send?), which determines whether the other end is ready to receive. Pins 2 and 5 are grounds.

Procedure:

1. Turn both computers on.
2. If you are connecting a Tandy 2000 to the Model 100, use a standard Radio Shack RS-232-C cable and null modem as configured above.
3. If you are using the EZ-232 interconnect system, plug a 102 (yellow) adaptor into the Model 100 RS-232-C port, then plug the complementary adaptor into your Tandy 2000. Now snap a phone cord into the EZ-232 socket, the other end into the remote adaptor.
4. Insert an MS-DOS or PC-DOS 2.1 (or higher numbered version) into drive A of the MS-DOS computer and press CTRL-ALT-DEL to reset.
5. Answer the date and time prompts.

On the Model 100:

1. After going to *TELCOM*, set Status to 37E1E (300 baud, 7 bits, even parity, 1 stop bit, X-ON/X-OFF enabled).
2. Press TERM (F4)

On the Tandy 2000 or Compaq:

1. At A> type BASIC.
2. When in BASIC, type the following command: OPEN "COM1: AS 1. This command opens up the first communications port in your MS-DOS computer and sets it at the default values of 300 baud, 7 bits, even parity, 1 stop bit.
3. At the OKAY prompt, type SYSTEM to leave BASIC.
4. At A> type CTTY AUX, press ENTER. The cursor and the prompt will disappear from the monitor of the Tandy 2000 and reappear on the Model 100 screen. The Model 100 has now become a terminal to the MS-DOS host. The MS-DOS host keyboard is disabled.
5. Type DIR on the Model 100 and you will get a disk directory from the host computer.

At this point you can perform standard DOS functions such as reading directories and creating or editing files.

To upload and download text files:

1. Uploading from the 100 to the MS-DOS computer:
   (a) At the A> prompt, type EDLIN filename.ext (e.g., EDLIN LOGON.100), press ENTER, then type in I for insert and press ENTER.
   (b) On the Model 100, press the F3 (Upload) key, answer the prompts, and when finished press CTRL-Z and ENTER. Type E to end the file; the Tandy 2000 or Compaq Plus (or Compaq) will write it on the disk.
   (c) At the Compaq's A> prompt, type DIR to check that the file has been recorded.
   (d) To see the file, respond to the A> prompt by entering TYPE filename (e.g., TYPE LOGON.100). The file will then be printed on the screen.
2. Downloading from the MS-DOS host to the Model 100:
   (a) In *TELCOM* on the Model 100, press F4 TERM, then type in type filename.ext (e.g., type *logon.100*). Before pressing ENTER, press F2 (Download) and type in filename.do (e.g., logon.do). Then and only then press ENTER twice.

Returning control to the MS-DOS machine:

1. Type in CTTY CON: on the Model 100.

Discussion: We found that this connection worked flawlessly when the hardware handshaking was correct. However, when we tried the same null modem setup (using a gender changer) on the Compaq Plus as we had on the Tandy 2000, we got a distorted directory and several mixed-up or aborted files; a message flashed Abort/Retry/Ignore. It simply didn't work. We discovered that the Tandy 2000 and the Compaq/IBM PC (using the IBM Asynchronous Communications Adaptor) use different handshaking signals across their RS-232-C ports, and thus required a different null modem configuration. The tip-off was a mixture of legible and distorted files, not necessarily a complete inability to communicate. A hardware handshaking problem may not necessarily freeze a connection or cut it short; it can simply mash up text. Consequently, you should always check your hardware handshaking before assuming you've got a software protocol problem on your hands.

We solved our handshaking problem with Compaq by going the easy route. We plugged the EZ-232 connectors in, fired up the machines, and the file transfers worked perfectly. See the discussion in Chapter 10 for wiring the RS-232-C ports to make this connection work without EZ-232, or see the Apple to Compaq connection, later in this chapter.

IBM PC to Macintosh (w/Word Star File Transfer)

Step-by-Step Direct Connection

General: You can swap text, binary, BASIC, *WordStar*, and *Multiplan* spreadsheet files between the Macintosh and the IBM PC through a special hook-up hardware/software package, *PC to MAC and BACK!* (dilithium Press, Portland, Oregon). The system can be used for linking two IBM PCs, two MACs, a Mac and a PC, or another computer with an RS-232 C serial port and communications software package.

This is an easy-to-use terminal communications and file transfer system that permits either dial-up or direct serial communications. We examined it during its beta test phase and, with the exception of a few ambiguities in the manual and a rather inconvenient method of reading transferred files, it worked well.

Specific Features: The system offers four separate modes of file transfer/error detection and correction at speeds of up to 9600 baud. They include: (1) a simple text mode, without error checking; (2) a "text with handshake" protocol that does ASCII transfer with X-ON/X-OFF flow control and auto-buffer saving; (3) XMODEM, the popular buffer-to-buffer error-checking protocol used by many software packages; and (4) a proprietary PC-to-Mac mode of transfer, which offers the ability to swap binary as well as text files. This is the preferred mode of transfer: when sending files directly from Mac to Mac, the mode handles the special internal formats of Macintosh files, including header information, the type of file, and how it is stored on disk. It's the only file transfer mode that will allow one Mac to transfer application programs to another Mac.

Problems: You must check and recheck many communications parameters on both sides before getting the connection to work. The system has a habit of returning to default configurations at the drop of a hat. You must reconfigure each time you try something new, or save configurations on disk.

Equipment Needed:

IBM PC, IBM PC XT, with a minimum of 128K RAM	Apple Macintosh personal computer
Asynchronous communications adaptor or internal modem with modular connector	128K RAM, a mouse, DB-9 phone and printer sockets as standard equipment
Two disk drives	
Microsoft Mouse optional	An optional modem (e.g., the Apple Modem 300/1200 equipped with adaptor cable)
A *PC to MAC and BACK!* adaptor cable (contains a DB-25 connector on one end, a null modem and a DB-9 connector on the other end)	
	1 disk drive minimum

Or

A cable you make up yourself (see description below)

<u>Software</u>

DOS 2.0 or greater	*MacWrite/MacPaint* (word processing/graphics package)
PC to MAC and BACK! communications diskette for the IBM PC	*PC to MAC and BACK!* microfloppy communications diskette for the Macintosh
Multiplan (optional)	*Multiplan* (optional)
WordStar (optional)	

Preparation: Unpack the *PC to MAC and BACK!* system and find the standard Macintosh computer cable. If you are doing a direct connect, plug the smaller end (the DB-9 male connector) into the phone or printer socket at the back of the Macintosh (both are serial ports). If you are planning to use the ImageWriter Printer, plug the cable into the phone socket, leaving the printer socket free for the printer cable.

Plug the other end of the cable, the DB-25 female connector, into your male communications card on the IBM PC or compatible. If you are connecting to a standard modem with a DB-25 female socket, you can use the male adaptor/null modem that comes in the package and attaches directly to the female end of the cable.

Now insert a backup copy of the *PC to MAC and BACK!* microfloppy diskette in the Macintosh and turn the computer on. You will also have to make a backup copy of the IBM diskette. The program documentation tells you how to do this.

Operation and File Transfer: Power up both computers now with *PC to MAC and BACK!* in the primary disk drive.

On the Macintosh, the program will immediately display the program main menu (the menus appear at the menu bar at the top of the screen). Options include File, Edit, Control, Connector, Baud, Rate, Mode, and Break. You'll also see a Terminal Mode prompt on the blank part of the screen, indicating the program is ready for you to set up your communications parameters.

Use the "point and click" operation of the Macintosh mouse to pull down each menu and make your appropriate selections. As a starter, choose Keyboard Print (the equivalent of local echo), Scrolling, and Auto Line Feed Off. You can always add line feeds if you need them when communicating with another computer; you may have to turn off smooth scrolling (a device that lets the computer automatically scroll text upward on the screen) when you communicate at rates faster than 1200 baud.

Now make your other selections. Move the screen pointer to the Connector menu and choose the appropriate socket (phone or printer socket). Now choose your Baud. Start at 1200. Switch to the Mode menu and you'll see four methods of file transfer. If you're communicating to the PC using the *PC to MAC and BACK!* diskette on both sides, choose the highest level protocol, called PC to MAC. With this mode you can transfer both ASCII and binary files back and forth with full error checking and correction.

For the time being, ignore the Break menu. You may need it later to send delays or halt control characters to a remote computer to get them to stop what they're doing and accept another command. The Break menu allows you to select the length of the break signal.

Now switch to the File menu and choose the Save Configuration option. That will store your parameters on disk; they'll automatically load next time you boot your *PC to MAC and BACK!* program.

On the IBM PC, fill in the date and time. At the systems A>, type PCTMAC and press the ENTER key. The communications program now begins. At the bottom of the first screen you'll see which of the two IBM communications channels has hardware installed for use. If you see, for example, the message COM1 Available, choose COM1 on your *PC to MAC and BACK!* Configure menu. You can switch to COM2 if you have another communications adapter card or modem thus configured in your IBM PC.

You'll now see a main menu offering a number of options controlled by the IBM PC function keys. Press function key F9 to access the Configure menu. Use the arrow keys on the right of the keyboard to position the highlighted window bar over the item you wish to choose. (You must move the right arrow key first to get downward movement.) Select communications settings that match those on the Macintosh. Choose the highest level protocol. Press F2 to save the parameters to disk; or F1 to return to the main menu.

Now type back and forth on both computers. If you can't see what you are typing on your screen, press the F3 function key and the keyboard print option will be turned on. Alternately, press F4 (remote echo) and the remote computer will echo back to your local computer the characters it's receiving on the screen.

You should get a completely clear transmission. If characters are garbled, recheck your communications parameters and make sure all hardware connections are correct.

File Transfer: To send a file from the PC to the Macintosh, press the F6 key on the PC and get a directory of the files on disk. The display will ask you to designate the appropriate disk drive. Regroup or change the directory by choosing the F7 key. Once you've got the name of your file, choose the F2 (Send File) key. The screen will display the mode of file transfer that you are using (PC to MAC, text with handshake, etc.). It will ask you to name your file; you can send multiple files by naming them at the prompt. If you are sending from a B or C drive, designate that by typing B:filename.EXT.

On the Mac, enter the File menu and click the Receive File option or, if you want to save your data to a different disk, choose the

Receive File [Select] option. The screen will ask you to insert the file name in a dialogue box. Click the Save option and that will begin the receiving process. The Mac screen will now flash a message saying it's waiting for the remote computer to send.

Press the ENTER key on the IBM PC to start the Send File process. Both screens will keep you apprised of the status of the connection. If errors occur, error messages will be displayed on screen; you may have to press the Break key function (F8) to stop the transmission, then the F5 key to Erase the screen and start over.

To Send a file from the Macintosh to the IBM PC: Press the Send File option in the File Menu on the Macintosh. A dialogue box will appear showing all the files you can send. Use the scroll bar to select the file you wish, and when it's displayed, move the mouse arrow to Open and click the button. Be sure the IBM PC is already ready to receive before doing this.

On the IBM PC, press F1 for Receive File. If you are in PC-to-MAC File Transfer Mode, the systems will automatically swap necessary file information; each file name is sent to the receiving computer automatically. If the transfer is in Text, Text with Handshake, or XMODEM mode, then the operator will have to name the file to be received. In XMODEM, a transferred file will not be displayed on the screen. Text, and Text with Handshake display the file on screen as it's being received. When the transfer is finished, the operator on the PC presses F1 to close the file and write it to the disk.

Reading Macintosh Files: By far the least convenient and least intuitive of processes in this connection, the Read File function requires the use of the *MacWrite* word processing program. When you press the Receive Files option on the File menu in the Mac, you must name the file in a dialogue box, then either save it to the PC-to-Mac disk or eject that disk and insert the *MacWrite* program disk. Open up the *MacWrite* file, and with the pointer in the text entry field, press the Mouse button once and then open the File Menu, pressing Open and getting a menu of data files. Select the one that has been sent, open it, and go into Save As in the File Menu, renaming the file under a different name and as Text only. Then and only then can it be retransferred to the PC disk.

Reading files on the IBM PC is much easier. Exit the program by pressing F10 (Exit to DOS), and at the A> prompt, type DIR (directory) and then type in the command A> Type (file name). The IBM PC will then print out the file on the screen. You can also dump the contents to a printer.

A *WordStar* File Transfer

The *PC to MAC and BACK!* program contains utilities to transfer and execute many BASIC programs from the IBM PC to the Macintosh. The documentation contains complete instructions for this process, which involves converting BASIC programs into ASCII, transferring them as text files, and then reopening and running them under Macintosh BASIC.

PC to MAC and BACK! also transfers *Multiplan* spreadsheets and *WordStar* files. Spreadsheet data are converted to an ASCII format through a universal file format known as SYLK, and then transferred to the remote computer, where it can be read and manipulated by the computer's own version of *Multiplan*.

We tested the *WordStar* conversion program that *PC to MAC and BACK!* offers. It will indeed take any document written in *WordStar* and convert it to a format that can be transferred to the Macintosh for complete editing. The secret is running a program that strips out all of the special control characters only *WordStar* recognizes. You run a program called WSCONVRT (*WordStar Convert*) that comes on the *PC to MAC and BACK!* diskette. The procedure runs like this:

1. In drive A of the IBM PC or compatible, insert *PC to MAC and BACK!* and press F10, which exits to DOS. In drive B, insert your *WordStar* diskette containing the files you wish to transfer.
2. Now, at the A> prompt, type WSCONVRT, pressing the ENTER key. Then type B: followed immediately by the file name, and press ENTER. The computer will request a different name under which the converted document will be saved. Press ESC when the conversion is complete.

You must then execute a second procedure to strip out line feed characters (*MacWrite* can't read them). Boot the communications diskette in drive A, as before, press F10, and at the A⟩ prompt, type CRLF, pressing the ENTER key. Your *WordStar* files should be in drive B. A list of five options will be displayed. Option 2 removes line feeds from the document. Save it under a different name.

After completing the conversions, you can swap files in the Text Transfer Mode. We successfully completed a file transfer using a direct-connect cable at 1200 baud, 0.2-milliseconds delay, with auto line feeds off. The entire procedure takes a few minutes, and will be a great boon to *WordStar* users who are now finding that Macintoshes are creeping into their offices. These programs are being incorporated, by the way, as generic utilities, with other communications programs for the Macintosh and IBM PC.

Cable Requirements for the Macintosh and IBM PC

Because PC-to-Mac software is available with or without specially configured cables, you can also choose to build your own. The following are the cable requirements as specified in the *PC to MAC and BACK!* documentation.

MAC to PC: The standard cable that comes with the package will achieve this connection.

Mac to Modem: Use a standard Apple Mac-to-modem interface cable (Apple part 590-9017-A) if you are using the Apple 300/1200-baud modem. For other types of modems using the 25-pin connector, you'll need the *PC to MAC and BACK!* standard cable with a 9-pin male connector on one end and a 25-pin female connector on the other, to which you attach an adaptor to the 25-pin connector and then hook that to most modems. The 9-pin connector plugs into the Macintosh phone socket jack or the printer socket.

Mac to Mac: For this connection, each Mac needs a standard Mac computer cable with the female-to-female null modem adaptor to mate the two ends together. The 9-pin connector hooks into the Macintosh phone or printer socket; the 25-pin connector hooks into the null modem adaptor.

PC to PC: You need a standard RS-232 communications cable as well as a standard null modem adaptor, which are available from most computer stores. The cable and adaptor are generally fitted with a 25-pin male connector on one end and a 25-pin female connector on the other. The null modem has a 25-pin female connector on each end.

Building Your Own

A PC-to-PC Direct-Connect: You need a null modem cable with a DB-25 female socket on each end. Pins 2 and 3 are crossed, with Pin 7 running straight as a signal ground.

```
        PC#1              PC#2
   Female DB-25P      Female DB-25P
        2 --------------------------- 3     (transmit data from 1 to 2)
        3 --------------------------- 2     (transmit data from 1 to 1)
        7 --------------------------- 7     (signal ground)
```

A Mac-to-Mac Direct-Connect: Use a cable with a DB-9 connector on each end; connect each to the phone socket in the back of the Mac. Transmit and receive pins must be crossed, as specified below:

```
  Mac #1 Connector   Mac #2 Connector      Function
       DP-9P              DB-9P
        3 --------------------------- 3     (signal ground)
        5 --------------------------- 9     (transmit 1 to 2)
        9 --------------------------- 5     (transmit 2 to 1)
```

Mac to Modem: Most modems have a female DB-25 connector. The Apple 1200-baud modem has a DB-9 female connector, for which a DB-9 male connector will be required. Below are the cable requirements for a DB-25.

```
   Mac Connector     Modem Connector     (DCE) Function
       DB-9P              DB-25P
        8 --------------------------- 1     (chassis ground)
        3 --------------------------- 7     (signal ground)
        5 --------------------------- 3     (transmit Mac to modem)
        7 --------------------------- 8     (carrier detect)
        9 --------------------------- 2     (data modem to Mac)
        2 --------------------------- 6     (data set ready)
        6 --------------------------- 20    (data terminal ready)
```

Macintosh-to-modem connecting cable.

Mac-to-PC Direct-Connect: You will need a DB-9 male plug on one end and, depending on your serial card on the PC, a male or female DB-25 plug on the other end. The pins on one end must be wired to a specific pin on the other end of the cable.

```
   Mac Connector      PC Connector        Function
       DB-9P              DB-25
        9 --------------------------- 2     (transmit PC to Mac)
        5 --------------------------- 3     (transmit Mac to PC)
        3 --------------------------- 7     (signal ground)
```

The Macintosh phone socket is a 9-pin female DB-9 connector that requires a male plug. Below are the signal names associated with the pins. Asterisks mark those associated with modem connection. The corresponding RS-232 signal names are shown at right.

Pin No.	Mac Signal Name	RS-232-C Signal Name
1	chassis ground	chassis ground (1)
2	+5 volts	+5
3*	signal ground	signal ground (7)
4	transmit data +	(TXD+)
5*	transmit data −	(TXD−) (3)
6*	+12 volts (+12)	DTR (20)
7	HSC input	DCD (8)
8*	receive data +	(RXD+)
9*	receive data −	(RXD−) (2)

Apple Macintosh to Radio Shack TRS-80 Model 100

Step-by-Step Direct Connection

General: You don't need to build elaborate cabling systems to get the Macintosh talking with other computers. The EZ-232 connectors will take care of the job for you—on the hardware end—and the new *MacTerminal* program will handle the details of your communications settings and text file transfer. *MacTerminal* is also configured to communicate with a Lisa using *MacTerminal* with *MacWorks*, any personal computer with the appropriate communications software, as well as an IBM or other mainframe computer. The documentation for *MacTerminal* contains complete instructions for setting up the Macintosh and transferring data back and forth to mainframes via an Apple Cluster Controller or the Apple Line as an intermediary.

Specific Features: *MacTerminal* not only communicates with personal computers, but also emulates three popular terminals: a DEC VT100, a TTY (Teletype), or an IBM 3278. The manual provides instructions on how to choose settings and do a hook-up. In addition, there's a good variety of protocols to choose from: not only X-ON/X-OFF, but the popular XMODEM protocol. *MacTerminal* documents can be saved as text only and then read by *MacWrite*; conversely *MacWrite* documents can be saved as text and sent to different personal computers that can't handle Mac's own special file formats. *Multiplan* documents can be saved as text using the SYLK format and transferred to other computers as a *MacTerminal* document.

Equipment:

Macintosh personal computer 128K with 1 disk drive minimum and mouse
EZ-232 adaptor (No. 301) for the Macintosh plus phone cord

Radio Shack TRS-80 Model 100
24K RAM
EZ-232 adaptor No. 102

Alternate: A null modem cable with the pin-out of Figure 11.4.

MacIntosh DB-9	Radio Shack DB-25
9	2
5	3
3	7
2	6
6	20

Figure 11.4

<u>Software</u>
MacTerminal microfloppy disk   *TELCOM* communications software

Procedure: Plug the EZ-232 adaptors into the DB-9 phone socket of the Macintosh and the DB-25 port of the Radio Shack. A phone cord passes between them. This will complete the hardware connection.

Access *TELCOM* on the Model 100 and set the status indicators at a minimum of 300 baud, 7 bits, even parity, 1 stop bit, and X-ON/X-OFF enabled (37E1E). If you wish to try a high-speed transfer, set your parameters at 88N1E (9600 baud, 8 bits, no parity, 1 stop bit, X-ON/X-OFF enabled). We tested file transfer and Terminal Mode communications at both of these speeds and found absolutely no difficulty. Press F4 for Terminal Mode.

Boot the *MacTerminal* disk and use the mouse to move the pointer to the disk icon saying "MacTerminal." Double click to open the icon. You'll now see a variety of icons in the *MacTerminal* disk window, including the *MacTerminal* applications icon, which looks like a telephone. Double-click, and you'll now open a *MacTerminal* document. (Or click the icon and choose Open from the File Menu.)

The menu bar at top contains all the commands to set up the type of terminal and communications parameters necessary. Use the mouse to toggle to each submenu. Choose the Settings submenu, then click and pull down the menu and choose the Compatibility Settings option. You'll now have a menu of communications parameters: point and click on the baud rate (e.g., 9600), bits per character, parity, X-ON/X-OFF handshake, connection type (options include Modem or Another Computer), and connection port (Phone or Printer). Click the appropriate settings, then confirm them by clicking the OK button. Now return to the Settings menu and choose the Terminal Type.

You'll get another big menu of options. Unless you are emulating a TTY or IBM 3278, choose the default VT100 setting. Other options appear highlighted: ANSI (referring to RS-232-C standards of the American National Standards Institute) and 80 column width (a 132 column width is also available). Choose Local Echo (half duplex), Auto Wraparound, and New Line (line feed), then click OK to save the settings.

Still under the Settings menu, choose the File Transfer option. You can choose your transfer method: XMODEM or text. (Remember: you can add a flow control protocol on the Text file transfer by choosing the X-ON/X-OFF option under the compatibility settings menu.) Under Remote System, choose Other if you're communicating to anything other than a Macintosh. You can also set delays between characters and lines in increments of anywhere between 0/60 and 60/60 second. Options exist to retain line breaks and word wrap the outgoing text. Press OK to save the settings.

Now type back and forth in terminal model (see Figure 11.5). You should get clear text. Save the settings in a *MacTerminal* document by accessing the File menu and choosing the Save As option (e.g., Sample.Text). You'll get a dialogue box in which you'll name the file and then save it to the disk drive.

Now begin file transfer. Load a document (text only) from *MacWrite* or write out a small document within the *MacTerminal* mode. Remove or delete any formatting or special dot commands or characters from the Model 100 text file and the Mac text file. Open up the File menu and choose the Send File option on the Mac. You'll see a dialogue screen, including lists of files. If you're transmitting to unlike computers, the files will be text only. Click the file you want and then click the Send button.

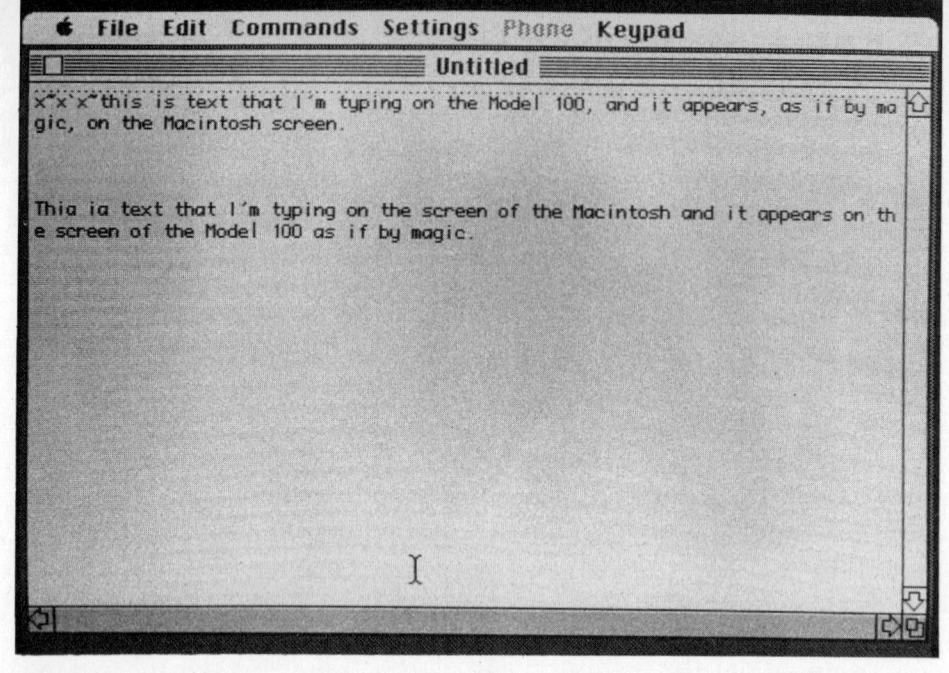

Figure 11.5 This is graphic proof that direct connections work. The picture could have been a setup, but it wasn't. Trust us. (*Photo: Stephen Ross*)

On the Model 100, press the download key (F2) and type in a file name at the prompt. Then press ENTER. Downloading will begin. To reverse the direction, choose the Receive File option on the File menu and give it a name. Then choose the upload key (F3) on the Radio Shack, type a file name, specify a width, and press ENTER. The file will be immediately sent to a disk. The file with the name will be on the disk you specified.

Compaq Plus to Apple II+

Step-by-Step Connection

General: This is a very common required connection. There are innumerable Apple computers in homes and offices around the country. Of course, as time passes, the IBM PC is becoming a *de facto* standard for the office. But there will be a need to transfer files from Apples to IBM PCs for some time.

There are a number of ways to accomplish this transfer. You can, first of all, subscribe to a mail service, like Source Mail or MCI Mail. With either one, use the file created on the Apple as a letter to yourself. Then, when you get to the IBM, call up and read your mail. You have just transferred the file. Alternatively, on MCI mail, don't send the file, just leave it as an unsent draft. Then when you get to the PC, read your unsent draft. You just transferred the file.

Second, get one of the commercially available file transfer programs. We've listed the vendors of many such programs in Appendix G. Third, try the direct connection in Figure 11.6.

Equipment:

Apple II
Apple II computer

CPS Multifunction Card
(This card has a clock, parallel port, and serial port. For this connection use the serial port)
RS-232-C cable, jumpered to the general solution outlined in Chapter 10

Compaq Plus
Compaq Plus computer (IBM PC XT-Compatible)

IBM Asynchronous Communications Adaptor configured as COM1:

After you have accomplished this connection, then boot up your software that will provide you with a control of the link. When we initially tried this connection, we thought that we could use the operating system on the Compaq Plus. MS-DOS has a copy command that's normally used for copying disk files, but it can copy any file from any logical device in the computer, theoretically. We found that using the Copy command with COM1 at 300 and at 1200 baud is chancy. Sometimes it works well, sometimes it doesn't work: it will stop at a random point in the transmission and close the file to which the information is being written. Nothing made this system work reliably, so we finally used *Telpac* (U.S. Robotics), which uses only the Transmit and Receive lines in the RS-232-C interface: it ignores handshaking lines. This software worked very well.

On the other side, all the terminal programs available to us are designed to work with a modem; none will work properly with a serial interface to another computer. So we wrote the *Sender* and *Receiver* programs listed in the last chapter to read a file and send, in one case, and to receive a file and store it in the other. The programs are in

```
   _____                           _____
       !                                    !
     2 +---\       /-----+ 2
       !    \     /      !
       !     \   /       !
       !      \ /        !
       !      / \        !
       !     /   \       !
     3 +---/       \-----+ 3
       !                                    !
       !                                    !
     4 +----!       !----+ 4
       !    !       !    !
       !    !       !    !
     5 +----!       !----+ 5
       !                                    !
       !                                    !
     7 +-----------------+ 7
       !                                    !
     6 +----!       !----+ 6
       !    !       !    !
       !    !       !    !
     8 +----!       !----+ 8
       !      \ /        !
       !       X         !
    20 +---/     \-------+ 20
       !                                    !
   _____                           _____
```

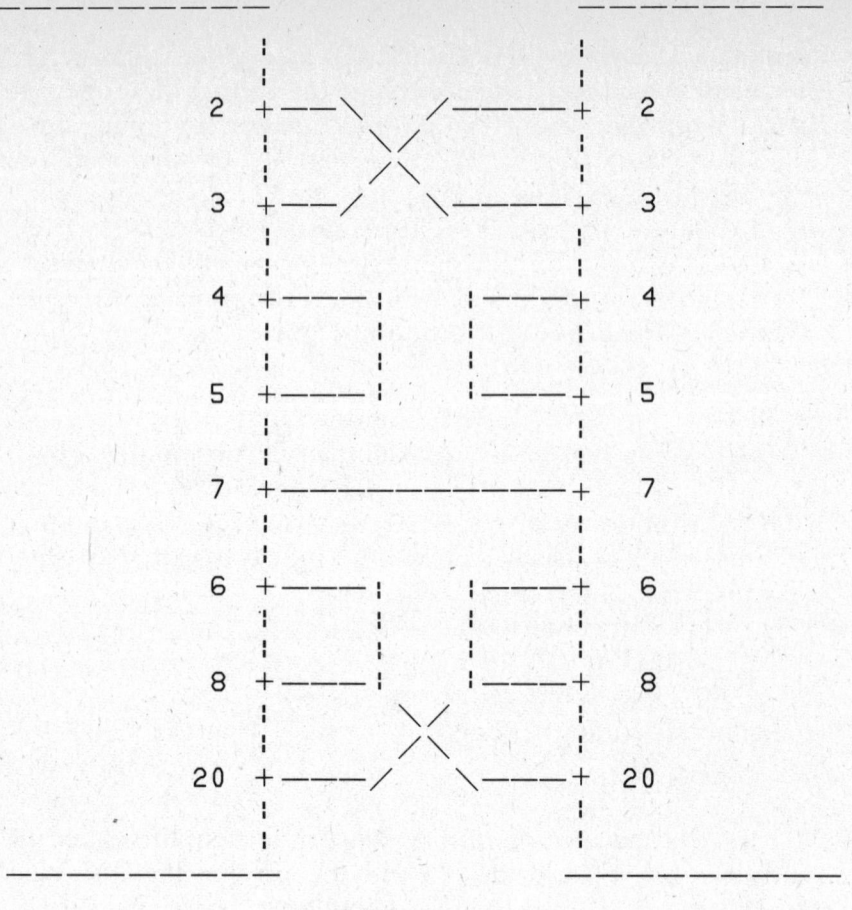

Figure 11.6

BASIC, which means we had to slow the transmission down for receiving. You can send from the Apple at 1200 baud with no problem, but receiving at that speed causes dropped characters. The solution is to insert pauses in the transmission from the Compaq, or write an assembly-language routine that will use interrupts to receive the data.

Software:

| Apple II | Compaq Plus (PC XT-Compatible |
| *Home Brew* Communications Program | *Telpac*, U.S. Robotics, Chicago, Illinois |

Boot both programs. On the Apple, the program will ask for information about the file to be sent/received. Answer, after the Compaq is ready to receive/send.

On the Compaq, boot the *Telpac* program. Type DEF to set communications parameters. This is an overly long and complex procedure requiring repeated changes to make the communications match those of the Apple. For example, the program will list the baud rates across the screen like this:

    1 Baud   110   150   300   600   1200   2400   4800   9600

It then asks you to choose the item to change, like baud rate, which has the number 1 next to it, by entering the number and pressing RETURN. Enter 1 and RETURN, and the screen will repaint, with the line now reading:

    1 baud   150   300   600   1200   2400   4800   9600   110

You have to go all the way around to get to 9600. The same holds true for other parameters.

Once that's done, then enter TERM filename. *Telpac* will open a Terminal-Save file, and go into Terminal Mode.

On the Apple, tell the program to send the file by entering the final Return after the character-count prompt. Apple will load the file into memory and then transmit. The screen monitors the status of communications.

You'll see the characters appear on the Apple II screen. If you have a lowercase adaptor, then the characters will be in lowercase. If not, they will look strange. Not to worry. Watch the Compaq screen to see the characters come across. They'll be fine.

To go the other way, boot the *Receiver* program on the Apple. In terminal mode in *Telpac* software on the Compaq, enter ESC-T. The program will prompt for a file name, such as A:STUFF.TXT. Enter the file name, and press RETURN. The program will now ask for transfer method: X-ON/X-OFF; user-defined prompt; or None. Choose the one that's appropriate, and press RETURN. The file will be transmitted. After transmission, the Apple will automatically save the file under the file name you already gave it.

CHAPTER 12
FILE COMPATIBILITY

- Binary Files and Other Mysteries • "Different" Text Files • Spreadsheet Files • Other Situations

COMMUNICATIONS BASICS

Application-Specific File: A file of information that has been written in some specified way by an application program. The program needs all files written in that specific way, or it cannot properly handle the information.

Binary Files: Files saved on disk as the representation of the memory space they occupied in the memory of the computer. Binary files are usually, but not always, compiled programs.

COM Files: Compiled programs saved under CP/M and MS-DOS are saved with a file name extension of .COM and are called "COM Files."

Random-Access File: A file to which the computer can have access at any point by receiving a specification called a pointer, which defines the record and field of information to be read or written. Random-access files are accessed more quickly, but take more space than sequential text files.

Sequential Text Files: Files in which information is accessed serially from the beginning of the file.

Now that you have your physical link firmly established, whether it's through a direct connection or with a modem-to-modem hookup, and you've taken care of data-link problems, like dropping characters, it's time to start thinking about using the data that comes across the line.

We've so far focused on transferring files made up of ASCII text characters. Furthermore, we've pretty much limited ourselves to discussions of plain, ordinary sequential text files—files that could be produced with a word processor—as opposed to those that could be produced with something else, like a database or a spreadsheet program. There are other kinds of files that you might want to transfer, and when you do, then the problems are a little different.

Binary Files and Other Mysteries

First, let us consider things such as binary files, like .COM files, or BASIC program files. In transferring these files, you only have one choice, and that is to use a program that gives you an error-correcting scheme for file transmission. That's because these files are saved in strict binary form, as in binary-code files, or in a packed form, as in BASIC-program files. These files defy translation without the use of the appropriate program to translate them. Therefore, if a transmission error is made, there's no way to detect it without some error-correcting mechanism. Most terminal programs without error correction will not even allow you to read such a file from disk for transmission.

"Different" Text Files

Of much more pressing concern for most people, though, is the simple problem of transmitting ASCII files that aren't necessarily sequential text files. Such files could be files that were saved by a database program in an unusual way. Or they could be files that were saved by a spreadsheet program, such as *1-2-3*, or *SuperCalc*, or the like. Alternately, they could be files that were saved by some other program using an unknown formatting scheme. Some applications programs, for example, use random-access file structures, files that have a very strict format as to the number of bytes in a field, fields in a record, and so forth. If you want to read these files from a disk, you need to know what their structure is before you can find the information stored in them. Such files define a parameter called a *logical record length* that tells the program writing them how many bytes to allocate to each record, and how many bytes to place into each field, or each portion, of a record. This means you can't use a plain old terminal emulator, like most normal communications programs, since these programs look for sequential text files, in which one character follows another, like soldiers in column formation on patrol.

Random access files are unusual in microcomputers, so we'll end the discussion of them here. If you run into one of these little monsters, then you'll have to be sure that your communications program can read them. Transend 2, for example, can. Many can't. But you can certainly do some things about the files that are written by special kinds of programs, like spreadsheet programs.

Spreadsheet Files

VisiCalc was the first of the spreadsheet programs, and the one credited, all by itself, with starting the microcomputer revolution. While you don't hear much about this program anymore—indeed, it's no longer being published—there are still plenty of people who use it. They may still be using it because they can't figure out how to transfer their spreadsheet files to more advanced spreadsheet programs, like *Lotus 1-2-3* or *SuperCalc 3*, which run on an IBM PC. Do they have to do away with all the data they've amassed in the form of *VisiCalc* spreadsheets when they make the switch?

Well, no. The really nice thing about *VisiCalc* is that it stores information in sequential text files. Moreover, Visicorp subscribed to applicable portions of the Microcom Networking Protocol, so that *VisicCalc* on one computer could read *VisiCalc* files written by another computer as long as the file could be transported to the second computer, and since the files are text files, that's no problem. So let's say that you have an Apple II+ and a *VisiCalc* program. You've amassed several floppy disks full of modeling information that you now want to get to *1-2-3*. What do you do about it?

A *VisiCalc* to *Lotus 1-2-3* File Transfer

The answer is simple. Use any of the communications methods we've discussed so far. Send the *VisiCalc* file over the telephone line through a modem to the PC, or send it through one of the electronic mail services, or over a direct connection. Save the file on the PC end in a file with a suffix of .VC. The translator in *1-2-3*, according to Lotus Development Corp., will read a .VC file that came from *VisiCalc*. Some *VisiCalc* functions will not be translated properly, but these are documented in the *1-2-3* manual.

While we're at it, we should point out that *1-2-3* will also read DIF files (those in the data-interchange format that was first popularized by *VisiCalc*) and *dBase II* files. It will also translate files from *1-2-3* to DIF and to *dBase* formats. So as far as getting a file from *VisiCalc* to *1-2-3*, or *dBase II* to *1-2-3*, there's no real problem. You just use whatever communications capability you have available, which we've discussed in the earlier chapters, and when the information is in the PC, then have *1-2-3* pick up the information in the spreadsheet.

Some of the information picked up will be read into the spreadsheet as *long labels*, labels that are too long to fit into one spreadsheet cell. An entire text file could be a long label, if you don't do anything to format the file. This term designates what *1-2-3* does with information it can't figure out how to allocate into its spreadsheet cells. (This isn't a problem with *VisiCalc* or *dBase II* files, but it can be a problem with other kinds of files.) Because of the long labels features, you can take data from these other kinds of spreadsheets and massage them for inclusion in *1-2-3*. Simply separate the data entries with commas, and place them into quotation marks. The commas count off the rows down the spreadsheet for *1-2-3*, and the quotes start and stop a data entry. You can either do this, or rely on conversion utilities built-in by your spreadsheet software publisher. In the case of *SuperCalc 3*, for example, its publisher, Sorcim/IUS, provides a utility program called SDI (Super Data Interchange) that will convert one of that program's .CAL files into a comma-separated value file, using a .CSV suffix. *Lotus 1-2-3* can then read the .CSV file. *Multiplan* also has a conversion program, by the way, to handle conversions into and out of its SYLK (Symbolic Link) file format to DIF and ASCII forms.

Other Situations

Software publishers must take care of other situations with conversion utilities built into their products. Remember that all the situations we've talked about here have to do with implementing the top layers of the OSI model: the applications and presentation layers. Handling these layers isn't really the province of the user, but of the software publisher. Generally speaking, it is the publisher who must provide application and presentation capability in communications—the file transfer and file-conversion utilities, in other words—as many microcomputer and mainframe publishers are now doing in the micro-mainframe context. In the cases just discussed—the transport of information from one spreadsheet to another—the publisher of the spreadsheet to which the data are to be imported has taken care of these higher layers. Unfortunately, there's no rule about this. Some just neglect the higher layer altogether, and some provide the service (file conversion, etc.), but it's expensive.

A good example is the provision of stock market information over public databases, like Dow Jones News/Retrieval. You can get a subscription to that stock database, and then get yourself a program called *Dow Jones Spreadsheet Link* that will automatically log on to the Dow Jones News/Retrieval database and get the information you want. The problem is expense, and on-line charges are quite high as well. Professional brokers go this route, as do many private investors, but it costs money. Is there a cheaper way?

There is. The UPI Unistocks system is available from The Source, for example. You call The Source and access Unistocks and then follow the instructions for downloading current quotes from the database, and the information starts flowing across your screen. The problem is that the information comes in a completely unformatted way, as 80-character strings, each of them terminated with a carriage return. The separate items don't even line up properly in columns, so you have to figure out what each of them is. Then you have to do something about getting them in a form that a spreadsheet will understand.

There are a couple of solutions to this problem. First of all, you can write a BASIC program to read the file you got from Unistocks, finding where each real value starts, and then putting that into a form that the spreadsheet can use.

You can use the same sort of approach to massage a file for incorporation into *SuperCalc*, or *1-2-3*, or *Multiplan*, or *dBase II*, provided that you know what the structure of the file is that the program will use.

Unfortunately, we can't tell you everything about this because the question of the application layer is a very big one, and could easily take up a full book on its own. The important thing to notice is that usually the information you need to accomplish a successful file transfer is buried in the program's documentation. You just have to dig it out, by reading and by experimenting with the files that a program saves.

There is another approach that's easier in one way, but more time-consuming. The information that comes in over the communications link is saved onto disk as an ASCII file, which means you can load it into a word processor. (*MultiMate* will require a conversion, but the program has a utility program included for that purpose, as does *DisplayWrite 3* from IBM, which also requires a conversion.) Once you have the information you got through communications in a word processor, you can then manually edit it. This is time-consuming, and if you are going to download stock information every day, the process might not be practical. But it can be done, and it doesn't require programming.

Our purpose at this point isn't to tell you everything there is to know about file transfer. There are lots of hidden traps. About the easiest way to make sure the file transfers is to use a program that's been provided for that purpose by the software publisher. Of course, you can write your own file conversion utilities, and while these are fun to develop, they'll take up some time and effort.

Finally, we should note that independent publishers also sell file transfer programs to go from Apples to IBM computers, from the PC to Macintosh, and so forth. A list of such programs is in Appendix D.

CHAPTER 13
NETWORKS

- Networking Introduction • A Proto Network • From Ideal to Real • Trade-offs • Size, Scope, and Topology •
- Points of Failure • Software vs. Hardware Compatibility • Costs and Flexibility

COMMUNICATIONS BASICS

Bandwidth: A term that refers to the number of signals that can exit simultaneously in a given communications medium. A medium that supports a wide number of signals is said to have a wide bandwidth.

Baseband: A communications scheme in which the information signals are transmitted in their natural format, without modulation, to a higher frequency, or a different frequency.

Broadband: A communications medium that will transmit a very large number of signals.

CSMA/CD: An acronym for Collision Sense, Multiple-Access/Collision Detection, a scheme that stops more than one station on a network channel from transmitting at the same time.

Gateway: In a local-area network, a gateway is the means of egress from the network to some other communications network.

Headend: The apparatus, in a broadband network, that serves as the origin of messages to stations, and the destination of messages from stations. The headend is like the master antenna in a cable-TV system. It retransmits messages it receives that are intended for other stations on the net.

RF: An acronym for radio frequency, the portion of the electromagnetic spectrum used for radio and television transmission.

Networking Introduction

Up until now we have been concentrating on point-to-point computer communications. Using either serial cables or modems to transfer data, we've seen the necessity of matching communications protocols in hardware and software to pace, transmit, and read files of data. The higher up our protocols have gone on the OSI "ladder," in fact, the more services we've gotten during communications.

But what if we want to connect together more than two computers? What about four, five, ten, or 1000? How can we get the same high levels of compatibility between groups of dissimilar machines? How do we control their conversations, and share common databases, printers, modems, and the telephone or cabling systems they use?

The answer is networks. *Networks* are systems for transporting information. They connect together computers, printers, hard disks, phones, facsimile machines, PBXs, and other communicating devices. They provide a way to integrate multiple electronic media—data communications, voice and video—over a single set of cables.

Networks are local or global. They can be arranged over small areas—an office floor or building, for instance—and large areas, like university campuses scattered around the world. There are worldwide networks, like the RCA Global Communications Network, which provide high-speed communications links over enormous distances.

Local Area Networks (LANs) are so dubbed because their geographical range is much more limited, say, from a few hundred feet to 250 miles or more. But local nets even apply to the four or five computers and a couple of printers tied together in a small office. They are systems for connecting and communicating, no matter what the size or scale.

A Proto Network

We can see the beginnings of a LAN concept in the home offices of an Ernest Mau or George Heidenrich, the two computer professionals who used a set of cables to swap data between several dissimilar personal computers and peripheral devices. If we were to suddenly imagine a system of permanent links, in which all the computers and printers in each man's office were connected together, and controlled through some sort of switching device, we would have the makings of a primitive LAN.

Such a LAN might attempt to connect three or four personal computers at their RS-232-C ports to a four-channel switch, which in turn would output to a single letter-quality printer. The switch would control which of the four computers could access the printer, so that all four computers could effectively share the resource without switching cables.

Or a single computer might be connected, through a switching system, to a modem, plotter, parallel printer, and letter-quality printer: one input to four outputs. This arrangement would permit the single computer to output its serial data to any of the four peripheral devices.

A still more elaborate scheme would hook numerous computers and peripherals together. This could be achieved in a comparatively simple way: by cascading a number of switches. If we were to join two or more switches together, for example, we could have eight channels instead of four. Creating a switching network, we would then attach four computers to the inputs of one switch, and then connect its output port to another four-channel switch, and finally connect that to a modem, plotter, and two kinds of printers. We'd get a system of eight devices—four computers and four peripherals—sending data back and forth in practically any permutation of computer/peripheral. And if we were to switch the arrangement slightly, we could get computers communicating directly to each other, assuming we'd handled the RS-232-C interface properly and configured the cables so that all could share common data and control signals.

The scheme we've just outlined exists. One particular manufacturer we know of (Micro-Module Systems, Inc., San Diego, California) has already developed the switches, cables, and the RS-232-C adaptors, called EZ-232, which we've already discussed (see Figure 13.1).

Figure 13.1 EZ-232 switch, which can be used to develop the beginnings of a local-area network. (Photo courtesy Micro-Module, Inc.)

If we were to add to this scheme some kind of simple software protocol—to ensure flow control between communicating devices, and to check for errors during transmission—we'd get a pretty effective resource-sharing system, and with no more cost than the price of the software itself, the switches, cables, and the RS-232-C connectors.

What we've described here is a "proto-network": not a full-blown local-area network scheme, necessarily, but an effective way to share data files and computer resources in a small setting. (See Figure 13.2). If we were to expand on that idea slightly, however, we'd probably touch on most of the elements of a classic LAN. These elements include a cabling system and a piece of hardware to regulate throughput—the effective rate at which data packets from each device are transferred on the system. In addition, we'd need a storage device for common files—a hard disk—sometimes known as a network server. We'd need protocols to check errors and do any necessary file conversion or reformatting. And certainly we'd want a controlling device to manage access to the ports on the system, and to avoid collisions of data.

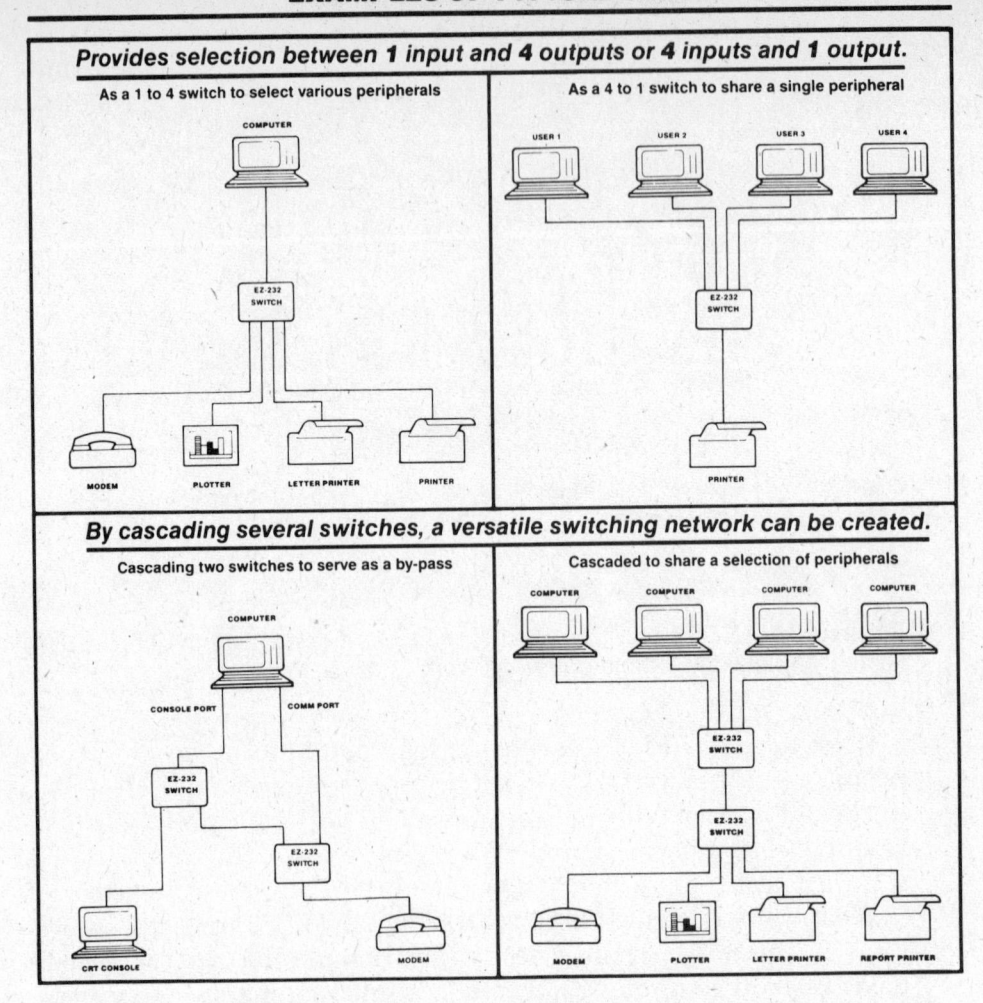

Figure 13.2 These are some of the ways that devices can be cascaded with a number of EZ-232 switches. (Illustration courtesy Micro-Module, Inc.)

From Ideal to Real

These basic elements make up the LAN. By definition, LANs ensure that every device on the system communicates with every other. LANs may integrate data, video, voice, and other signals by using some kind of special cabling: twisted pair, fiber optic, or coaxial. Some LANs, however, are equipped to carry computer data only. LANs also vary by their arrangement of devices (network topology or architecture), by the hardware technology they employ, and by the sets of standard protocols they use. Networks can be centralized or distributed, and offer a variety of transmission speeds, bandwidths, and access methods.

Obviously, sorting through this hodgepodge of elements is a confusing and difficult chore. There are probably as many LAN announcements today as there are viable products; many of them amount to no more than "vaporware." In addition, costs and capabilities of LANs vary a great deal. On the one side are the smaller nets and store-and-forward systems that are primarily designed to bring office automation services to limited numbers and types of microcomputers: systems like the Omninets (Corvus Systems), Ethernets (Xerox), and Arcnets (Data Point) of the world. These provide computer resource sharing, electronic mail, and basic physical- and data-link-layer compatibility.

On the other side are the large-area LANs, some of which offer open system architecture for plugging in future devices, as well as broadband (cable television) technology capable of transmitting along multiple data paths. Systems like Sytek Inc.'s LocalNet and Ungermann-Bass's Net/One are configured to connect thousands of computers/workstations together in one or more buildings or campuses. Several now offer gateways into IBM SNA/SDLC and other networks.

Discerning which kinds of nets might be applicable to your particular need isn't all that mysterious. What's important is to put technical mumbo jumbo aside and figure out how exactly you wish to use the LAN.

Do you need, for example, to hook together a wide range of personal computers—IBMs, Apples, Osbornes, TRS-80s, TI Professionals, DEC Rainbows—and other workstations or terminals? Or are you connecting up one family of computers? That issue will immediately narrow your range of choices. Do you need very fast throughput, or is data speed a secondary consideration? Is your network area within a small building or office, or does it span several campus buildings and include connections to remote networks? Will the primary thrust of use be the sharing of peripherals—printers, hard disks, and the like—or do you need a sophisticated layer of software to exchange files and programs between the workstations on the net? Do you need peer-to-peer communication, or will your primary communication link run between terminals and a host database?

Asking these kinds of questions early will focus your search for a LAN. It will also help you sort out vendor claims and hype, and eliminate a lot of contenders simply on the basis of net size, types of computers that are connectable, and software services provided.

Where to begin? Start by composing a list of all the things you think appropriate for your LAN.

You know, for example, that any good system should allow computers to share files easily. You may also want the system to make efficient use of printers, modems, and plotters. Ideally, you'd want to have a system so complete that different personal computers, workstations, and large systems (minis and mainframes) could share data files and even applications programs. It would be wonderful, for example, to find a LAN that would let us swap 10 megabytes worth of spreadsheets and word processing files already written in *1-2-3* or *MultiMate*, for example, without having to rewrite them in another format for different computers. It would be miraculous to run a *WordStar* word processing program on your Osborne Executive, and then dump your documents to the network server where an IBM PC, also equipped with *WordStar*, could pick up those files, then read and edit them without any problem. It would be wonderful if we could use a network not only for all these things, but also to swap messages, hold on-line computer conferences, and access data on other networks asynchronously or synchronously as needed. How's that for a wish list?

Well, we think it's terrific and complete. We suggest that you insist on a vendor's demonstration of products, as well as clear explanations of what the networking hardware and software can and cannot do. If the vendor gives you an ambiguous answer, like "We've announced our intention to . . ." or "third-party software vendors are working on that . . ." or "it should be coming along any day now," then press hard until he gives you the facts. When you are satisfied he can offer no more than half what you want, begin weighing carefully his grab bag of inferior offerings. Shop around. Price out competing technologies. Chances are you will have to sacrifice some element of productivity as you lay your foundation for a LAN. The trick is to find a network that will let you add on software and hardware services as they become available, or as you can afford them.

Trade-offs

In truth, you face no small dilemma here. LAN technology today offers a significant trade-off in services. Much of the technology is nascent and/or promised, and standardization has not been achieved.

Thus the current trade-offs involve the size and scope of the net (range of products—single vs. multivendor), open vs. closed architecture, low vs. high levels of software compatibility, distance vs. speed of data exchange, single vs. multichanneled communication, and different levels of reliability. Secondary trade-offs involve issues like channel access and allocation, and bandwidth, as well as methods of net security (lockout features, passwords, and so forth) and flow control. Practically every net that is strong in one or two areas is weaker in others. There is no one perfect network to meet everybody's needs.

Size, Scope, and Topology

The first issue, net size, is associated with the network configuration. There are three basic types of networks (with many variations): star; ring, or loop; and bus. Star configurations can be quite large: they are based on a centralized computing facility branches to remote sites. The sites may be dumb or smart, meaning the processing and communications control is either completely centralized or distributed among the workstations or microcomputers.

Time-sharing and telephone systems—private branch exchanges (PBXs) and computerized branch exchanges (CBXs)—are examples of star networks. In a PBX, for example, a PBX switch acts as a central, intelligent node. In CBXs, data and/or voices are shuttled from the remote sites to the central node via single communications lines. PBX and CBX capabilities are converging rapidly in today's networks. The clear advantage of the "hub" or star configuration is that they make point-to-point communications easy. Protocol conversion can be centralized in the central node, eliminating the need for complex network interfaces. The central node, or network controller, may also provide gateways to remote networks. This kind of arrangement is ideal for companies primarily involved in micro-to-mainframe links—getting at centralized databases using protocols that support micro-mainframe communications.

In contrast, ring topologies offer more distributed control. Rings connect network devices in a closed loop, with each device attached to those on its right and left. Ring topologies often work well with smaller numbers of computers. They demand some way of controlling traffic and access to, and allocation of data on the system, however. Many rings and loops use token-passing technology to handle the problem.

In token passing, a bit pattern, called a token, is passed around the ring. A computer gains exclusive access to the channel when it grabs the token. It sends its data in packets, then passes the token onto other nodes when it finishes transmitting. The receiving computer knows it's got to grab onto the data because it recognizes a destination address attached to the received packet. The receiver marks the packet as delivered, and sends it back to the transmitter. When the source station retrieves the packet, it marks it empty and sends it back into the ring, where another computer can pick it up and start the process over again.

Loop technologies are variations on rings; they may offer a central control node that handles the data traffic through communications polling or perhaps through time-division multiplexing (TDM). Both are ways to divide available time slots so that each user on the network gets equality or priority access. Polling does it by periodically querying each user location whether it wants to transmit. TDM allocates a set time period to each location.

Whatever the traffic-control method, though, rings and loops offer some clear advantages. Rings, for instance, provide high speed and efficient avoidance of data collisions. There is no need for centralized control, since control is distributed equally. Moreover, network interfaces tend to be low cost, though custom interfaces onto the network are required.

In the case of looped topologies—including the polled networks with a central computer in control, in which each computer is interrogated in sequence by the central node to see if it has information to transmit—connections are also low cost. The master controller on the system can move data off the local net onto other networks. But the disadvantage is central-controller dependence—the whole loop is inoperative if the central controller fails.

The third major configuration, bus topology, offers the widest variety of possibilities for network size. Configured so that computing devices and peripherals attach to a central backbone—a coaxial, fiber-optic, or ribbon cable—bus networks can be expanded to fit a room, building, or building-complex size. Moreover, control is distributed. As a signal traverses the backbone, every connection on the system listens; the signal contains a destination address. Collision of messages is avoided through the use of token passing or another technique, called "carrier sense multiple access with collision detection" (CSMA/CD). With CSMA/CD, a station that want to transmit listens to the network. If there are no other stations talking, then the one that wants to talk can do so. When collisions are detected, the station that transmitted first jams the network to make sure that all stations are aware of the collision. Each station then waits a set length of time before retransmitting.

Since the bus cable is passive, network operation continues even when nodes fail. And unlike ring topologies, computers on a bus network don't have to repeat or forward messages intended for other nodes. Consequently, there is no delay associated with retransmitting messages at each intervening node. Computers are thus relieved of network responsibility on that level.

Bus networks have gained increasing popularity in the United States in recent years. Systems like Ethernet, Omninet, and many others use backbone technology; in Omninet, for instance, the backbone is composed of a twisted pair of wires. Whatever the cabling media, though, bus systems, including those that use coaxial cable, require a piece of hardware called a terminator at the end of each network cable to satisfy the electrical properties of the cable, and a translator unit. The cable either contains forward and return paths on a single wire, or a double wire system; that is, one wire for forward signals and one wire for returning signals.

Star, ring, and bus are not the only topologies available, however. Hierarchical computing networks exist that have computers connected to computers connected to other computers.

In addition to these, simpler networks exist: a computer attached to a terminal is an example of a point-to-point network. Multipoint networks use a central intelligent node and several connected workstations. So-called unconstrained topologies are often made up of multipoint or point-to-point computer connections linked together. The long-haul packet-switching networks are examples of unconstrained topologies. These networks grow and assume new configurations based on customer and switching demands. However, the unconstrained arrangement may not be as suitable for most conventional LANs, because greater networking intelligence is required of each node to route data. This often results in delays in communications, and adds costly overhead to the node.

Points of Failure

Configurations are not as significant as the advantages/disadvantages they bring to the user. A star network, for example, onto which other LANs can be linked, is often the way to go when a large company desires an intelligent hub for communications/data processing, and data streams are flowing primarily from remote station to hub and back again. Star networks usually offer low cost per connection, and many types of equipment hook into the network with relative ease.

But the salient disadvantage of a star is that, without backup techniques, it harbors single-point failure. In other words, when the central hub goes out, the entire network goes out. Bus networks don't have that problem. But bus networks aren't designed for centralized control. Ring networks, in contrast to stars and buses, are wonderful for a small but stable set of users. Access methods are easy, and network interfaces are usually cheap. But each station must be active on the network: this is a single-point failure system also. When one station is out, the entire system goes out, unless bypass circuitry is part of the station. In addition, most rings require custom interfaces. Each different device requires one of them, and adding or deleting devices on a ring may be a problem for a company that wants to prewire a building because it plans for more computing devices to be added in the future.

So you can see that the configuration issue is a trade-off, and it's only one trade-off when you consider the problem of network size. Another trade-off is physical cabling, its power, cost, and the bandwidth of frequencies the cable can carry. In general, a small LAN extended over an office or a single building will require less bandwidth than a large LAN distributed over several buildings or campuses. A baseband system—an Ethernet or Arcnet, for example, which uses an unmodulated signal shunted along coaxial cable—is usually restricted to distances of less than a mile. Broadband systems—like Sytek's LocalNet 40 or Ungermann Bass's Net/One—in contrast, are usable at distances of 5 miles or more.

Baseband technology is used exclusively for LANs, and it has thus far provided more office automation products and dedicated network server devices than the other technologies. Baseband technology is based on the idea that all network devices listen and talk on the same communications channel.

Unlike broadband systems that split signals into different frequency bands, and in which the frequency bands can coexist, something like the way the FM and AM band coexist for radio and television broadcasting, baseband technology relies on using the whole wire to transmit a signal that is never modulated. Access to a baseband system is accomplished not through a modem but a *transceiver*, a device that takes the signal from a computer or peripheral on the net and forms it into a usable network packet with source and destination addresses, in addition to the data themselves. The bandwidth is kept deliberately wide to send high data volumes down the pipe quickly. Transmission speeds have to be high, because only one message can be on a baseband cable at a given time. Though either coaxial or twisted pair cables can be used as the physical medium in baseband technology, twisted pair is cheaper, but is more susceptible to noise than coaxial. And, practically, it is not used for the same kinds of distances as coaxial, and usually is attached to fewer network nodes.

Broadband technologies, in contrast, are generally wide-area technologies; they subdivide the frequency spectrum into multiple channels; within a single channel the system may use multiplexing schemes to subdivide frequencies further. More frequencies means more power and distance. Broadband is like cable TV—you can get 40 to 60 channels onto the coaxial cable. Voice, data, and video can travel on broadband systems, giving it added advantages. Two channels are required, inbound and outbound. Devices in a broadband system transmit along the inbound channel directed at the headend; outbound data leaves the headend after being modulated onto a different frequency. Each broadband system, furthermore, has a *guard band*—a range of frequency that separates inbound and outbound channels; it uses an RF modem to modulate digital pulses into analog signals.

What you should know about broadband vs. baseband technologies extends beyond these simple distinctions, however. For one thing, there is enormous variation in size and possible user connections within either technology. A Corvus Omninet, for example, is designed for 64 network nodes and several different kinds of microcomputers: it's a baseband, shared-bus system that uses twisted pair wiring. ARCnet, a coaxial-based star/bus topology, also baseband, can handle 255 devices in any one net. Xerox's Ethernet supports 1024 connections. And there is similar variation in broadband systems: Wang Laboratories' WangNet, for example, supports up to 62,535 connections—it's an enormous bus-configured LAN. Protean Associates ProNet, a logical ring topology, but also broadband, supports no more than 255 connections. And IBM's new PC Network, which is nominally a broadband network, isn't designed for large-area characteristics. It may, however, ultimately tie into IBM's announced large-scale token-ring LAN through a gateway. According to one LAN expert, Omri Serlin, President of Itom International, Inc., in Los Altos, California, IBM put restrictions on the electrical characteristics of the PC Network so it could be installed by users; so baseband and broadband do not necessarily define net size.

It's important, therefore, to look beyond the labels when determining matters of LAN size and appropriateness. A good rule of thumb is to choose a LAN that will accommodate both a reasonable speed of data transfer and enough devices to support as many users as you know you'll have, plus a reasonable number of additions that are bound to come over time. A reasonable LAN data speed, measured from the user's perspective, (not in terms of the absolute speed of the network) is about 10 characters per second. Another way to say that is that a network should deliver 10 characters per second to a screen, counting all the network overhead. Practically speaking, though, both baseband and broadband systems can do better than that: actual speeds approaching 19.2K bps are typical of low-speed broadband LANs, and higher speeds are readily available in such systems. Baseband systems, with dedicated interface devices, may do even better.

In contrast, twisted pair technology tends to be slower; its data rates are often in the 1200- to 4800-baud range. PBXs, using digital technology and twisted pairs, can transmit at 19.2K bps. Fiber-optic technology, with the highest bandwidth (500 Mbit/s), offers the potential for the fastest transmission. But technical problems with cable splicing and tapping technology so far have curtailed the use of fiber optics in many distributed LANs. Fiber optics is thus considered the LAN technology of the 1990s.

A Fiber-Optic Promise

Though fiber-optic systems are still used mainly for high-speed point-to-point communications, rather than distributed LANs, the technology is progressing rapidly. In 1984, AT&T announced its open-architecture LAN, called the Information Systems Network (ISN), which uses both twisted pair and fiber optics, notably optical fiber gateways to numerous PBXs, which link voice and data together; moreover, the system operates at a bandwidth of 8.6 Mbps over twisted pair or optical fiber. Protocol converters and a link to AT&T's powerful Ethernet-based LAN, called 3B net, ensure connection of a wide variety of micros, minis, and mainframes, including the MS-DOS and PC-DOS family, which can operate on the net with AT&T's own Unix-based minicomputers.

The final choice of cabling medium is often determined in a very simple way: companies either choose PBX topology and hence twisted pair technology, or they choose coaxial cable and either broadband or baseband technology. The choice of broadband is clear when the user wants multiple channels and types of media transmission, including video and voice. It is also clear when a large and diverse number of computing devices must be attached to the network. The choice for baseband, on the other hand, is often made in the more intimate LAN settings, where office automation services, such as central data vaults and file serving, are prime requirements. Generally, most baseband systems are designed to support only one or a few computer products, which can be a drawback for companies seeking nets to connect a wide variety of equipment.

In fact, scope and range of product support is crucial in every LAN choice. After all, what's the use of a network if half of your personal computers, printers, and ASCII terminals can't be connected to it? It's a problem, and although many vendors are attacking the problem today with a variety of interfacing schemes, a number of these vendors still haven't gotten the interfaces quite to work as they should. And still others are hanging on to single-vendor or single-computer family concepts. Apple Computer's AppleTalk, a local-area network released in 1985 for the Apple Macintosh, is a prime example. Other single-vendor LANs include AppleNet (for Apple IIs and IIIs), XODIAC (Data General Corp.), PCNET (Orchid Technology), Tandy ARCnet (Tandy Corporation, for TRS-80 computers), DEC Ethernet (Digital Equipment Corporation), HPLAN 9000 (Hewlett-Packard Co., an Ethernet-compatible LAN for HP 9000 microcomputer), and PCnet (Santa Clara Systems, Inc., for the IBM PC), among others. IBM has also announced a number of different nets for its cluster of personal computers, terminals, mini, and mainframe products.

As pressure to find links to different systems grows, however, single-vendor strategies will take a back seat to those supporting multiple products. Xerox's Ethernet, a kind of *de facto* baseband standard, for example, is now equipped to handle a wide range of micro and terminal equipment; a number of third party-vendors compete to produce off-the-shelf Ethernet-compatible components. Bridge Communications, Inc., for example, manufactures communications and gateway servers that link microcomputers and other serial devices to Ethernet through the RS-232-C and RS-422 interfaces. Some of these products are shown in Figures 13.3 and 13.4. The company also provides links that offer local-area network services like resource sharing in addition to separate gateways into IBM SNA host environments, the VAX environment, and the X.25 Public of Private data network, and other Ethernet networks.

Corvus Systems, Inc., manufacturers of Omninet, a resource-sharing system that now boasts E-mail, has gone another way. Its network

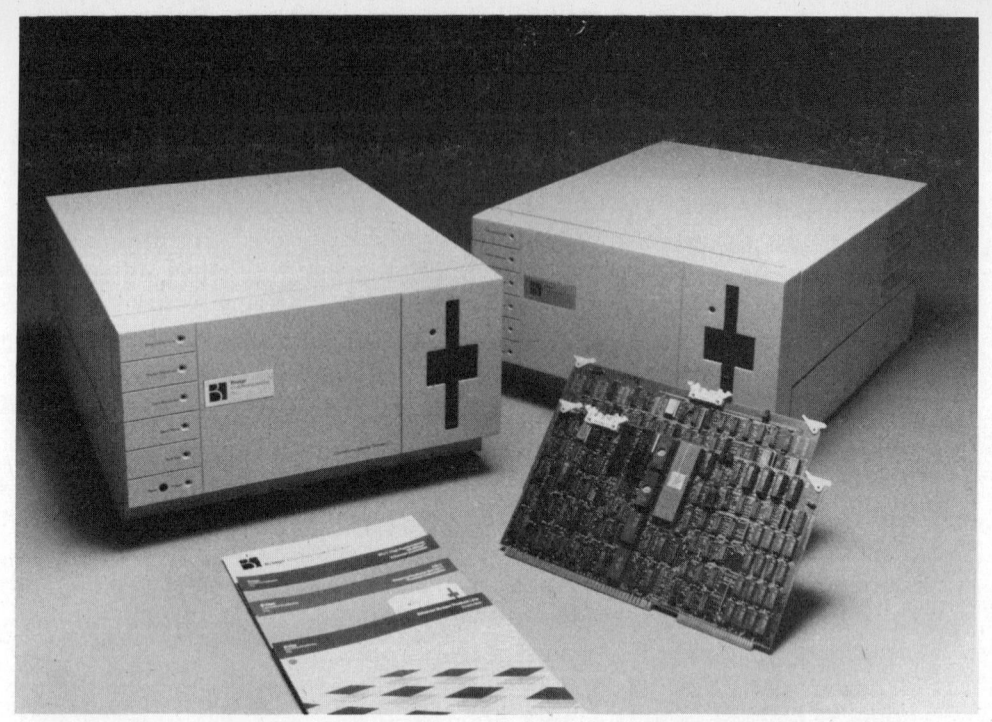

Figure 13.3 Bridge Communications' Ethernet products connect the Ethernet network to a variety of non-networked devices, and to public data networks.

supports several different microcomputers, among them the IBM PC and XT, DEC Rainbow 100, TI Professional, Zenith Z-100, and the Apple II, IIe, and III, in addition to its own Corvus Concept workstation. It has, however, maintained stricter control over the sharing of peripherals, limiting the range of devices to Corvus Winchester disk drives, printer servers, and Corvus Bank or Corvus MIRROR back-up devices.

Some systems are choosing one or two main players to connect together: Nestar System's Plan:4000, for example, now incorporates an ARCnet-compatible network for both Apple II, III, and IBM PC. Davong Systems, Inc., has designed a MultiLink IBM-compatible hard disk system that connects the IBM PC or XT with devices using CP/M and Concurrent CP/M-86 operating systems. Net/Plus, by Interlan, Inc., connects over a dozen micros and four minicomputers together.

Many LAN manufacturers are finding it to their advantage today to develop standard interfacing strategies for their LANs rather than machine-specific interfaces. Ungermann-Bass's Net/One, Network Interface Unit, for example, is designed to support devices ranging from the RS-232-C serial interface to the RS-449/422, V.35, IEEE-488, V.35, and the IBM PC bus, among others. In addition, the unit supports a number of software protocols. The company also provides a separate Net/One Personal Connection line of products exclusively for the IBM PC that will interface with its Net/One LAN. This kind of strategy is growing in appeal throughout the LAN marketplace; as vendors develop products that cater to standardized RS-232-C and other interfaces, they can naturally hope to bring more devices into their LAN interconnection schemes.

Software vs. Hardware Compatibility

Hardware compatibility, which we've been talking about so far, is not the most important compatibility issue for networks; software compatibility is. In general, people can find some kind of customized or off-the-shelf hardware solution to get computers connected on a net. A vendor or consultant could design an RS-232-C or RS-449 connector,

Figure 13.4 Local-area network hardware from Bridge Communications.

or you could do it yourself. At least you could get your data and handshaking signals interfaced to a LAN cable or transceiver. The real problem, as we learned from industry consultant Omri Serlin, is that your software protocols, as well as hardware, must understand each other before you can communicate programs or data to the other net devices.

Serlin says the problem is twofold. If you want to connect many computers of different kinds, the first requirement is that they must all understand the basic low-level disciplines, specifically the data-link layer, and the physical layer. Then you run into the higher level protocol issues. If you were using *WordStar* on one computer, and transferred that file onto another, then both machines had better understand the *Wordstar* control codes if they are to print or display the document properly—and that gets into the applications layer. Computers have to understand each other in terms of the higher layers. But today there aren't very many commonly accepted standards in those areas.

Just like individual microcomputers, nets of computers must conform to layered architecture standards. They need the same kinds of protocols defined theoretically in the OSI model or IBM's SNA. But most networks don't follow either of those architectures. In fact, says Serlin, most systems stop at layers 1 and 2; some may provide the essentials of layer 3, network routing, if needed, and some will provide services in layer 4, transport control, which amounts to error handling, recovery of errors, flow control, and packet information. These basic layers of services are provided in most LANs. The higher layers— session control, presentation, and applications software—are very often missing. Serlin says that companies like 3-COM or Interlan or other Ethernet suppliers provide the medium and interfaces and data-link layer. The software that provides data to the network delivers messages and receives messages without understanding what it's handling. Yet this content ignorance must be done away with if applications are to be exchanged among different pieces of hardware. If, for example, you want to transfer *Lotus 1-2-3* files to a different machine running a graphics program that outputs to a presentation-quality plotter, you'd need an applications bridge that understands both formats to massage the data into a form the graphics program could use.

There are some remedies for this kind of problem. Some LAN vendors are looking toward third parties to write applications software, and some, like Nestar Plan:4000 and the Sytek networks, are providing their own layered software solutions that go to the session level of services and beyond. In addition, many of the popular applications programs for IBM PCs are being upgraded for use on networks; Lotus's *1-2-3* and *Symphony, MultiMate, dBase III, Samna*, and *Wordstar 2000* will likely be compatible with the IBM PC Network in the near future. The new IBM PC net, based on Sytek network technology, goes nearly to the applications layer, Omri Serlin adds. A prime issue for buyers, he says, is not only to consider the elementary connectivity issues of the LAN, but the higher level protocols as well. You should know exactly what software applications and data files can be exchanged among computers.

Costs and Flexibility

Although we don't think present-day LANs can provide all the software services to meet practical needs, we're optimistic that day is coming. Obviously, choosing LANs that offer open software and open hardware architectures that may eventually incorporate a much greater variety of services is preferable to choosing prepackaged LANs that offer a closed architecture and little room for growth. However, your particular applications will determine the best LAN for your needs. You may, for instance, choose a relatively limited architecture because you know that the services you need are distinct and unaltering. You may be a freelance writer or engineer, for example, who uses a simple network technology to run a small business. Needs almost always change. So, if you're investing in a true LAN technology, choose one with flexibility—preferably with component support from several vendors.

Finally, a few items related to technical things and cost. You should know that every LAN implements a form of message flow control. Whether your LAN uses a simple ACK/NAK, or X-ON/X-OFF, or something known as the EIA Reverse Channel signal method (an electrical signal in the RS-232-C interface that ensures flow control), make sure that a flow-control protocol exists. If the network devices have data buffers and have flow-control features independent from microcomputers on the system, then the two connections may run at different speeds during a session, which enhances the flexibility of the system. Parallel data transfers can also use a flow-control function in hardware. In large organizations, nets should implement a standard synchronous protocol to interface properly with large systems.

A second technical item is collision detection: the token ring vs. CSMA/CD alternatives. Both are being standardized by the IEEE 802 Committee (LANs). Whether one is superior to the other is a matter of fervent technical debate—again, not within the realm of this chapter. The point about them for you is this: you really don't care what the particular collision-detection and avoidance scheme is, so long as there is one. More important is the question of the suitability of the network's architecture to your particular needs.

The problem of cost in LANs is a much thornier issue, though. Vendors generally "sell" their LANs by providing rough figures that are based on estimated per-connection costs. Those kinds of figures can be terribly misleading, however, since getting networks up and running often involves hidden costs: consultants, special hardware and software adaptations, etc. Indeed, even the so-called $50 AppleTalk Connection ToolKit may be a misleading figure, according to some consultants. If a user must hire a consultant to set up a LAN, then the per-connection cost of $50 goes out the window. Incidentally, most LAN's per-connection costs run between $350 to $1000 or more, although the cost is dropping rapidly.

Much of the controversy about cost is centered in the physical cabling media, but again, the obvious may be misleading. Though twisted pair wiring is, at this time, cheaper than coaxial cable, and coaxial cheaper than fiber optic, prices have to be weighed against what is already available in any given building environment. For example, if a large organization wants a twisted pair PBX-based LAN, but already has coaxial cable installed, it might be much cheaper to add LAN hardware based on a coaxial connection rather than starting over with hundreds of new telephone circuits. And in large-area LANs of several buildings or more, cabling costs for competing technologies come out just about equal when users start from scratch.

There are therefore two ways to know how much a LAN will cost. You must have it designed by a good engineer or grill competing vendors and contractors for bids on all their components. Here's a general rule of thumb: you will pay more than you expected to. One mile of coaxial trunk cable, for example, can cost as much as $10,000. Component costs must also be considered in light of consultant costs. You should talk to as many consultants as possible to find out how much configuration, customizing, and start-up time and money would be required. Almost all LANs require service and support throughout their working life, so service contracts with vendors may be preferable to going it alone.

The cost issue grinds down finally to LANs that meet your needs.

Overspending on broadband systems when you have a tiny office area to cover is probably a waste of money. Scrimping on a baseband system when you need more is also throwing money away. Before you invest in any LAN, you should investigate cheaper alternatives. You may be able to buy prepackaged E-mail services from a vendor, or simply buy electronic mailboxes on The Source or other public database. Some developers are now producing cheap file servers, print-queuing devices, and other office automation tools. An example is the Quadram Interfazer universal controller/buffer. It provides a vault for either serial or parallel data input from up to eight personal computers and will store the input in a buffer and output it on a first-in, first-out basis.

Don't forget, if you have a network need, your company MIS manager or data processing specialist might be able to rig up a micro-to-mainframe link with some data storage on the host. You may be able to switch and swap files with peers using an ordinary RS-232-C asynchronous connection with a modem or cable, using the host as intermediary. Micro-mainframe links are the subject of the next chapter.

IBM PC Network Options

When it comes to numbers and types of LAN technology, products, and announcements, IBM is unsurpassed in its power to excite and confuse the marketplace. Between 1983 and 1985, IBM announced its intention to support no less than five full-blown networking schemes, several of which are incompatible at present, but all of which IBM promises will ultimately fit into its Systems Network Architecture (SNA), a comprehensive set of layered communications protocols defining how IBM computer systems interface with one another.

The IBM LAN announcements included the Communications Products Division's much-ballyhooed Cabling system, a twisted pair configuration meant to provide the physical medium for a forthcoming token-ring network. This network, IBM says, will connect different departments, workstations, and computer systems over large areas. It will carry both voice and data and is scheduled for release sometime in 1986. Analysts see the token-ring net as IBM's future networking standard.

Another LAN, offered by Entry Systems Division, is IBM PC Network. This is a coaxial-cable broadband network designed to link IBM PCs together. The net will allow users to share files and

Networks 249

printers, send E-mail messages, and access applications programs and databases in large IBM System/370 computers. Unlike the proposed token-ring LAN, however, PC Network employs CSMA/CD collision detection and avoidance technology, which is incompatible with the cabling system/token-ring network. Software for the PC Network, released in the Spring of 1985, proved difficult to use and could not support popular applications such as *Symphony* and *dBase II*. Dampened sales and lack of consumer enthusiasm ensued. Many analysts speculated that PC Network was a stopgap only, and eventually would be orphaned by IBM in favor of its large-area token-ring standard.

Yet another announced LAN, which IBM describes as an intended LAN for factory automation (the product is sponsored by General Motors), will use a "broadband token-bus network." Like PC Network, it is incompatible with the proposed large-scale token-ring network. IBM has been sketchy about further details.

IBM has had software and hardware development problems during the course of product announcements. A LAN interface chip, under development by Texas Instruments, and intended for the token-ring LAN, was reportedly delayed due to the unexpected difficulties in implementing standards set forth by the IEEE 802.5 Committee. Industry consultants also cite IBM's problems in developing software that provides adequate user menus and network management and performance measures.

Whatever the problems, IBM has both ignored and reflected the general confusions in the marketplace. It has argued that the industry is in search of more than one type of LAN—and IBM, as always, will be there to oblige with a variety of products. This approach has worked well in supplying its customers with diverse—and not totally integrated—computer products. It remains to be seen whether the same approach will work in communications.

CHAPTER 14
THE MICRO-TO-MAINFRAME LINK

- The Mainframe Connection • Basic Dilemmas • Needs and Standards • Essential Terminology • Physical Connection • Types of Conversions • Common Characteristics • Limitations •Applications Interface Links • Universal Links • The Future? • One Final Word

COMMUNICATIONS BASICS

BCD: Binary-coded decimal, a coding in which each group of 4 bits represents one of the digits 0 through 9.

Cluster Controller: A piece of equipment that controls a number of terminals, called a cluster.

Floating-Point Real Values: Numbers expressed as whole number parts with digits following a decimal. In a computer, they are stored as a mantissa and an exponent.

Integer Values: Numbers having no decimal part.

Logic Unit 6.2: An SNA building block that will allow for advanced program-to-program communications between dissimilar computers and peripherals in the IBM operating environment.

Virtual Disk File Transfer: File transfer between a micro and mainframe in which the mainframe stores an exact image of the microcomputer's floppy; the microcomputer communicates with the mainframe as though it were accessing its own physical disk drive

X.25: A CCITT standard for packet-switching networks; implements layers 1 through 3 of the OSI model.

The Mainframe Connection

Small-computer users get power and anonymity from a link to the mainframe: a virtually unlimited data source combining problem-solving capability with the remoteness of "the big machine out there." Hooked to terminals, minis, or microcomputers locally or hundreds of miles away, mainframes can seem out of sight, out of mind.

Since mainframes can apply reasoning rules to solve complex problems, as well as integrate, store, and retrieve vast amounts of data, they are considered to be the most vital of corporate computing resources. Links to "live" (current) mainframe data files from the personal computer and its 32-bit derivatives (the "supermicro" generation) will be the thrust of communications technology and interest well into the 1990s. And the micro-mainframe link will wed the advantages of both machines: the analytic and report-writing capabilities of the micro, and the data-storage and number-crunching capabilities of the mainframe.

Basic Dilemmas

At present the micro-mainframe link is still in its infancy. Mainframes are multitasking, obey much more complex transmission rules, communicate in different symbolic codes, and structure their information differently than micros. Micros, by virtue of limited memory and processing power, use less complicated communications and data-formatting procedures. But if they are linked to mainframes, micros must be outfitted to exchange data in formats acceptable to the mainframe, and to obey the data-access, security, and communications procedures of the host. These requirements hold true even if software is written to make the mainframe interface more like communicating directly with a micro applications program, such as *Lotus 1-2-3* or *dBase III*.

The problems of fulfilling the mainframe's requirements for

communications are not small. Mainframes were never designed to communicate with micros, or to exchange data and instructions interactively between micro and mainframe-resident applications programs.

Selective access to mainframe data, and the conversion of those data to forms compatible with micro and mainframe applications, are two of the most important link challenges. First, the micro must be selective in accessing data; otherwise, it will be overwhelmed by mainframe files containing billions of bytes of information. Once access is achieved, through some kind of physical link, the mainframe must understand what the user means by requesting a file (or subset of a file) of data. The data must be moved down to the personal computer, and then put into a format that makes sense to the micro application program in use. For example, if you move a personnel record on the mainframe to a *dBase II* application on the micro, the link program must put the information into a form compatible with *dBase II*'s input format; that is, the information "fields," the categories of data, and the punctuation (e.g., commas) required to delimit each field. By the same token, budget data moved down from the mainframe to a *Lotus 1-2-3* spreadsheet must be converted into a Lotus file; that is, the micro must be equipped with a program to insert the numeric data and categories into the proper spreadsheet cells.

How are these conversions achieved? Each of them requires separate formatting (and sometimes software/hardware additions) and connection expertise. At times, the conversions required can be complicated. For example, packed numeric fields in mainframe VSAM files, a particular kind of mainframe file structure, must undergo conversions into ASCII character strings, BCD, floating-point real values, or integer values in order to transfer data between the mainframe and micro applications program. The storage formats for these values tend to vary from application to application on the micro, and the conversions must be made accordingly.

In addition, information that is captured or input on the microcomputer and transported up to the mainframe requires at least some form of conversion or "preprocessing" prior to integration with the host database. (Most of the analysis and final processing occurs on the host.) An ASCII-to-EBCDIC (Extended Binary-Coded Decimal Interchange Code) code translation is an example of preprocessing. Code translation can be simple when documents are uploaded to the mainframe, especially if there is little formatting information in the text. But if documents are swapped between micro and mainframe-resident word processing applications, and specialized formatting codes are embedded in the document, then a series of conversions may be required to enable the host system to interpret correctly the micro program's formatting codes.

Needs and Standards

Whatever the kinds of conversion, certain basic questions about need and appropriateness exist. Why implement a micro-mainframe link to begin with? What kind of link is required? What kinds of information will be transferred and massaged? The costs of interactive links are high, ranging from $300 for a single micro software package to more than $75,000 for a micro-mainframe "two package" solution with hardware. In large corporations, pressures to get into mainframes often exceed immediate, and even medium-term benefits. At what point does the need for accessing corporate data exceed the hassles of setting up a link, troubleshooting it, and ensuring procedures to maintain security and data integrity? Why should managers access mainframes when they can lock up all the analytic data they need on hard disk? Why not use a cheap electronic mailbox on a public database (e.g., The Source) rather than implement a complex networking solution through the host? Establishing needs and priorities is important, and should drive technical and purchase decisions.

Once the need has been established, though, technical questions naturally follow. A chief one revolves around standards issues. Micros must recognize and run with mainframe communications standards. In the IBM world, the emerging *de facto* standard for mainframe communications, especially in the Fortune 1000, is IBM's Systems Network Architecture (SNA), the set of protocols that defines how IBM computers and peripherals interact with each other. Terminals linked to IBM hosts under SNA can work interactively with mainframe applications programs, and micros attached to hosts will have similar capabilities through the SNA scheme by implementing the same communications protocols as terminals.

In the non-IBM world, especially in Europe, the emerging communications standard is OSI (Open Systems Architecture, which we've already discussed in detail), whose layered protocols are still being defined by the International Standards Organization and the Consultative Committee on International Telegraphy and Telephony (CCITT). Several proprietary vendors are now "migrating" their communications networks toward OSI compatibility. For example, companies like Digital Equipment Corporation (DEC) and Honeywell are shortly to implement OSI-level four transport protocols in their networks, DNA/DECnet and DSA, respectively. In addition, both IBM and non-IBM vendors are offering products and interface options to X.25, the communication standard for high-speed digital packet-switching networks, which implement the essential functions of OSI layers 1 through 3.

Logical Unit 6.2

Of particularly keen interest worldwide today is the potential impact of an SNA building block called Logical Unit (LU) 6.2. The unit is the basis of what IBM calls Advanced Program-to-Program Communications (APPC). Under LU 6.2, micro and mainframe programs can exchange data in such a way that one program can do specialized work while the other manages the work, or two peer programs on different machines can share data interactively. Some analysts see LU 6.2 as the beginning of real distributed data processing in multicomputer environments. At this writing, IBM has yet to implement LU 6.2 capability on its personal computer, but plans to release an expanded version of its 3274 cluster controller (a controller that sits between the host and the terminals or PCs on an SNA network and directs data transport and message routing). The controller will link up 128 devices, including the IBM PC, and also support LU 6.2 capability. Industry reports indicate it will provide a direct link to the mainframe, rendering obsolete many of the current micro-to-mainframe products. APPC ability will also enable PCs to communicate with each other through the controller, bypassing the host entirely.

At present, though, the state of micro-to-mainframe links remains in flux. Vendors, unsure of IBM's future communications product strategies, haven't settled on link standards of their own. A few have begun to implement their own versions of LU 6.2, hoping they will be "upward compatible" with IBM communications products. But most have stuck within the realm of proprietary link architectures.

Corporate computer managers, in turn, have voiced confusion about link products. Slow to purchase and test links, they have generally limited their uses to one or two "must do" traditional applications: shuttling budget or banking transaction data from a host or minicomputer to a PC, for example, or downloading selected personnel files from a host to a PC for manipulation and writing of reports.

The confusion has made it difficult, on all sides, to properly define what links can and can't do. But there are distinct differences between links, and different kinds of software/hardware combinations offer a variety of functions and capabilities.

Essential Terminology

A *link*, for example, can refer to a simple physical connection: the wire, cable, or phone transmission medium that attaches your personal computer to a mainframe. A link may also refer to a *terminal emulator*—a circuit board that slots into your personal computer, attaches to a phone line or coaxial cable, and mimics the characteristics of a mainframe-linked terminal. Another type of link is a *protocol converter*—a device that lets you switch from slow, asynchronous communications to the ultrafast, precisely timed synchronous communications that mainframes use.

Links also refer to software. There are packages called *applications interface links* that let PCs download and manipulate data from selected applications programs on the mainframe. Another kind of link, the *database interface link*, gives micros access to different (or one kind of) mainframe database files. The more sophisticated of these use generic file reading and writing capabilities, in which the mainframe piece of the link can read a wide variety of mainframe database files and convert the data into formats compatible with *1-2-3, Symphony, dBase II, VisiCalc*, or other popular micro-analysis tools. Each of these options has disadvantages and benefits. Some software packages do very simple file transfers and terminal emulation; others begin to approach "interactive" and integrated applications.

Physical Connection

It's necessary to establish a physical and data link between micro and mainframe. The alternatives for these links are limited: either get a mainframe to communicate asynchronously (like a micro) or do the reverse—outfit the micro to communicate synchronously, like a terminal communicating to the mainframe.

Synchronous communications is a much faster and more accurate form of communications; it is the primary means of communications for mainframes, and is designed for high-volume data transfer. Engineers design specialized modems and software to handle synchronous communications, usually by employing a *blocked protocol*, in which the mainframe obeys sets of rules that precisely time transmissions and send out entire screenfuls of data in big bursts.

In contrast, microcomputers communicate asynchronously, sending information over wires in bytes, one bit at a time. Each byte is framed by start and stop bits, and usually a parity bit, which provides a small measure of error checking. The speed of communications (except for direct-connect techniques) is generally much slower than mainframes. The error rate is higher, also, and asynchronous modems thus far cannot communicate at the speeds synchronous protocol calls for— 19,200 baud or higher.

Types of Conversions

Whichever ways communications take place, a protocol conversion is in order. With asynchronous links, the mainframe is forced to obey the same communications rules that micros use. The mainframe is outfitted with a preprocessor (often a software package) that converts its internal code (all IBM mainframes, for example, use EBCDIC, which is an 8-bit code that generates 256 unique characters) to the standard ASCII character set. The mainframe is also equipped with an RS-232-C serial port(s) on its front-end processor. Attach a modem to the port, run some communications software, preferably with an error-checking protocol, and mainframes can communicate with micros in ASCII.

Another method of protocol conversion is asynchronous to synchronous, beginning with hardware changes on the micro end. IBM PCs, PC ATs, and the family of compatibles, for example, can be outfitted with terminal-emulation circuit boards and software for synchronous communications. These systems, when properly configured, mimic or "emulate" the characteristics of common IBM 3270 terminals, which connect via coaxial cable, twinax, or dial-up line to IBM System 370 mainframes. They communicate with the mainframe either in IBM Bisynch or SDLC (Synchronous Data Link Control) communications protocols, two of the most popular in the IBM operating environment. Other types of terminal emulator boards and software mimic the popular IBM 5250 terminals and the DEC VT100 smart ASCII terminals, which connect, respectively, to the IBM System 34, 36, and 38 minicomputers, and the DEC VAX 11/780 superminis, among others.

> ### SNA/SDLC: Networked Communications
>
> Emulator boards that enable PCs to hook into IBM Systems Network Architecture (SNA), implement SNA/SDLC layered communications protocols. Under normal operating conditions, computers in an SNA environment will enjoy a branching configuration, rather than "point-to-point," as is common in asynchronous communications. This means that communications can take place between the host and many computing devices simultaneously or in sequence. The SNA network contains multiple communications lines and, upon each line, one or more network controllers, each of which are connected to several PCs (with emulators) and terminals. The controllers act like a "traffic cop" for data, receiving messages, in the form of data packets, which are routed from the mainframe and specifically addressed to the control unit and an attached terminal or PC. The control unit locks onto the packets, then reroutes them to the specific computer/terminal recipient. This arrangement makes for much greater communications and data processing efficiency: fewer dedicated phone lines are required, and the mainframe can consequently "poll" literally hundreds of controllers and thousands of computers, giving each a chance at access into the network.

Common Characteristics

Whatever the configuration, terminal-emulator systems for PCs display common characteristics. They provide a basic physical and data-link-layer solution in addition to some limited file-transfer intelligence. For example, Digital Communications Associates, Inc.'s (Norcross, Georgia) popular terminal emulator board, the Irma Decision Support Interface (in Figure 14.1), lets users access mainframe files in the IBM VM/CMS and MVS/TSO operating systems/file structures. Additional mainframe conversion software isn't needed; the emulator presents a request for these files in a format the mainframe computer can accept. Each emulator board (one per computer) is slotted into a free slot on the IBM PC or compatible; it connects directly to a communications controller via coaxial cable. A software package is added, allowing the user to select a number of keyboard options (including choices for different color support, light pens, etc.), and to save downloaded files

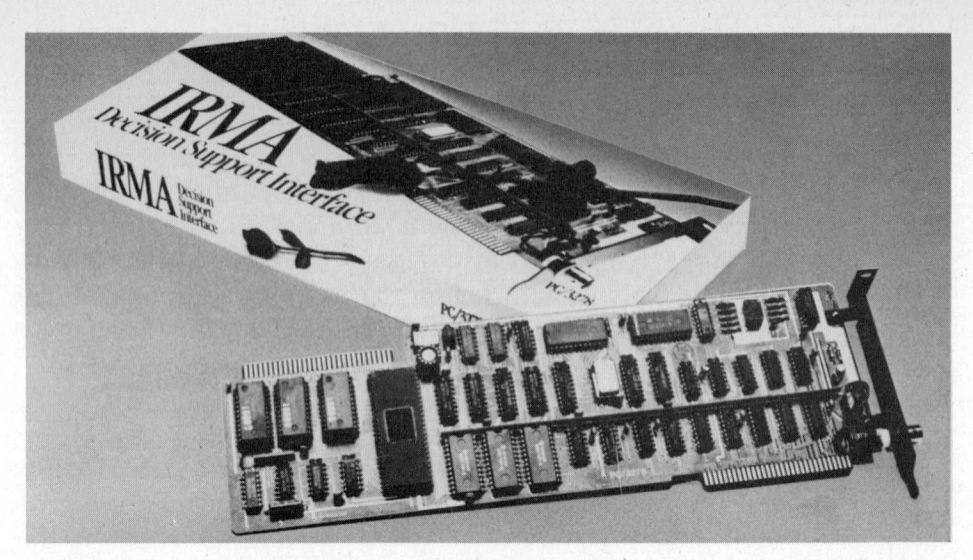

Figure 14.1 The Irma Decision Support Interface is a micro-to-mainframe link for the IBM Personal Computer and compatibles.

in ordinary text or binary format. Users can switch, on-line, back and forth from normal microcomputer applications to the 3270 "terminal" mode.

In recent months, DCA and other communications companies have expanded the capabilities of their terminal-emulation products. Some now provide for remote dial-up links into the 3270 terminal environment (see Figure 14.2), while others are reported to be developing boards with APPC (Logical Unit 6.2) capability. The leader in emulator products, Digital Communications Associates, has produced a converter called Irmalette—actually an asynchronous communications card—which is installed in the remote PC and attached to an asynchronous modem using ordinary RS-232-C control signals; the modem then dials into the network via the Irmaline, a stand-alone protocol converter that takes ASCII data and switches it into 3270 synchronous protocol. Irmaline is installed directly at a controller site, and is linked to the controller by coaxial cable. The advantage of this kind of system is that different types of microcomputers, such as Apples or DEC Rainbows, can now dial into the network environment and communicate in ASCII, their data automatically converted into the synchronous protocol the mainframe computers can understand.

Other types of emulators are giving PCs the ability to run more than one mainframe program at a time, and to convert data into usable micro applications formats. For example, Techland Systems, Inc., of New York City, manufacturers of the famous Blue Lynx line of termi-

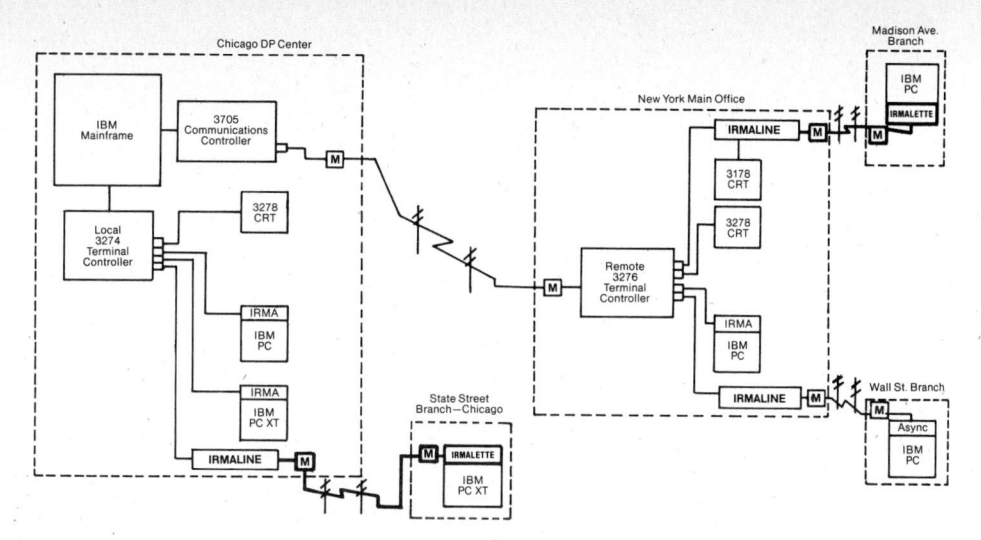

Figure 14.2 This is an example of how synchronous and asynchronous communications hardware can be used together to create a diversified communications network.

nal emulators (for IBM 5151 and 3270 terminals, among others), has developed multiple program access capability, so that a user can switch back and forth between sixteen full mainframe screens. A separate utility, called Data Reader, takes downloaded data and formats them for spreadsheets and databases. It grinds away and produces a *Lotus 1-2-3* file, a *VisiCalc* file, or a *dBase II* file.

Limitations

Despite these and other capabilities, terminal emulation is still a comparatively limited link strategy. It provides pure connectivity to the mainframe, but with few exceptions, downloaded mainframe data must be reformatted for use with specific micro applications programs. Whereas some programs or emulators already contain conversion utilities to accomplish this task, most don't, and the user may be forced either to view the data without making changes or write a program to complete the reformatting chore. Otherwise, the data may just sit there, in unusable form, and must be rekeyed into the applications program. This makes the mainframe link virtually useless.

Better and more sophisticated software links are on the horizon, however. Some of the simpler ones are actually file-transfer programs. One type of program allows the user to perform "virtual disk file transfer" from micro-to-mainframe; another type allows for automated data entry into existing host applications.

The first kind, virtual disk file transfer, refers to archival storage of micro data on the mainframe. A virtual disk system allows the mainframe to copy the image of a micro floppy onto a host disk librarian program, a program that keeps track of complete microcomputer disk images. Consequently, transferring a file between micro and mainframe is very much like swapping files between two floppy disk drives on the microcomputer.

A virtual disk system is implemented in two parts: the disk librarian and a virtual disk device driver. The librarian may come with options to configure each disk image to different sizes: 360 kilobytes or 5 or 10 megabytes, for example. The device driver, in contrast, is actually a PC-resident program that manages the interface with the microcomputer operating system (like MS-DOS). It is the driver that lets the mainframe virtual disk image appear as a physical disk drive to MS-DOS. Files are then transferred; a simple copy command is all that's required. But no conversions of data take place, and therefore micro data can't be integrated with any host applications. (Some virtual disk products, however, offer optional conversion packages that allow an interface to host programs.)

Another file-transfer link, automated data entry, allows selective uploading of micro files into existing host applications. The software on the micro side works with terminal-emulation hardware and software, and the program reads data from a micro file and feeds them through the emulation program as though they were coming from the keyboard. Such a system works well in simple ASCII text file transfer to a host text editor, but users must be equipped to reformat micro files, if necessary. They must also be familiar with the screen format of the host application, and perform any required conversions of data before uploading to the host.

A third kind of file transfer uses interactive and integrated applications on both micro and mainframe. An interactive application is a two-package product for the micro and the mainframe. Such products will enable a host accounting module to interact with a complementary module on the micro, as an example. The user is able to store and validate data entries, ship them to the host, or pick exactly which fields of a data record should be downloaded from the mainframe. Interactive packages usually include security features, a menu-driven interface, as well as data-conversion utilities designed to translate files from applications programs on the mainframe to the most popular PC applications programs.

In essence, interactive links penetrate the higher layers of the OSI model. Implementing file-transfer protocols, they download specific mainframe file subsets and convert them into formats that similar PC applications can manipulate. The links may also offer on-line help, and employ English-like query tools to aid in the extraction of mainframe files. Some links, like PC/FOCUS (Information Builders, Inc., New York), are actually database management systems combining mainframe querying capability with a micro report-writer and applications development tool.

Like most other links, the PC/FOCUS software relies on a terminal emulator board (Irma, for example) to establish the basic physical connection with the host. Data can then be downloaded using synchronous protocols, and then sorted on the micro.

Applications Interface Links

PC/FOCUS isn't alone. Vendors are seeking applications interface links between their proprietary mainframe packages and the micro itself.

But whereas some manufacturers have used a proprietary or "exclusive" link between their mainframe and micro-resident packages—an example is Management Science America's (Atlanta, Georgia) Executive Peachpak II with ExpertLink, which links the micro to mainframe data stored in MSA's host accounting module—others are beginning to see the wisdom of creating more generic or "universal" links with an open communications architecture. Generic links give the micro user more flexibility, greater access to mainframe files, and more analytic capability on the micro.

Universal Links

As a class, the higher level links read a variety of mainframe file structures and are equipped to reformat data in host files to structures used by the most popular microcomputer applications. Processing chores may be split between PCs and mainframes, a kind of "shared intelligence" scheme. These links are often dubbed *general link* products or *database interfaces*, since some of them allow the user to access mainframe databases without necessarily being familiar with the mainframe data dictionary. Examples are Micro Tempus's Tempus-Link (Montreal, Quebec, Canada), InfoCenter Software's iLink, and the

Answer series from Informatics General Corp. (Canoga Park, California), called Lotus/Answer, dBase/Answer, and VisiAnswer.

The Answer series uses "two-package" link technology. But it exemplifies the broader based file-reading approach. The link includes a host data extraction package, Answer/DB, that will read virtually any file written in the common mainframe file structures, such as IBM's IMS, Cullinet Software Inc.'s IDMS, Cincom Systems' Total, or Software AG's Adabas, for example. The corresponding micro packages let the user decide, off-line, which kinds of data to look at. Select the conditions, fields, and types of data sorting desired, then send the completed request via the Irma or similar board to the mainframe, where it is executed according to a priority assignment. The downloaded data are loaded on the PC into formats that *VisiCalc*, *dBase II*, *III*, *Friday1!*, *Framework*, and *Lotus 1-2-3* applications programs can use. (Informatic General's Micro/Answer Toolkit allows the micro user to develop his own applications and then download data to them.)

Another link, Cullinet Software Inc.'s GOLDENGATE package, exemplifies a variation on this strategy. The $795.00 package is a stand-alone integrated series of PC applications which, according to its producers, can be equipped with a direct upload and download capability to Cullinet's own mainframe product, the Information Center Management System (ICMS). This package summarizes data on the mainframe and presents them in a format that is understandable to PC users who are unfamiliar with corporate mainframe languages. Given the proper commands, Cullinet's mainframe package, like some of the more general links, can read databases like IBM's IBM and DL/1, as well as data produced by outside sources. The file summaries are then converted into Cullinet's own IDMS/R format. This capability, combined with a microcomputer link, called InfoLink (an add-on to the GOLDENGATE package), enables PCs to exchange files and talk to one another using IBMs as host. The GOLDENGATE package, however, does not offer access to popular micro applications programs (such as *Lotus 1-2-3*), a problem Cullinet says it will remedy with new interfaces to *1-2-3* and *Symphony*.

The Future?

There's so much new technology being developed in the mainframe link arena that our functional categories may well be supplanted in the near future. For the micro user of today, the uncertainties of the link marketplace pose some unusual problems. Do you wait, or not? Is it better to plunge in, buying a mainframe data-extraction package running in the range of $30,000 to $150,000, and pay hundreds to thousands of dollars for a corresponding micro package, as well as $750 to $1300 for a terminal emulator? Or do you hold back for less expensive and more technologically consistent solutions in the future?

In some cases, you may not have the option of waiting. Pressure from users within a company may force an early decision. And usually the decision is made by a group: managers, technical specialists, and mainframe systems people who know the capabilities of the mainframes and are intent on keeping their corporate data well secured from as many people as possible, including you.

For now, one of the most reliable micro-to-mainframe links is readily available for most large computers—the asynchronous link. Even though such links are relatively slow, some asynchronous mainframe ports can be set to run at speeds of 9600 baud, full duplex, using X-ON/X-OFF flow-control protocol. Asynchronous links allow several different types of microcomputers to tie into the mainframe system, and are generally cheaper to implement than leasing a full-time line for synchronous communications. In fact, if you have comparatively small amounts of data to transport, and speed is not paramount, then communications in ASCII may be ideal.

The synchronous decision, on the other hand, begins to look better when you're talking high-volume data traffic, and have needs for high-speed service and networking. In that context, the terminal-emulator solutions and small local nets might be useful. Emulation lets busy managers and executives tie into corporate databases occasionally without requiring full-time 3270 terminal emulation. And PCs are frequently less expensive than dumb terminals. Many of the important applications and database interface links require 3270 emulation to work; some organizations require synchronous communications links to ensure a high-level of data security and integrity. (Asynchronous communications, in general, do not provide the level of security that synchronous-based protocols do.)

One Final Word

We wish we could tell you that mainframe systems and micros will eventually integrate seamlessly with each other. Many vendors are promising that and more. But promises are just that; and for now we should remember that micro-mainframe links are like early versions of the telephone or telegraph. The nitpicking points of operation have yet to be refined, but the systems offer immense potential for handling data. As the evolution of links continues, it may be necessary to take the machinery of the past and discard it—or make it speak to the future in ways we might have never expected.

Our advice? Research links thoroughly before making any purchase decision. Decide on your needs, and then detail the types of data conversions required. Make a list of the specific personal computer and host software applications from which data will be extracted and transferred. Ensure that the list includes any data formats with which the applications can interface (DIF, SYLK, etc.).

Then talk to your mainframe systems people. Make a list of data security requirements, decide who should be locked out, who should gain access to files, and at what level (entire file, record, or field). Evaluate your intended users, their degree (or lack) of technical expertise. And only then investigate vendor products. What kind of systems support do they offer? Can they demonstrate the link in action? Do they offer on-sight inspections of their products? Is their link architecture proprietary or open? Will it support popular communications protocols? Can you get names of companies using the product, and talk to them? How long has the company been in business? Learning from experienced users is the best way to avoid the pitfalls. But expect them anyway.

In short: Your time and research, and the input of informed users, will make link products easy-to-use and universal in the best sense of the term. In the meantime, brace yourself for a challenge: the micro-mainframe link is the most difficult of direct connections, but it is also the most rewarding. With better products and inventive services, it's only a matter of time before the gap between micros and mainframes is closed.

APPENDIX A
ASCII CODE CHART

Decimal	Hex	00 / 00	16 / 10	32 / 20	48 / 30	64 / 40	80 / 50	96 / 60	112 / 70
0	00	nul	dle		0	@	P		p
1	01	soh	dc1	!	1	A	Q	a	q
2	02	stx	dc2	"	2	B	R	b	r
3	03	etx	dc3	#	3	C	S	c	s
4	04	eot	dc4	$	4	D	T	d	t
5	05	enq	nak	%	5	E	U	e	u
6	06	ack	syn	&	6	F	V	f	v
7	07	bel	etb	'	7	G	W	g	w
8	08	bs	can	(	8	H	X	h	x
9	09	ht	em	)	9	I	Y	i	y
10	0A	lf	sub	*	:	J	Z	j	z
11	0B	vt	esc	+	;	K	[	k	{
12	0C	ff	fs	,	<	L	\	l	|
13	0D	cr	gs	-	=	M	]	m	}
14	0E	so	rs	.	>	N	^	n	~
15	0F	si	us	/	?	O	_	o	rub

To use the chart, look at the numbers along the top. The decimal or hexadecimal representation of an ASCII character is found by adding the number along the side to the number at the top. For example, the numeral "6" is ASCII 54, found by adding 6 to 48.

APPENDIX B
KEYBOARD CONVENTIONS FOR ASCII CODES

It is usually possible to input an ASCII control character from the keyboard of your microcomputer. Control codes are not printing codes—they don't represent letters, numbers or punctuation marks. Instead, control codes control things like printers and modems. A CTRL-J, for example, is interpreted as a line feed (ASCII 10).

The codes shown in this chart are the common control codes. To input these codes, hold the CONTROL key down *at the same time* as you strike the letter key. These combinations work on most, but not all, computers that have a control key on their keyboard.

What to Type	Dec	Hex	Char
CTRL-@	0	00	NUL
CTRL-A	1	01	SOH
CTRL-B	2	02	STX
CTRL-C	3	03	ETX
CTRL-D	4	04	EOT
CTRL-E	5	05	ENQ
CTRL-F	6	06	ACK
CTRL-G	7	07	BEL
CTRL-H	8	08	BS
CTRL-I	9	09	HT
CTRL-J	10	0A	LF
CTRL-K	11	0B	VT
CTRL-L	12	0C	FF
CTRL-M	13	0D	CR
CTRL-N	14	0E	SO
CTRL-O	15	0F	SI
CTRL-P	16	10	DLE
CTRL-Q	17	11	DC1
CTRL-R	18	12	DC2
CTRL-S	19	13	DC3
CTRL-T	20	14	DC4
CTRL-U	21	15	NAK

What to Type	Dec	Hex	Char
CTRL-V	22	16	SYN
CTRL-W	23	17	ETB
CTRL-X	24	18	CAN
CTRL-Y	25	19	EM
CTRL-Z	26	1A	SUB
ESC	27	1B	ESC
N/A	28	1C	FS
CTRL-SHFT-M	29	1D	GS
CTRL	30	1E	RS
N/A	31	1F	US

Some of the names are a little strange, and no one really uses them any more. For example, ETB means End Transmission Block, and SUB is SUBstitute. They came from the days of Teletype machines. The codes we're interested in are DC1 and DC3, because they start and stop text transmission from many time-sharing services; BEL, because it beeps a computer's speaker; SUB, because it closes a CP/M or MS-DOS file; and the standard printer controls, LF, FF, HT, CR, and VT.

APPENDIX C
RS-232-C PIN ASSIGNMENTS

Pin Number	Circuit	Description	Direction
1	AA	Protective Ground	None
2	BA	Transmitted Data	To DCE
3	BB	Received Data	From DCE
4	CA	Request to Send	To DCE
5	CB	Clear to Send	From DCE
6	CC	Data Set Ready	From DCE
7	AB	Signal Ground	None
8	CF	Received Line Detect	From DCE
9	—	For Testing	
10	—	For Testing	
11		Unassigned	
12	SCF	Second Received Line Detect	From DCE
13	SCB	Second Clear to Send	From DCE
14	SBA	Second Transmit Data	To DCE
15	DB	Transmit Signal Timing	From DCE
16	SBB	Second Received Data	From DCE
17	DD	Received Signal Timing	From DCE
18		Unassigned	
19	SCA	Second Request to Send	To DCE
20	DC	Data Terminal Ready	To DCE
21	CG	Signal Quality Detect	From DCE
22	CE	Ring Indicator	From DCE
23	CH	Rate Detector	To DCE
24	DA	Transmit Signal Timing	To DCE
25		Unassigned	

APPENDIX D
FILE-TRANSFER SOFTWARE VENDORS

Access Telecommunications Corp., 60 Shore Dr., Burr Ridge, IL 60521 (312) 920-7920. *Product:* File-transfer program for TRS-80 Model 100 to IBM minicomputers.

Alpha Software Corporation, 30 B Street, Burlington, MA 01803 (800) 451-1018. *Product: The Apple-IBM Connection.*

dilithium Press, 921 S.W. Washington, Portland, OR 97205 (800) 547-1842. *Product: PC-to-Mac and Back!*

Vertex Systems, Inc., 6022 W. Pico Blvd., Los Angeles, CA 90030 (213) 938-0857. *Product: Xeno Copy Plus 3.0, Apple Turnover, 80-Mate,* and *Hypercross* (TRS-80 to IBM).

Woolf Software, 6754 Eaton Ave., Canoga Park, CA 91303 (213) 703-8112. *Product: Move-it.*

APPENDIX E
LOCAL-AREA NETWORK VENDORS

Baseband Vendors (Servers and Networks)

Apple Computer Inc., 20525 Mariani Ave., Cupertino, CA 95014 (408) 996-1010. *Product:* AppleTalk (supports 32 Macintosh computers and peripherals).

AST Research, Inc., 2121 Alton Ave., Irvine, CA 92714 (714) 863-1333). *Product:* AST-PCnet II (twisted-pair cable).

Bridge Communications, Inc., 10400 Bubb Rd., Cupertino, CA 95014 (408) 446-2981. *Product:* CS/100 communications server; CS/1-SNA; CS/1-X.25; GS/1; NCS/100. (Products are communications and gateway servers that support Bridge Communication's Ethernet local area network. Supports Blast communications software for CP/M, MS-DOS, ADS, Unix, and VMS.)

Corvus Systems Inc., 2100 Corvus Dr., San Jose, CA 95124 (408) 559-7000. *Product:* Omninet (supports Corvus Concept, Apple II, IBM PC, DEC Rainbow 200, TI Professional, Zenith Z100, PC XT, Ti Professional). *Connections:* 64.

3Com Corporation, 1390 Shorebird Way, Mountain View, CA 94043 (415) 961-9602. *Product:* ETHERSHARE (supports IBM PC, Apples); manufacturers Ethernet interface card, software; all 3Com products operate on the Ethernet network.

Datapoint Corp., 9725 Datapoint Dr., San Antonio, TX 78284 (800) 344-1122. *Product:* ARCNET (supports Datapoint computers as well as computers that implement ARCnet chip technology. Nestar, Tandy, Wang, Davong, Interactive Systems/3M, and Lobo have announced implementation or intentions to implement). *Connections:* 255 maximum per network.

Hewlett-Packard Co., 1820 Embarcadero Rd., Palo Alto, CA 94303 (415) 857-1501. *Product:* HP LAN 9000 (supports HP 9000 microcomputer/Unix-based, 32 bit; Ethernet-compatible network). *Connections:* unknown.

Nestar Systems, Inc., 2585 E. Bayshore Rd., Palo Alto, CA 94303 (415) 493-2223. *Product:* PLAN: 4000 (supports IBM PC and Apple II, III; implements ARCnet Resource Interface Module (RIM) to serve as network controller). *Connections:* 64. PLAN: 3000 (supports IBM PC, Apple, and computers from Nestar; provides file server). *Connections:* 250 microcomputers.

Sperry Corp., PO Box 500, Blue Bell, PA 19424 (215) 542-4213. *Product:* Usernet (supports Sperry PC; other MS-DOS computers). *Connections:* 63.

Standard Microsystems Corporation, 35 Marcus Blvd., Hauppauge, NY 11788 (516) 273-3100. *Product:* COM 9026 Local Area Network Controller (LANC) (an ARCnet local area network controller). *Connections:* 255.

Tandy/Radio Shack, 1700 One Tandy Center, Fort Worth, TX 76102 (817) 390-3011. *Product:* TRS-80 ARCnet (supports Tandy TRS-80 Model 12, Model II computers and peripherals). *Connections:* 255.

Ungermann-Bass, Inc., 2560 Mission College Blvd., Santa Clara, CA 95050 (408) 496-0111. *Product:* Net/One (supports IEEE-488, RS-232-C, RS-499/422, V.35, Asynch, Bisynch, SDLC, and other popular protocols; user has option to choose Ethernet-compatible, thin-coaxial baseband, broadband, or fiber-optic technology). *Connections:* 2,400 maximum.

Xerox Corp., PO Box 1600, Stamford, CT 06904 (203) 329-8700. *Product:* Ethernet (supports RS-232-C; DTE interface). *Connections:* 1024 maximum.

Broadband Vendors

Concord Data Systems, Inc., 303 Bear Hill Rd., Waltham, MA 02154 (617) 890-1394. *Product:* Token/Net (supports DTE interface, V.35; RS-449). *Maximum connections:* unknown.

The Destek Group, 830 C East Evelyn Ave., Sunnyvale, CA 95131 (408) 737-7211. *Product:* DESNET (supports DTE interface; RS-232-C, 8- and 16-bit parallel). *Connections:* over 350.

International Business Machines, Inc., Information Systems Group, Old Orchard Road, Armonk, NY 10504 (914) 765-9600. *Product:* PC Network (supports IBM PCs, XTs, portables, and ATs). *Connections:* 1000.

Interactive Systems/3M, 3980 Varsity Dr., Ann Arbor, MI 48104 (313) 973-1500. *Product:* ALAN (supports DTE interface; RS-232-C). *Connections:* 248.

Proteon, Inc., 24 Crescent Street, Waltham, MA 02145 (617) 655-3340. *Product:* proNET (supports DTE, RS-232-C, and IEEE-488).

Santa Clara Systems Inc., 1860 Hartog Dr., San Jose, CA 95131 (408) 287-4640. *Product:* PCnet (supports IBM PC). *Maximum connections:* 64,000.

Sytek, Inc., 1255 Charleston Rd., Mountain View, CA 94043 (415) 966-7300. *Product:* LocalNet (supports DTE; RS-232-C). *Connections:* 24,000 maximum.

Ungermann-Bass, Inc., 2560 Mission College Blvd., Santa Clara, CA 95050 (408) 496-0111. *Product:* Net/One (DTE interface, RS-232-C, and a variety of others—see baseband vendors). Net/One offers the option of broadband cabling technology, as well as fiber optic and baseband. *Maximum broadband connections:* 36,000.

Wang Laboratories, Inc., 1 Industrial Dr., Lowell, MA 01851 (617) 459-5000. *Product:* WangNet (supports DTE interface, RS-232-C, RS-449). *Connections:* 62,535 maximum.

Other LAN Vendors

Applitek Corp., 107 Audubon Rd., Wakefield, MA 01880 (617) 246-4500. *Product:* Unilan (universal local network; supports baseband, broadband, or fiber-optic cable; RS-232-C, RS-449 asynch, bisynch, or SDLC; uses Unilink multipurpose protocol). Broadband version supports 200 terminals.

AT&T Information Systems, Parsippany, NJ 07054 (800) 833-9333. *Product:* Information Systems Network (ISN; supports PBX/twisted pair or fiber-optic wiring; uses open architecture; supports 3B minicomputers that can be connected to an Ethernet-based LAN; linkage of IBM, IBM-compatibles with Unix-based 3Bs; also protocol conversion to IBM hosts). *Maximum connections:* unknown.

Davox Communications Corp., 6 Continental Blvd., PO Box 328, Merrimack, NH 03054 (603) 424-4500. *Product:* DavoxNet (2 workstations and a twisted pair local network, which emulate IBM 3270 terminals; uses twisted pair instead of coaxial to transmit voice and data signals simultaneously to an IBM 3274-compatible controllers). *Maximum connections:* unknown.

APPENDIX F
MICRO-TO-MAINFRAME LINK VENDORS

Link Software

Cullinet Software, Inc., 400 Blue Hill Drive, Westwood, MA 02090-2198 (617) 329-7700. *Product:* GOLDENGATE (for microcomputers); Information Center Management System (ICMS) (micro-to-mainframe link; can draw summarized information from IDMS/R, as well as from external sources. Information can be downloaded to GOLDENGATE for massaging with productivity tools. Supports IBM PC.

Decision Resources Corp., 1701 K Street, N.W., Washington, DC 20006 (202) 296-0770. *Product:* Customized software link between Lotus software and Issco Inc. (San Diego) *Tel-A-Graf* presentation-quality mainframe graphics software; designed for IBM PC, XT, AT, the Portable, and 3270 PC family.

Informatics General Corp., 21031 Ventura Blvd., Woodland Hills, CA 91364 (818) 887-9040. *Product:* Visi/Answer, dBase/Answer, Lotus/Answer (for micros); Answer/DB for mainframe. Three micro packages massage data extracted selectively from mainframe; can load data directly into the *VisiCalc*, *dBase II*, and *Lotus 1-2-3* formats, respectively.

Information Builders, Inc., 1250 Broadway, New York, NY 10001 (212) 736-4433. *Product:* PC/FOCUS (micro); FOCUS (mainframe). PC/FOCUS is a fourth-generation language and applications development that allows microcomputer operators to develop mainframe queries, write reports, and build local databases. IBM PC XTs and compatibles.

International Business Machines, Inc., Information Systems Group, 900 King St., Rye Brook, NY 10573 (914) 934-4488. *Product:* Personal Decision Series (PDS), for microcomputers; asynchronous communications to IBM VM/CMS and MVS/TSO systems. Attachment/370 (mainframe package); Attachment/36 (minipackage). PDS's software module, *The Data Edition*, can download information from selected IBM System/370 mainframes and IBM System/36 minis using the complementary host attachment packages.

Management Science America, Inc., 3445 Peachtree Rd., NE, Atlanta, GA 30326 (404) 239-2000. *Product:* Executive Peachpak II with ExpertLink; provides link to host data within the package's accounting modules.

Mathematica Products Group, Inc. (Martin Marietta Data Systems), 12 Roszel Rd., PO Box 2392, Princeton, NJ 08540 (609) 799-2660. *Product:* RamLink with Ramis II. Micro-mainframe link to Ramis II database management system.

McCormack & Dodge Corp., 1225 Worcester Rd., Natick, MA 01760 (800) 343-0325. *Product:* PC Link. An applications interface software tool that lets the micro ship data from selected mainframe applications software.

Micro Tempus Inc., 440 Dorchester Blvd., W. Suite 300, Montreal, P.Q., Canada (514) 397-9512. *Product:* Tempus-Link (for microcomputers). Provides a link to a subset of mainframe database software that the microcomputer can download and manipulate. IBM PCs and compatibles.

Terminal Emulators (hardware & software)

AST Research Inc., 2121 Alton Ave., Irvine, CA 92714 (714) 863-9913. *Product:* AST-5251/11. Allows PC/AT/XTs, portables, and compatibles to link to IBM System 34/36/38 minicomputers. Emulation of standard IBM 5251/11 display terminal.

CXI Inc., 3606 W. Bayshore Rd., Palo Alto, CA 94303 (415) 424-0700. *Product:* PCOX board.

Digital Communications Associates, Inc., 303 Technology Park, Norcross, GA 30092 (404) 448-1400. *Product:* Irma, Irmaline, Irmalette, Irmalink File Transfer Software (a series of communications boards, modems, protocol converters, and software products designed to make IBM PC, PC XT, and compatibles emulate IBM 3278/79 terminals).

Forte Data Systems, 2205 Fortune Dr., San Jose, CA 95131 (408) 945-9111. *Product:* Forte board.

Techland Systems Inc., 25 Waterside Plaza, New York, NY 10010

(212) 757-7700. *Product:* Blue Lynx family of terminal emulators. Boards and software emulate IBM 3270 and IBM 5251 terminals.

Software Only (Emulation; Micro/Host Communication)

Cappcomm Software Inc., One World Trade Center #1453, New York, NY 10048 (212) 938-5702. *Product: smarTelex* (S version). Transforms a PC into a telex workstation.

Computer Toolbox, 1325 E. Main St., Waterbury, CT 06705 (203) 754-4197 *Product: Intellicom.* Transfers ASCII and binary files between IBM PC and information services, mainframes, and microcomputers.

Cosmos, PO Box AH, 123 Ferntree Dr. W., Morton, WA 98356 (206) 496-5974 *Product: R/NET; R/Upload. R/NET* is a smart terminal program that emulates the ADDS Regent 100. *R/Upload* lets the IBM PC transmit data from a DOS file to a local or remote minicomputer using the PICK operating system.

The Datalex Company, 650 5th St. #406, San Francisco, CA 94107 (415) 541-0780. *Product: Passport.* Corporate communications package that allows for error-free transmission of ASCII or binary files between IBM PCs and host computers such as IBM/CMS, NCSS, DEC-10 and DEC-20, HP 3000, and PRIME.

IBM, PO Box 1328, Boca Raton, FL 33432 (800) 322-4400. *Product: IBM 3101 Emulation.* Enables an IBM PC to emulate an IBM 3101 terminal.

Persoft, Inc., 2740 Ski Lane, Madison, WI 53713 (608) 233-1000. *Product: SmarTerm/PC* Model TE125-FT. Enables an IBM PC to function as a DEC VT 125, VT 100, VT 101, VT 102, or VT 52 terminal.

APPENDIX G
COMMUNICATION SOFTWARE VENDORS

Apple Computer Inc., 20525 Mariani Ave., Cupertino, CA 95014 (408) 996-1010. *Product: Access II* (Apple IIe, IIc).

AT&T, Parsippany, NJ 07054 (800) 833-9333. *Product: Softcall* (PC-DOS, MS-DOS, AT&T PC 6300).

Buttonware, PO Box 5786, Bellevue, WA 98006 (206) 746-4296. *Product: PC-Dial* (IBM PC).

Byrom Software Inc., 2400 W2900 N, Vernal, UT 84078 (801) 789-4807. *Product: BSTAM* (PC-DOS, MS-DOS, CP/M).

Cawthon Scientific Group, 24224 Michigan Ave., Dearborn, MI 48124 (313) 565-4000. *Product: Computer-Telex-Link*; *Computer-Phone-Link* (for PC-DOS, MS-DOS, CP/M-86 16-bit, CP/M MP/M 8 bit).

Commodore, 1200 Wilson Dr., Westchester, PA 19380 (215) 431-9100. *Product: EasyCom-64* (COM).

Communications Research Group, 8939 Jefferson Hwy. Baton Rouge, LA 70809 (504) 923-0888. *Product: BLAST* (Micro, mini, mainframes, from DEC, DG, IBM, Wang, AT&T, NCR, Prime, Altos, Sperry, Apple, MS-DOS, CP/M, Unix).

Compuview Products, Inc., 1955 Pauline Blvd. Suite 200, Ann Arbor, MI 48103 (313) 996-1299. *Product: Modem-86* (CP/M-86, MS-DOS).

Corporation for Distributed Systems, 17440 Dallas N. Pkwy. Dallas, TX 75252 (214) 380-0671. *Product: COM-80* (HP Series 80).

Digital Marketing Corp., 2363 Boulevard Circle, Walnut Creek, CA 94595 (415) 947-1000. *Product: Micro Link II* (most personal computers).

Direct*Aid Inc., PO Box 4420 Boulder, CO 80306 (303) 442-8080. *Product: Direct*Connect*; *The Impersonator*; *LawSearch* (IBM PC, XT, AT, and compatibles).

Dow Jones Software, PO Box 300, Princeton, NJ 08540 (609) 452-2000. *Product: Dow Jones Straight Talk* (Macintosh).

Dynamic Microprocessor Associates, 545 Fifth Ave. New York, NY 10017 (212) 687-7115. *Product: ASCOM* (IBM PC and compatibles).

Ebert Personal Computers, 4122 S. Parker Rd., Aurora, CO 80014 (303) 693-8400. *Product: TBBS* (MS-DOS 2.0; CP/M-80; TRS 1, III, 4 with DOS Plus, L-DOS, NEWDOS-80).

Epson America, 2780 Lomita Blvd., Torrance CA 90505 (800) 421-5426. *Product: EpsonLink* (EPS HX-20).

Ferox Microsystems Inc., 1701 N. Fort Myer Dr., Arlington, VA 22209 (703) 841-0800. *Product: Logon* (IBM PC and compatibles).

Freeware, The Headlands Press, Inc., PO Box 862, Tiburon, CA 94920 (415) 435-9775. *PC-Talk III* (IBM PC and compatibles).

Frontier Technologies Corp., PO Box 11238, Milwaukee, WI 53211 (414) 964-8689. *Product: Compac* (IBM PC, XT, and compatibles).

General Datacomm Industries, Inc., Personal Computers Products Group, Middlebury, CT 06762-1299 (203) 574-1118. *Product:* General Datacomm Communications Software (PC-DOS, MS-DOS).

Hawkeye Grafix, 23914 Mobile St., Canoga Park, CA 91307 (818) 348-7909. *Product: Commx* (CP/M-80, CP/M-86, MS-DOS, PC-DOS, Turbo-DOS).

Hayes Microcomputer Products, 5923 Peachtree Industrial Blvd., Norcross, GA 30092 (404) 449-8791. *Product: Smartcom II 2.1* (MS-DOS, PC-DOS, TI PRO, Wang, HP 150, Compaq, Corona, Columbia, Televideo, DEC Rainbow).

Hewlett-Packard Co., 11000 Wolfe Rd., Cupertino, CA 95014 (408) 725-8111. *Product: AdvanceLink* (HP Touch).

IE Systems, Inc., 112 Main St., PO Box 359, Newmarket, NH 03957 (603) 659-5891. *Product: ACCULINK* (IBM PC and compatibles).

Lindbergh Systems, Inc., 95 Nagog Hill Rd., Acton, MA 01720 (617) 263-5049. *Product: Omniterm, Omniterm Plus* (IBM PC, XT, AT, and compatibles; Tandy 2000; TRS-80 Model 4).

Madison Computer, 1925 Monroe St., Madison, WI 53711 (605) 255-5552. *Product: McTerm 4000, 8000; McTerm 64* (COM 4000, 8000; COM).

Mark Of The Unicorn, Inc., 222 3rd Street, Cambridge, MA 02142 (617) 576-2760. *Product: PC/InterComm* (PC-DOZ, Z-DOS).

Microcom Inc., 1400 A Providence Hwy., Norwood, MA 02062 (617) 762-9310. *Product: ERA-2*; *Micro/Terminal* (IBM PC; Apple, Macintosh).

Microcorp, 913 Walnut St., Philadelphia, PA 19107 (215) 627-7997. *Product: Intelliterm* (IBM PC, XT, AT, *jr*, and compatibles; TRS-80 III, 4).

MicroPro International Corp., 33 San Pablo Ave., San Rafael, CA 94903 (415) 499-1200. *Product: TelMerge* (enhancement for *WordStar*; PC-DOS).

Microstuf Inc., 1000 Holcomb Woods Pkwy., Suite 440, Roswell, GA 30076 (404) 998-3998. *Product: Crosstalk; Crosstalk XVI* (CP/M; MS-DOS).

Microft Labs., Inc., PO Box 6045, Tallahassee, FL 32314 (904) 385-1141. *Product: MITE* (CP/M-80, CP/M-86, MS-DOS, PC-DOS, Mac).

Novation Inc., 20409 Prairie St., Chatsworth, CA 91311 (213) 996-5060. *Product: Comm-Ware* (comes bundled with its AppleCat II modem, Apple).

Persoft, Inc., 2740 Ski Lane, Madison, WI 53713 (608) 273-6000. *Product: SmarTerm 100*; *SmarTerm 125*; *SmarTerm 40* (IBM PC, XT, AT, PC*jr*, and compatibles).

Quadram Corp., 4355 International Blvd., Norcross, GA 30093 (404) 923-6666. *Product: QuadTalk* (comes bundled with the firm's modems for most personal computers).

Sanyo Business Systems Corp, 51 Joseph St., Moonachie, NJ 07074 (201) 440-9300. *Product: Sanycom* (MS-DOS; CP/M; Sanyo Machines).

Softronics, 3639 New Getwell Rd. Suite 10, Memphis, TN 38118 (901) 683-6850. *Product: Softerm 2* (Apple II, II+, IIe, and IIc, Franklin, BASICs); *Softerm PC* (IBM PC, XT, AT, and compatibles).

Software Publishing Co., 1901 Landings Dr., Mountain View, CA 94043 (415) 962-8910. *Product: pfs: Access* (IBM PC; Apple).

Southeastern Software, 7743 Briarwood Dr., New Orleans, LA 70128 (504) 246-8438. *Product: DataCapture 5.0* (Apple II+); *DataCapture IIe* (Apple IIe, IIc); *DataCapture III* (Apple III); *DataCapture PC* (IBM PC, XT, and compatibles).

Supersoft Technology, PO Box 1628, Champaign, IL 61820 (217) 359-2691, (217) 359-2691. *Product: Term II* (CP/M-80).

Tandy/Radio Shack, 1700 1 Tandy Center, Fort Worth, TX 76102 (817) 390-3011. *Product:* Tandy markets a variety of communications software products for its computers. See Tandy computer centers for details.

Televideo Systems, Inc., 550 E. Brokaw, San Jose, CA 95112 (408) 971-0255. *Product: TeleAsynch* (CP/M, MS-DOS, PC-DOS).

Transend Corp., 2190 Paragon Dr., San Jose, CA 95131 (408) 946-7400. *Product: Transend I* (Apple II+, IIe, IIc); *Transend PC COMplete* (PC-DOS, MS-DOS); *Transend PC Pipeline* (PC-DOS, MS-DOS); *Easycom/Easygo* (Apple II+, IIe, IIc).

United Software Industries, 1880 Century Park East, Los Angeles, CA 90067 (213) 556-2211. *Product: ASCII Express* (Apple II+, IIe, IIc, Franklin, Basis); *ASCII Pro* (PC-DOS, MS-DOS); *ASCII PRO-80* (CP/M-80); *ASCII Express ProDOS Version* (Apple II+, IIe, IIc); *ASCII Express P-Term The Professional* (Apple under Pascal); *ASCII Express Z-Term The Professional* (Apple under CP/M).

U.S. Robotics, 1123 W. Washington Blvd., Chicago, IL 60607 (312) 733-0497. *Product: Telpac* (PC-DOS, MS-DOS 2.0 and up).

VM Personal Computing, 475 Fifth Ave. Suite 411, New York, NY 10017 (212) 686-1450. *Product: RELAY* (IBM PC and compatibles).

Westico Inc., 25 Van Zant St., Norwalk, CT 06855 (203) 853-6880. *Product: ASCOM* (CP/M-80, CP/M-86, PC-DOS, MS-DOS).

APPENDIX H
A COMMUNICATIONS DIARY

The following is the step-by-step direct-connect diary of Ernest Mau, a writer and technical specialist from Aurora, Colorado. Mau spent a number of years transferring programs and text between CP/M, Apple DOS, and MS-DOS computers. His experiments began in 1980, when he first converted a $15,000 MITS/Pertec 300/25 Business System (based on the old MITS Altair 8800b microcomputer) from its own limited 32-sector, hard-sectored drives to a soft-sectored version for CP/M. Mau was able to locate an implementation of CP/M 2.2 for the Altair that would run without hardware modification. His source: Gary Shaffstall, International Software Service (13050 W. Cedar Drive, #15, Lakewood, CO 80228), who helped Mau begin his series of direct connections.

Stage 1: From Altair DOS to Altair CP/M

I purchased Shaffstall's software, together with specialized software that would read CP/M-based programs from standard soft-sectored diskettes (8-inch SSSD), and re-recorded the programs onto my own 32-sector diskettes using my existing hardware. Shaffstall also had conversion programs to adapt BASIC programs written under the MITS BASIC system so they would run under Microsoft's MBASIC.

With the aid of these specialized programs, I made my move into the world of CP/M, salvaging all custom programs I had written under BASIC and all existing word-processing files.

Stage 2: Altair CP/M to Apple CP/M

During the second quarter of 1981, I acquired my second computer—an Apple II+ equipped with a Microsoft SoftCard and a California Computer Systems 7710a Asynchronous Serial Interface card (RS-232-C). Since I was already using CP/M-based software, I wanted the Apple primarily as a backup system and had little interest at the time in Apple DOS. . . .

As a backup system, I felt it was necessary to have the Apple storing many of the same word processing text files, programs I had developed under BASIC, and data files for those programs as were stored on the Altair CP/M system. I had about 2 megabytes of material to move—too much to retype. So I began to look for ways to transfer disk files directly from one machine to another.

At the time, modems, networks, and similar applications were almost unknown in the microcomputer industry. . . . My only obvious path was to cable one computer directly to the other through their RS-232-C ports and arrange some way for the machines to talk to each other and exchange files. Local dealers, especially those for Apple machines, were no help at all. They claimed it couldn't be done or they tried to sell me outrageously expensive consulting services. . . .

Luckily, I thought again about my friend Gary Shaffstall. He had developed a set of custom programs he called LINK (or variations such as ALINK for the Apple and PLINK for another machine). Though not the highly sophisticated communications programs we can find today, they were designed to use a software protocol for machine-to-machine data transfers . . . where one machine would read a file and send the ASCII characters to an open capture buffer in the other machine, from which the buffer could be stored as a disk file. There was also a more formal provision to send and receive files directly from one disk to another without going through the capture buffer—even with an error-checking protocol.

I immediately purchased the programs for a nominal cost. On the way home, I stopped at a computer store and had them make a 100-foot RS-232-C cable with all 25 leads wired straight through (pin to pin at either end) for about $45. For another $5, they bolted two DB-25 connectors back-to-back (male-to-female) and soldered some wires so that pins 1, 4, 5, 6, 7, 8, and 20 fed straight through, while pins 2 and 3 (transmit and receive) crossed over. Known as a 2–3 crossover, the connector arrangement is shown in Figure 1-A:

Cabling the CCS 7710a interface in the Apple to the 2SIO interface in the Altair, I was unable to make the machines communicate. However, I thought back to an incident about a year earlier when my regular printer had failed, as well as a replacement printer. . . . A service technician had been called in, determining that several of the signal lines were not active in the Altair. By strapping leads, he made the computer and printer work, forcing needed signals to appear present by simply tapping another continuous signal on another line.

Male	Female	Function
1 ------------------------ 1		Chassis Ground
2 ------------------------ 3		Receive Data
3 ------------------------ 2		Transmit Data
4 ------------------------ 4		Request to Send
5 ------------------------ 5		Clear to Send
6 ------------------------ 6		Data Set Ready
7 ------------------------ 7		Signal Ground
8 ------------------------ 8		Data Carrier Detect
20 ---------------------- 20		Data Terminal Ready

Figure 1.A

That much I remembered, but I couldn't recall which leads were involved or what pins he had strapped.

I then made several short wires with small test clips I bought at a local electronic supply house. With those, I began shorting pins. I knew that the data leads on pins 2 and 3 should not be shorted, and I guessed the grounds on pins 1 and 7 shouldn't either. That left pins 4, 5, 6, 8, and 20 to play with. After several hours (or experiments), the two computers began to exchange data. I looked at the test leads and saw that I had shorted all five pins (4, 5, 6, 8, and 20) together. No handshaking lines were active—all were carrying a constant signal seen by the computers at either end of the cable (Figure 1.B).

With that success I was able to solder permanent jumpers onto my jury-rigged adapter, as shown in Figure 1.B. I didn't know it at the time, but this one connector was to become my standard, almost universal connector for intercomputer communications among several more machines. Basically, it just eliminates the handshaking capabilities

```
 1 ------------------------ 1
 2 ------------------------ 3
 3 ------------------------ 2
 4 ---------- X ---------- 4    Pins 4, 5, 6, 8, and 20 strapped
                                 together,
 5 ---------- X ---------- 5    Pins 2 and 3 crossed
 6 ---------- X ---------- 6    Pins 1 and 7 straight through
 7 ------------------------ 7
 8 ---------- X ---------- 8
20 ---------- X ---------- 20
```

Figure 1.B

from the interfaces by making each computer think each handshaking line is present at all times.[1]

Stage 3: Morrow Decision 1 to Apple CP/M

In mid-1982, I was forced to abandon the Altair system. Service was unavailable and the machine was becoming less and less reliable. There was no problem finding a replacement—a Morrow Decision 1 (S-100 bus, CP/M system) with 8-inch, double-sided, double-density 1.2-Mbyte floppy disk drives. But, the disk drives once again were incompatible, and I had over 150 Mbytes stored in the Altair that had to be salvaged. I immediately contacted Gary Shaffstall again. Could he modify his LINK program for the Decision 1? Sure! It took a week or so, and some considerable testing to accommodate the three-port Morrow Multi-I/O board and its difficult-to-program 8250 ACE devices, but it was done. I used the same jury-rigged connector (Figure 1.B) as I had used between the Altair and the Apple. Best of all, I was able to transfer data between the Altair and the Morrow, between the Apple CP/M and the Morrow, and between the Apple CP/M and the Altair with the same set of compatible programs, the same cabling, the same command structure, and the same degree of reliability. Transfers between the Apple and Morrow, however, remained somewhat slow, being limited by the 1200-baud effective display rate of the Apple screen.

Stage 4: Decision 1 CP/M to Apple DOS

Shortly thereafter, I came up with a new need. For many years, I have had a sideline business selling word games to puzzle magazines. For a long time, it was a profitable business, with the S-100 computers (Altair and Morrow Decision 1) being able to work from standard data and programs I'd written. The programs printed copies of the printed puzzles, which I then would have to work by hand to develop a suitable answer key for the publications. Even with the computer able to

---

[1]*Note:* Mau's solution differs slightly from our general solution presented in Chapters 9 and 10.

generate the puzzles in under half a minute apiece, working the answer keys by hand was taking too much of my time.

I realized I could program the Apple, using its graphics capabilities, to work the answer keys and print them automatically. But the Apple was too slow and had too little disk storage space.

The obvious alternative was to have the Decision 1 generate the puzzle and transfer data in ASCII form to the Apple for graphic work. The problem was that I needed to use programs like Apple's *DOS Toolkit*, which work under Apple DOS and not CP/M. Thus far all my data transfers had been CP/M to CP/M, and I lacked any software to go CP/M to Apple DOS. But I had seen a program that comes on Apple DOS's 3.3 diskette, called *MAKE TEXT*; I realized it could be adapted, without too much difficulty, to accept data from the RS-232-C interface, buffer it into memory, and write out a disk file when finished. The buffer wouldn't "care" where the data originated as long as they were delivered at a rate the receiving computer could handle. Furthermore, I might be able to write a simple BASIC program on the Decision 1 to read a disk file line by line, sending the contents to a printer. By cabling the printer output to the input port of the Apple, I should be able to make the Decision 1 think it was simply making a hard copy of the disk file when, in fact, it would be filling a buffer in the Apple.

For initial tests, I used the same connector (Figure 1.B) as before, but moved the cable from the Morrow's spare port to the printer port. Not surprisingly, the connection worked. Just by doing a DIR command routed to the printer (with a {Control} P under CP/M on the Morrow), I could send an entire disk directory to the Apple buffer.

I then set about writing the BASIC program for the Morrow and modifying the *MAKE TEXT* program in the Apple. The results are shown in Figures 1.C and 1.D. There are several important points about these programs:

First, I can use them at speeds up to 1200 baud, with the delays built into the transmitting program of the Decision 1 sufficient to keep from overrunning the Apple screen display. (*See Mau's case study in Chapter 3 for details.*)

Second, no provision is made to stop data transfer should the Apple memory be filled. Therefore, the amount of data transferred must be small enough to fit into the Apple memory at one time—not a problem in my applications.

Third, the FRE command in the Apple is used to force something known as a "string-space garbage collect" at a convenient time—immediately after a file is written out on disk. This keeps the Apple from

```
10 CLEAR
15 REM Identify start of file transfers stored in
sequential order
20 INPUT"Starting WF No. ";NN
30 INPUT"Type (CAW or WF):",AA$:IF AA$<>"CAW" AND
AA$<>"WF" THEN 30
40 S$=AA$+MID$(STR$(NN),2)
50 OPEN"I",1,"B:"+S$
60 PRINT S$
70 FOR X=1 TO 100:IF EOF(1) THEN 180
80 REM read a line from disk file
90 LINE INPUT#1, SS$
100 REM Output the line to printer port (remote
Apple computer)
110 LPRINTSS $
120 REM Delay after line to prevent overflowing
Apple buffer
130 FOR Y=1 to 60:NEXT
140 NEXT
150 REM Close file & use long delay to allow
Apple to store
160 REM data to its disk and perform a forced
string-space
170 REM garbage collect procedure.
180 CLOSE:FOR Z=1 TO 36000!:NEXT
185 REM Increment file number and proceed to
transmit next file
190 NN=NN+1:GOTO 40
```

Figure 1.C

pausing for such cleanups at disastrous times, for example, when the Morrow Decision 1 is sending data.

Incidentally, I've modified these programs to move simple ASCII text files from the Decision 1 to the Apple for use with word processors. I haven't, however, bothered to write programs to move data from Apple DOS to the Decision 1, simply because I don't have transfer needs in that direction.

Stage 5: Adding a Morrow Micro Decision MD3

By mid-1983, I needed yet another computer. The one I selected this time was the Morrow Micro Decision MD3. Again, a CP/M machine, but not an S-100 bus. It was incompatible with all my other equipment.

```
10  DIM A$(1000):I = 0
11  INPUT "Starting WF No. ";NN
20  D$ = CHR$ (4): REM CTRL D
30  HOME : TEXT
55  PRINT D$;"IN# 2"
70  I = I + 1
90  PRINT "#";I;": ";
100 INPUT " ";A$(I)
110 IF A$(I) < > " " GOTO 70
120 PRINT : PRINT D$; "IN# 0"
130 N$ = "WF" + STR$ (NN)
140 PRINT D$;"OPEN ";N$,D2"
150 PRINT D$"DELETE ";N$
160 PRINT D$;"OPEN ";N$
170 PRINT D$;"WRITE ";N$
180 PRINT A$(1)
190 FOR J = 2 TO I - 1
200 PRINT CHR= (34) + A$(J) + CHR$ (34)
210 NEXT J
220 PRINT D$;"CLOSE ";N$
229 NN = NN + 1
230 X = FRE (1):I = 0: GOTO 20
```

Figure 1.D

I called Gary Shaffstall to discuss modifications, but this time, we agreed that I should try to get some commercial software, especially since I was planning to buy more computers. This time I purchased Woolf Software's *Move-It* package. I use it now for most of my inter-computer communications. There are other programs available, but the *Move-It* program is available for many types of computers, including my MD3, the Decision 1, and Apple CP/M. There's even a version for PC-DOS. Best of all, the protocol system used in *Move It* tests as error-free when running wide open at 19,200 baud over a 100-foot RS-232-C cable running between the MD3 and the Decision 1. Hardware handshaking isn't required, so my universal connector, once again, worked perfectly well in this application.

I also moved to MD3 a copy of the BASIC program I had used for transferring puzzle data from the Decision 1. With that step, either or both the Decision 1 or MD3 could now generate puzzles, and the Apple could do the graphics under Apple DOS for both CP/M machines. In fact, by that time, the Apple was relegated to a minor unit serving only to graph puzzle answer keys, to test software and to handle networking communications when the other machines were busy. I had recently acquired my first modems and modem-oriented telecommunications program as a result of writing for CompuServe's *Online Today* magazine. I was beginning to spend a lot of time with telephone data communications.

Now, though, I had good communications links between all the machines. If I developed or captured data on one machine, I could quickly and conveniently move it to the other.

Stage 6: Adding a Compaq Portable Computer (IBM PC-Compatible)

The next acquisition, in late 1983, was a Compaq portable computer, bringing me into the PC-DOS/MS-DOS operating system for the first time. Although I haven't equipped this machine with an 8-bit coprocessor and CP/M-80 yet, I will eventually: there are occasions when I need to move things like word processing text files between the Compaq and the other computers.

Once again, my standard connector and cable usually works, though I use conventional modem-style communications programs to transfer the data. Things like VM Computing's Relay or virtually any public-domain XMODEM protocol program will suffice for many of my transfer needs. Since quantities of data moving through this machine are small, speed is less of a consideration, and I'm usually content to send files across the communications interface at 1200 or 2400 baud.

The one thing I do have to be careful of is to avoid programs that rely on hardware handshaking in an IBM PC. There are many of those that work fine in conjunction with typical modems, but tend to malfunction when used in a direct connection to another computer lacking those signals.

For emergencies, I also use a Mountain Computer RS-232-C Configuration Adaptor, which allows me to quickly switch the wires from a full-handshaking to a no-handshaking setup and to cross and uncross the send and receive lines as needed.

Modem Solutions

For the most part, these direct connections have satisfied my needs for intercomputer communications within my own office and working environment. However, for the past two years, I've been involved in telephone communications. As an editor for *Online Today* magazine, I send and receive all materials via sections of the CompuServe system. I also have used MCI Mail extensively for dealing with other publications, and have frequent need to access local RCP/M and BBS setups to acquire information and public domain software.

Therefore, each of my active computers now is equipped with its own modem, 300 and 1200 baud, and a variety of communications software, both from public domain and commercial sources. I even have a program, *TermExec*, that uses XMODEM protocol under Apple DOS.

Most modem communications are straightforward, requiring little if any attention to cabling irregularities, since modem connections are pretty well standardized unless the software requires hardware handshaking with the modem (some do).

However, I often need to move files associated with modem communication from one computer to another. Typically, I may write or edit an article on either the Morrow Micro Decision 3 or Compaq, but store it in my "archive" on the Decision 1, which has a greater disk storage capacity. The transfer can be accomplished in any of three ways. First, I can send the files to the remote public database, later accessing those files from the second computer. Another way is to transfer data directly with a cable, but that involves switching connections, changing software, and otherwise interrupting my workflow. A third way is to send the files to the remote system through one modem and capture it simultaneously for another of my computers through a second modem. This one comes as a surprise. I hit upon it while transmitting ASCII files informally (no protocol) to the CompuServe system from my Micro Decision. I was sending data via a Universal Data Systems 212 A/D modem. Because my files were text without protocol, I was getting a character-by-character echoback from the remote system.

To take advantage of this, I used a Y tap on my telephone cord, connecting the UDS 212A/D to one leg and a Hayes Smartmodem to the other leg. The Smartmodem in turn hooked up to my larger Decision 1 microcomputer. I set the Smartmodem into its "monitor incoming" mode, suppressed its generation of carrier signals, and dialed the number from the UDS 212A/D. On connection, I used the Micro Decision to initiate file storage on the remote computers. Before starting the actual transmission, however, I had the Decision 1 open a capture buffer. Once I started the transmission from the Micro Decision through the UDS modem, I found that the Smartmodem and its Decision 1 computer were receiving only the echoback being returned on the telephone lines. Smartmodem/Decision 1 totally ignored the outgoing data; thus I was recording single (not double) characters.

SELECTED BIBLIOGRAPHY

Books and Manuals

AT&T Bell Laboratories. *Vision of the Future.* Bell Telephone Laboratories, Murray Hill, N.J., 1984.

Campbell, Joseph. *The RS-232-C Solution.* Sybex Books, Berkeley, Calif., 1984.

CompuServe, Inc. *Consumer Information Service User's Guide.* CompuServe Inc., Consumer Information Services Division, Columbus, Ohio, 1984.

CompuServe, Inc. *CompuServe Information Service VIDTEX 4.0 Standards for Intelligent Terminal Emulator Programs.* CompuServe, Inc., Columbus, Ohio, 1983.

Digital Equipment Corp. *Introduction to Local Area Networks.* Digital Equipment Corp., Maynard, Mass., 1982.

Electronic Industries Association, Subcommittee TR 30.2, EIA Standard EIA-232-D, April 1985.

Glasgal, Ralph. *Techniques in Data Communications.* Artech House, Inc., Dedham, Mass., 1983.

Glossbrenner, Alfred. *The Complete Handbook of Personal Computer Communications.* St. Martin's Press, New York, 1983.

Hogan, Thom. *Osborne CP/M User Guide,* 2nd ed. Osborne/McGraw-Hill, Berkeley, Calif., 1982.

Madron, Thomas W. *Local Area Networks in Large Organizations.* Hayden Book Company, Hasbrouck Heights, N.J., 1984.

Shapiro, Neil L. *The IBM PC Connection.* Micro Text Publications/McGraw-Hill, New York, 1983.

Source Telecomputing Corp. *User's Manual.* Source Telecomputing Corp., McLean, Va., 1983, 1984, 1985.

Articles

Bannister, Hank. "IBM's PC Network: The Scramble Begins." *InfoWorld,* April 22, 1985, pp. 15–17.

Campt, David W. "Protocol, Protocol, Who's Got the Standard?" *Data Communications,* August 1984, pp. 60–64.

Chin, Kathy. "Time Running Out for Mainframe Link Vendors." *Communications Week,* May 27, 1985, pp. C1–C8.

Dryzmkowski, Frank, and Dave Goodman. "Connectors—The Missing Link in EMI Suppression." *Computer Design,* August 1984, pp. 77–84.

Emmett, Arielle. "Micro-to-Mainframe Links." *Popular Computing,* August 1985, pp. 71–73, 126, 128.

Gabel, David. "Swapping Data." *Personal Computing,* September 1983, pp. 104–118.

Martorelli, William. "SNA: After 10 Long Years, Something to Celebrate." *InformationWEEK,* April 22, 1985, pp. 23–29.

Passmore, L. David. "The Networking Standards Collision." *Datamation,* February 1, 1985, pp. 98–108.

Pearson, Gregory. "Anatomy of a Microcomputer Protocol." *Data Communications,* March 1983, pp. 231–239.

Pearson, Gregory. "The Microcom Agreement." *PC World,* May 1984, pp. 103–108.

Pearson, Gregory. "Microcom Networking Protocol." *Micro Communications,* August 1984.

Scott, Geoff, "The Problem with Standards." *Link-Up,* August 1984, pp. 44–51.

Simpson, Richard. "Stepping into File Transfers." *Micro Communications,* June 1985, pp. 32–36.

Stone, Paula S. "Micro to M'Frame Blues." *Datamation* (OEM ed.) February 15, 1985.

Witten, Ian H. "Welcome to the Standards Jungle." *Byte,* February 1983, pp. 146–166, 170–178.

(P) PLUME (0452)

COMPUTER GUIDES FROM PLUME

☐ **THE NEW AMERICAN COMPUTER DICTIONARY by Kent Porter.** The acclaimed reference on the language of computer, revised and updated to reflect the rapidly changing computer scene, with 2,400 entries. A Comprehensive A-Z reference source, it covers every term one needs to know to buy and use a computer. (256534—$8.95)*

☐ **ALMOST FREE COMPUTER STUFF FOR KIDS by Linda Gail Christie and Gary Bullard.** Hundreds of companies across the country offer a tremendous array of products for computer fun and educational challenge at startlingly low prices—or even no cost—if you know where to write. This book tells you all the things you can get and provides the send-away-for coupons you need to enjoy special discounts on everything from software to T-shirts. (255619—$9.95)*

☐ **THE COMPUTER FREELANCER'S HANDBOOK: Moonlighting with Your Home Computer by Ardy Friedberg.** This practical guide will show you how you can use your personal computer for extra income. Step-by-step advice, a wealth of real-life success stories, and inspiring ideas offer all the information you'll need for choosing the right home-based business, figuring prices, attracting customers, and growing as much and as fast as you want. (255627—$10.95)*

☐ **DATABASE PRIMER: AN EASY-TO-UNDERSTAND GUIDE TO DATABASE MANAGEMENT SYSTEMS by Rose Deakin.** The future of information control is in database management systems—tools that help you organize and manipulate information or data. This essential guide tells you how a database works, what it can do for you, and what you should know when you go to buy one. (254922—$9.95)†

☐ **BEGINNING WITH BASIC: AN INTRODUCTION TO COMPUTER PROGRAMMING by Kent Porter.** Now, at last, the new computer owner has a book that speaks in down-to-earth everyday language to explain clearly—and step-by-step—how to master BASIC, Beginner's All-Purpose Symbolic Instructional Code. And how to use it to program your computer to do exactly what you want it to do. (254914—$10.95)*

*Prices higher in Canada.
†Not available in Canada.

To order use coupon on next page.

ⓟ PLUME

CREATIVE COMPUTING

(0452)

☐ **MACINTOSH GRAPHICS. From MacPaint to Your Own Graphics Programming on the Macintosh. Gordon Mann.** Covering MacPaint, MacDraw, and the graphics commands of Apple's own versions of BASIC and Pascal, this is a one-stop reference book for anyone who wants to do anything with Mac graphics. (255708—$16.95)

☐ **COOKBOOK OF CREATIVE PROGRAMS FOR THE IBM PC AND PCjr: Projects for Music, Animation, and Telecommunications. Robert Rinder.** This collection of innovative and useful programs is designed to help novice and experienced programmers alike explore the fascinating world of sound and graphics on the standard-setting computers from IBM. (255724—$14.95)

☐ **COMPUKIDS: A Parents' Guide to Computers and Learning. Felicia Antonelli Holton.** A clear, informative, entertaining guide for parents on using computers to learn about other subjects. (255600—$9.95)

☐ **THE EASY-DOES-IT GUIDE TO THE IBM PCjr. Barbara Schwartz.** The ultimate "reader-friendly" book on the IBM PCjr, explaining what it can do, how to use it, and how to service it. (254892—$8.95)

☐ **THE COMPUTER LOG: The Best Thing Next to Your Computer by Howard Hillman.** If you use a computer, you need *The Computer Log*. The carefully planned logs and directories in this oversized organizer will help you find those crucial numbers, codes and lists you often need at a moment's notice as you work at your computer. Some features: task and activity log, on-line database directory, electronic mail service directory, repair service directory, software inventory, vendor directory, and much, much more. Finally, one place for all your information! (256488—$12.95)

Prices slightly higher in Canada.

Buy them at your local bookstore or use this convenient coupon for ordering.

NEW AMERICAN LIBRARY
P.O. Box 999, Bergenfield, New Jersey 07621

Please send me the PLUME BOOKS I have checked above. I am enclosing $_____ (please add $1.50 to this order to cover postage and handling). Send check or money order—no cash or C.O.D.'s. Price and numbers are subject to change without notice.

Name_____

Address_____

City_____ State _____ Zip Code _____

Allow 4-6 weeks for delivery. This offer is subject to withdrawal without notice.

Ⓟ Plume (0452)

PLUME/WAITE COMPUTER GUIDES

☐ **Introducing the TRS-80® Model 100, by Diane Burns and S. Venit.** This book, intended for newcomers to the Model 100, offers simple step-by-step explanations of how to set up your Model 100 and how to use its built-in programs: TEST, ADDRSS, SCHEDL, TELCOM, and BASIC. Specific instructions are given for connecting the Model 100 to the cassette recorder, other computers, the telephone lines, the optional disk drive/video interface, and the optional bar code reader.
(255740—$15.95)

☐ **Mastering BASIC On the TRS-80® Model 100, by Bernd Enders.** An exceptionally easy-to-follow introduction to the built-in programming language on the Model 100. Also serves as a comprehensive reference guide for the advanced user. Covers all Model 100 BASIC features including graphics, sound, and file-handling. With this book and the Model 100 you can learn BASIC anywhere! (255759—$19.95)

☐ **Games and Utilities for the TRS-80® Model 100, by Ron Karr, Steven Olsen, and Robert Lafore.** A collection of powerful programs to enhance your Model 100. Enjoy fast-paced, exciting card games, arcade games, music, art, and learning games. Help yourself to practical utilities that let you count words in a text file, turn your Model 100 into a scientific calculator, show file sizes, and generally increase your Model 100's usefulness, and your own grasp of programming. (255775—$16.95)

☐ **Practical Finance on the TRS-80® Model 100, by S. Venit and Diane Burns.** The perfect book for anyone using the Model 100 in business: investors, real estate brokers, managers. Contains short but powerful programs to perform production planning, and access financial and other information from CompuServe® and the Dow Jones News/Retrieval® service. (255767—$15.95)

☐ **Hidden Powers of the TRS-80® Model 100, by Christopher L. Morgan.** This amazing book takes you deep inside the Model 100 to reveal for the first time how it really works. You'll learn about the amazing power buried in the ROM, and how to use this power in your own programs. You can print in reverse video, prevent any screen lines from scrolling, dial the telephone from BASIC, control external devices from the cassette port, and discover many other fascinating secrets hidden within your Model 100. (255783—$19.95)

All prices higher in Canada.

To order, use the convenient coupon on the next page.

PLUME

Look for these forthcoming Plume/Waite titles on the Macintosh®:

(0452)

☐ **Games and Utilities for the Macintosh® by Dan Shafer.** Thirty exciting games and useful utility programs in Macintosh Pascal, ready for you to type in and run. Something for everyone, from "Crypto-quotes," "Parachute Man," and "Logic Probe," to sort routines and icon and menu constructors. Full-sized and expertly written, these programs are not only entertaining and useful, they are also a valuable education in the finer points of Macintosh programming. (256410—$18.95)

☐ **Hidden Powers of the Macintosh® by Christopher L. Morgan.** This unique, authoritative book takes you behind the Mac's user-friendly facade and shows you how the machine *really* works. Starting simply, the book explains all you need to know to write serious application programs; including QuickDraw and Toolbox routines, windows, pictures, bit maps regions, events, menus, files. RAM and ROM organization, and much more. Essential for serious programmers, this is the book Apple should have written. (256437—$24.95)

☐ **Basic Primer for the Macintosh® by Emil Flock and Miriam Flock.** Apple's own Macintosh Basic is one of the best-structured, fastest, easiest-to-learn versions of Basic ever developed. Using entertaining, carefully graded programming examples, this book takes the complete novice from simple one-line programs to full mastery of the language. Later chapters cover such advanced topics as sound, files, and using the Mac's QuickDraw and Toolbox routines. (256399—$17.95)

☐ **Assembly Language Primer for the Macintosh® by Keith Mathews.** Many serious application programs must be written in assembly language, which alone has the speed and versatility to handle tough problems. Assuming no previous knowledge of assembly language, this book shows you, in easy, step-by-step style, how to master 68000 code, and at the same time, how to access all of the Mac's features from your programs: windows, the mouse, text editing, and more. (256429—$24.95)

Prices slightly higher in Canada.

Buy them at your local bookstore or use this convenient coupon for ordering.

NEW AMERICAN LIBRARY
P.O. Box 999, Bergenfield, New Jersey 07621

Please send me the PLUME BOOKS I have checked above. I am enclosing $_____ (please add $1.50 to this order to cover postage and handling). Send check or money order—no cash or C.O.D.'s. Price and numbers are subject to change without notice.

Name _____

Address _____

City _____ State _____ Zip Code _____

Allow 4-6 weeks for delivery. This offer is subject to withdrawal without notice.